D0046728

American Images of Soviet Foreign Policy

American Images of

Soviet Foreign Policy

An Inquiry into Recent Appraisals from the
Academic Community

by William Welch

New Haven and London, Yale University Press

1970

Designed by John O. C. McCrillis,
set in Garamond type,
and printed in the United States of America by
the Carl Purington Rollins Printing-Office of
the Yale University Press, New Haven, Connecticut.

Distributed in Great Britain, Europe, Asia, and
Africa by Yale University Press Ltd., London; in
Canada by McGill-Queen's University Press, Montreal; and
in Mexico by Centro Interamericano de Libros
Académicos, Mexico City.

To Katharine

Contents

Tables and Figures

Preface

This book is about the ways in which the American academic community looks at the activities of the other major protagonist in the great international drama of our age. Its prime concerns are what the various images or perceptions are that have been developed by this community, how well founded they are, what may be done to improve them. Strictly speaking, it refers only to such images as, delineated in works dated 1959–68, were developed by their beholders in the decade 1955–65 and hence may be described as late-Dulles or early-Rusk. But the community's perceptions in this decade being, I believe, not so different from those of the preceding decade or those of the late-Rusk or Vietnam period, the volume's conclusions can reasonably claim to reflect academia's thinking on Soviet policy over the entire postwar span.

The undertaking arises out of a vague but long-standing dissatisfaction with this thinking. It has seemed to me for some time, on cursory examination, that we who aspire to a certain amount of expertise in the field have not been fulfilling our functions as well as we might. Those functions, I hold, include fashioning a body of knowledge firmly grounded and of wide acceptance. But quite a bit of what individuals present as knowledge firm and above challenge turns out, even on superficial scrutiny, to have little support, and the sparseness of propositions of wide acceptance is a secret to none. To determine whether the suspicion of inadequacy in respect to method is justified, and, if this is so, to suggest improvements in that method and ways of increasing the consensus—these are the purposes of the more extended analysis that constitutes the book.

There is a second, more practical reason for writing. Beyond improvement of knowledge for its own sake lies improvement of its uses to others. I hold we should be fashioning a solid body of knowledge about Soviet external conduct not only to satisfy our own curiosity, but to serve the needs of others, which in this case most notably means the needs of the officials of our government responsible for dealings with the Soviets. Looked at from the other side, the makers of our foreign policy should be able to count on us for well-based, uniform answers to the questions they must put on the nature of Soviet conduct. They should be able to look to us for well-based, uniform answers to the question of how addicted to the military instrument the Soviets have been, how prone or not prone to violate their obligations, etc. This kind of thing, it seems to me, they have so far been unable to get from us. In fact, it seems to me they have been able to count on us for little more than what they can get from the more thoughtful of journalists, or from study on their own. To these further conclusions cursory examination leads. To determine whether they too are justified, and if so, to suggest remedies for the situation, constitutes further reason for the undertaking.

Every one of us these days is supposed to have what is called, for lack of a longer and more barbarous phrase, a "methodological commitment." He is supposed to be committed to a historical approach, committed to a traditional approach, committed to a behavioral approach, but in any case committed. As shall become clear, I believe in rigor in the definition and application of concept; I believe in reducing such complex phenomena as state, party, etc., and their various attributes to the observable acts of individuals; I believe in conscious and conscientious attention to questions of method. And all of this, I suppose, puts me in the camp of the behavioralists.

At the same time, I also hold that there is a limit to which it is advisable to push the mind in its effort to correct its procedures; I hold that close, prolonged, detailed concern with method soon reaches a point of diminishing returns, where additional increments to the validity of the product no longer offset increments of time and mental labor expended, and where explanation of what one is about turns from being faintly interesting to mildly tedious, from mildly tedious to outright offensive, and, when accompanied by the kind of terminological obscurantism which seems at times to creep into such discussion, from outright offensive to absolutely repulsive. I believe that in order to get on with the task at hand one should feel free at times, and at points, to indulge an occasional hunch or insight, taking care only to describe it as such to the reader. I think that in reporting results one should feel at liberty, if only in the interest of livening the presentation, to express on occasion one's immediate, direct feelings toward the subject at hand, indulging the value judgments so deprecated by some. In fact, I think that without doing these things we shall eventually bore ourselves to death. In this general connection it is most important, I think, to remind ourselves that the counsel of perfection is the enemy of achievement. And all of this, I suppose, puts me closer to the traditionalists.

My "methodological commitment" is therefore to something that lies between those of traditionalist and behavioralist. I think of this middle way as a first-level refinement of common sense. And, since that which goes under the name of "scientific method" is *au fond* a refinement of common sense, I consider my commitment also a commitment to science. But all this, as I shall have occasion to mention later, is purely an affair of names, and as such it is not very important. What is important is the reality sought for—and the success with which the efforts undertaken in the following pages approximate that reality.

My emotional commitment is to an image of Soviet external conduct which stands on the border of the Hard and Mixed (Hard-Soft) ranges of the continuum worked out in Chapter 2—say, at point 6 on the 10-point scale. Following my own recommendation addressed in Chapter 8 to the improvement of consensus, I have tried to contain the influence of this bias and prevent its interfering with observance of rules of proper procedure. Whether I have succeeded in this, and whether, for instance, my finding of the superior substantiation of the Hard and Mixed images considered below rests solely on the rules of proper procedure—these, of course, are for others to judge.

There is one last observation that I would make before turning to acknowledgments. My book is a critique of the "images" which are its subject matter. And in the course of criticizing I render many an unfavorable judgment on the works containing the images and, indirectly, the men who wrote the works. These unfavorable judgments, I am especially anxious to make clear, are to be understood as applying within a very narrow, circumscribed frame of reference only. They apply only to the thought of the authors as contained in the works in question, and not to their thought as a whole. They apply, moreover—and this point I shall have occasion to repeat several times—only to that thought as judged on the admittedly stringent standards set up in this text with an eye to *its* ultimate objective, and not on the standards which the author may have set up for himself with an eye to *his* objective. The adverse judgment on some of the histories considered in the text, for instance, therefore means only that I do not find in these histories what I am looking for and expected might be there, not that I do not find what the author promised would be there. Correlatively, the work upon which an adverse judgment is rendered for failure to perform the function in terms of which this text's standard of judgment runs may very well perform the function for which it was intended. Moreover, and in any case, all adverse judgments to one side, I wish to say here that I should have been proud to have written almost any of the works hereinafter reviewed.

This book, as indeed all books, is indirectly the product of many minds and many hands. It is a pleasure as it is a duty to acknowledge as much, and to thank those who contributed most. Among institutional contributors I wish especially to thank The Washington Center of Foreign Policy Research, which in appointing me a research associate in 1957–58 gave me the time needed to do the first thinking on the subject, and the University of Colorado, which in granting me a faculty fellowship in 1967–68 gave me the time to do the bulk of the research and some of the writing. Among individuals who helped and exhorted and supported there stands out first of all the late Arnold Wolfers, director of the research center above mentioned at the time of my association, and earlier Sterling professor of international relations at Yale, always a thinker and a gentleman of the first rank who was unfailing in his encouragement to follow the line of thought here carried to a conclusion. Others who helped greatly, and much more than they could have known, are my early teachers: Payson Wild, today vice-president and dean of faculties at Northwestern University, who through his lectures to students in international law at Harvard in the '30s taught me to respect and to strive constantly for lucidity in the organizing and presentation of ideas; the late Cecil Driver of Yale, teacher and lecturer extraordinary, who could bring order into the most complex and confused of materials and charge with excitement discussion of the dullest of political philosophies; the late Whitney Griswold of Yale, who although remembered by others mainly as president of that august institution, for me will always stand first as loyal friend, supporter, and stimulating mentor, whose wit and gift for colorful language made discussion of serious and professional matters an affair of endless delight as well as instruction; and Robert M.

MacIver, professor emeritus of political philosophy and sociology at Columbia, who among many other things taught me the value of wrestling with the meanings of elusive abstract concepts until they had been pinned down and made crystal clear and distinct. I gladly acknowledge a considerable debt too to my father-in-law, Elliott Dunlap Smith, one-time chairman of the department of economics at Yale and, later, provost of the Carnegie Institute of Technology, who constantly urged the importance of starting the business of exposition and explanation not from the point which was most convenient to the expositor or which seemed right from the point of view of pure logic, but from the point at which the reader would seem most likely to catch on, and who constantly urged the virtues of brevity and reconcilement to a product short of impossible perfection.

As for more recent contributions, I want publicly to express my thanks to two colleagues at the University of Colorado, Professor William Safran of the department of political science and Professor Kenneth E. Boulding of the department of economics, who generously read and criticized individual chapters. I acknowledge with great appreciation the work of Eloise Pearson, typist extraordinary who spent days of uncomplaining work putting the manuscript in shape. And I record with much gratitude the many and varied services of my research assistant, Miss Dorothy Nuttall, who in addition to performing ably in that position cheerfully did a thousand and one miscalled "little things" that in sum make for a big difference in the quality of an end product.

My final acknowledgment appears in the form of the dedication of the book, and I shall say no more here save that that dedication carries with it a deep and lasting affection.

W. W.

Boulder, Colorado
January 15, 1970

PART I: DESCRIPTION

CHAPTER 1

The Literature in Survey

That Americans have different ideas of what the USSR is and does is a truth verifiable on the most casual inspection of the outpourings of press, radio, and other media of communication. As a quick review of cartoons will suggest, for some Brezhnev sprouts horns and bears a close resemblance to Lucifer himself, for others he is the faceless administrator of unmatched efficiency and ruthlessness, while for still others he is, despite his Communist affiliation, the affable business competitor, a sort of *bourgeois malgré lui* toward whom the proper attitude is a mixture of wariness and respect. Yet a fourth though smaller group sees him as the earnest if ham-handed knight errant questing for peace. The corporate or most commonly held idea has over time shifted back and forth across this spectrum.[1]

Americans of academic connection too have different ideas of what the USSR is and is about, and this observation too is verifiable on casual inspection. To use their own language, members of this elite conjure up and develop divergent images of the state that is their common subject. More particularly, they conjure up and develop divergent images of how that state behaves toward other states—of its foreign policy or, as I prefer, external conduct.[2] The corporate academic image of the USSR and its external conduct also has shifted with the years back and forth across the spectrum.

To describe such of these images of Soviet external conduct as were

1. For an interesting survey, see Peter G. Filene, ed., *American Views of Soviet Russia, 1917–1965* (Homewood, Ill.: Dorsey Press, 1968).
2. I prefer "conduct" and shall employ it more often than "policy" because it is the broader term, and I believe we should be trying to get at behavior in all its breadth. However, I consider the more common "policy" (which I use in my title) as virtually synonymous, and writers who use it students who have in mind roughly the same phenomenon as I.

framed in the recent past, or 1959–68;[3] to identify precisely the points
of difference between them; to assess their soundness or unsoundness;
to suggest ways and means of producing likenesses more faithful to
the original and bringing what exist more nearly into a single focus—
these are the tasks which I have set myself in this book, the chapter
at hand initiating the inquiry by surveying the broad features of the
pertinent literature.

A SAMPLE OF LEADING WORKS

The literature in question is vast, taking diverse forms.[4] Besides
that of book or monograph dealing squarely with the subject or with
near-equivalents like Soviet foreign relations, it takes the form of
works dealing with the subject as part of a larger one: works on Soviet
government, on Soviet society in general, or on the Communist Party
of the Soviet Union; works on the foreign policies of a number of
nations or on international politics and relations in general; works on
the Soviet Bloc or on the Communist movement as a whole. It appears
as compilations of documents with prefatory essays. A significant part
of it is cast in the shape of articles: articles found in periodicals of
related focus like *World Politics* and *Foreign Affairs,* like the *International
Studies Quarterly* and the *Journal of Conflict Resolution,* like
Problems of Communism and the *Slavic Review,* or like the *Survey*
and *Soviet Studies* of British publication; articles which may subsequently be gathered into collections with running commentary. Its
authors come from a number of disciplines, writing from a number of
different perspectives, in a number of different idioms. They have a
wide variety of institutional connections and come from a wide variety
of social backgrounds.

3. So defined because 1959–68 is the decade immediately antedating the
writing of the bulk of this manuscript. I bring in some material of later
date in the context of the discussion of possible improvements dealt with
in Part III, especially Chapter 6.

4. For bibliographies the reader is directed to: Thomas T. Hammond, ed.,
Soviet Foreign Relations and World Communism (Princeton: Princeton University Press, 1965), of which more anon; Paul L. Horecky, ed., *Russia and
the Soviet Union* (Chicago: University of Chicago Press, 1965), especially
Part VII; and, for a brief one of recent date, that found at the back of Jan
Triska and David D. Finley, *Soviet Foreign Policy* (New York: Macmillan,
1968), pp. 440–73.

In consequence of this vastness and diversity, a survey that is to be more than superficial must proceed, if it is to proceed at all within acceptable limits of time and space, by invoking some sort of sampling device. And if the survey is to proceed soundly in service to the ultimate end of suggesting improvements in the images contained in the literature, it must begin by selecting a manageable sample of that literature that may fairly claim to be representative of its best.

As a rough-and-ready way of obtaining such a sample I have taken a bibliography already at hand that covers publications through 1963 —Thomas Hammond's massive *Soviet Foreign Relations and World Communism;* extracted therefrom such books published in 1959–63 as are or contain academicians' treatments of the subject at once comprehensive and of some length; and completed the list by taking such works from the bibliographic sections at the end of periodicals of related focus, most notably *Problems of Communism* and the quarterly *Foreign Affairs,* as were published in the years 1964–68 and seemed to me to share the features of the Hammond selections.[5] By a comprehensive treatment I understand one that is "general," and "general" in the two senses of covering many aspects of Soviet conduct rather than one or two alone (as "aims" or "military strategy" or "treaty-making") and of covering conduct toward many or all other nations rather than one or two only (Germany, China) or a single region (the Middle or Far East). In classifying a treatment as "general" or not I have taken as controlling, with minor modifications, inclusion of the related book within Hammond's Part I, the contents of which are similarly defined.[6] By treatment of some length I understand one that makes up the whole or a significant part of the book that contains it as against a single chapter or article. The rough presumption here is that the more complete and extended a job, the more thorough and better all around.

Table 1 is the result of this operation. Sixteen of its 22 titles are the

5. Bibliographic sections of *Foreign Affairs* that were culled are those labeled "General" and "Eastern Europe and the Soviet Union."

6. Part I is defined (though more implicitly than explicitly) by the plurality of geographic areas and aspects of foreign relations covered, Part II being differentiated on the grounds of being confined to works primarily on one area or country, Part III to works on a single aspect such as ideology, military power, etc.

TABLE 1

Soviet External Conduct: A Sample of Leading Works Containing Recent Treatments by American Academicians[a]

Author(s)	Full Title	Place	Publisher	Year
Bouscaren, Anthony T.	Soviet Foreign Policy: A Pattern of Persistence	New York	Fordham U.	1962
Dallin, David J.	Soviet Foreign Policy after Stalin	Philadelphia	Lippincott	1961
Fleming, Denna F.	The Cold War and Its Origins: 1917–1960[b]	Garden City, N.Y.	Doubleday	1961
Gehlen, Michael P.	The Politics of Coexistence: Soviet Methods and Motives	Bloomington	Indiana U.	1967
Goodman, Elliot R.	The Soviet Design for a World State	New York	Columbia U.	1960
Halle, Louis J.	The Cold War as History	New York	Harper & Row	1967
Kennan, George F.	Russia and the West under Lenin and Stalin	Boston	Little, Brown	1961
Kintner, William R.[c]	The New Frontier of War: Political Warfare, Present and Future	Chicago	Regnery	1962
Kulski, Wladyslaw W.	Peaceful Coexistence: An Analysis of Soviet Foreign Policy	Chicago	Regnery	1959
Librach, Jan	The Rise of the Soviet Empire: A Study of Soviet Foreign Policy[d]	New York	Praeger	1965
Lukacs, John	A New History of the Cold War[e]	Garden City, N.Y.	Doubleday	1966
Mosely, Philip E.	The Kremlin and World Politics: Studies in Soviet Policy and Action	New York	Vintage	1960

TABLE 1 *(Continued)*

Author(s)	Full Title	Place	Publisher	Year
Overstreet, Harry[f]	The War Called Peace: Khrushchev's Communism	New York	Norton	1961
Schuman, Frederick L.	The Cold War: Retrospect and Prospect[g]	Baton Rouge	Louisiana State U.	1967
Schwartz, Harry E.	The Red Phoenix: Russia since World War II	New York	Praeger	1961
Shulman, Marshall D.	Beyond the Cold War	New Haven	Yale U.	1966
Shulman, Marshall D.	Stalin's Foreign Policy Reappraised	Cambridge	Harvard U.	1963
Strausz-Hupé, Robert[h]	Protracted Conflict[i]	New York	Harper & Row	1963
Triska, Jan F.[j]	Soviet Foreign Policy	New York	Macmillan	1968
Tucker, Robert C.	The Soviet Political Mind: Studies in Stalinism and Post-Stalin Change	New York	Praeger	1963
Ulam, Adam B.	Expansion and Coexistence: The History of Soviet Foreign Policy 1917–67	New York	Praeger	1968
Wolfe, Bertram D.	Communist Totalitarianism: Keys to the Soviet System[k]	Boston	Beacon	1961

a. Compiled by process described in text from Thomas T. Hammond, ed., *Soviet Foreign Relations and World Communism,* and from the bibliographies at the back of *Foreign Affairs* and the reviews in *Problems of Communism.*

b. Two vols.

c. With Joseph Z. Kornfeder.

d. Rev. ed., 1st ed. appeared in 1964.

e. Third ed., expanded, of *A History of the Cold War* (1st ed., 1961; 2nd ed. 1962).

f. And Bonaro Overstreet.

g. Second ed.; 1st ed. appeared in 1962.

h. And William R. Kintner, James E. Dougherty, and Alvin J. Cottrell.

i. Harper Colophon ed.; 1st ed. appeared in 1959.

j. And David D. Finley.

k. Rev. ed. of *Six Keys to the Soviet System* (1956).

most recent editions of what the editors of the Hammond bibliography, with minor modifications, inferentially consider to be or to contain the kind of treatment sought for the years 1959–63.[7] The remaining six (Gehlen, Halle, Librach, Shulman's *Beyond the Cold War*, Triska and Ulam) are 1964–68 publications noted in the bibliographic sections referred to (and especially that of *Foreign Affairs*) that appear to have the same features as the Hammond 16. The 22 in sum accordingly represent for purposes of this inquiry the leading exemplars of the literature under scrutiny—and stand, if you will, for the best of recent American academic studies of the subject. And it is upon them that attention will henceforth center.

The credentials of Table 1, which comprise the credentials of bibliographies and authors besides the credentials of the principles of selection set forth above, are thoroughly respectable. Those of the Hammond bibliography are impeccable. The Hammond describes as its general aim the choosing of works of greatest value to scholars, and it implies, on the negative side, the objective of eliminating "ephemeral works, polemical tracts, and books which deal with the subject only tangentially."[8] "Value to scholars" in turn is judged by such qualities as information contained, comprehensiveness, reliability,

7. The modifications referred to are the exclusion from consideration, on various grounds of insufficiency of scope and length as indicated, the following Hammond entries: A5, John Armstrong's *The Politics of Totalitarianism* (1961), which in centering on internal political history gives small attention to external affairs; A6, Terence Armstrong's *The Russians in the Arctic* (1958), because of its obvious geographic limitation; A43, George Kennan's *Soviet Foreign Policy 1917–1941* (1960), because its 115-page introduction to a collection of documents for the period covers ground better covered in his book of the following year; all titles of sections B and C, which are confined temporally to the four years 1917–21; F14 and F16, Herbert Feis's *Between War and Peace* (1960) and *Japan Subdued* (1961), because of the temporal narrowness of their subjects; F20, Matthew P. Gallagher's *The Soviet History of World War II* (1963), because it centers on Soviet appraisals of Soviet conduct; G2, Zbigniew Brzezinski's *The Soviet Bloc* (1961), which concentrates almost exclusively on Soviet relations with other Communist countries; and G117, the Columbia-Harvard Research Group's *United States Foreign Policy: USSR and Eastern Europe* (1960), which as a study conducted for the Senate Committee on Foreign Relations has so practical an orientation as to be sharply distinguished from the other listings.

8. Hammond, *Soviet Foreign Relations and World Communism*, p. viii.

and objectivity, and representativeness of various views.[9] More than one hundred Sovietologists participated directly or indirectly in the editing, including many figures of renown in the field.[10] While the product is not without flaws, one finds it hard to quarrel with the summary judgment entered by a British review—namely, that the work is one of "outstanding merit."[11] The credentials of *Foreign Affairs* and Henry Roberts, until recently its chief bibliographer, I assume hardly need defense, as I assume also of *Problems of Communism* and its editor (Abraham Brumberg).

The credentials of the authors in Table 1 are also impressive. The 21 individuals comprising this group[12] have almost without exception had extensive associations with one or more of the country's top institutions of higher learning—Harvard, Yale, Columbia, Princeton, Pennsylvania, Duke, California, Stanford, etc. Again, they have at one time or another almost all held posts with the federal government, the younger ones (Gehlen, Goodman) and those of less orthodox views (Fleming, Schuman) being the principal exceptions. Mosely served during the war and immediate postwar periods on a number of important coordinating committees of the Allied powers. Kennan spent years as a foreign service officer in Moscow and headed State's Policy Planning Staff under Acheson, besides serving for various periods as ambassador to the USSR and Yugoslavia. Halle also served on State's Policy Planning Staff, Tucker also as a foreign service officer in Moscow. Shulman and Wolfe have held important posts with the State Department, Kintner an assignment with the National Security Council, Strausz-Hupé a consultantship with the Department of the Army. Kulski and Librach were members of the Polish diplomatic service before emigrating to this country. Harry Schwartz, once an intelligence analyst in Washington, has for years been also a professional member of an institution scarcely less prestigious than government itself—the *New York Times*. Almost all, again, are the authors of numerous books on Soviet affairs or connected topics.

Table 1 is not without its faults. The method on which it is based,

9. Ibid., p. ix.
10. Ibid., pp. 1161–73.
11. *Times Literary Supplement,* August 26, 1965.
12. The number excludes co-authors (Kornfeder, Bonaro Overstreet, Cottrell, Dougherty, and Finley).

culling bibliographies for work containing comprehensive and extended studies, would no doubt scandalize the physicist or chemist as a method of sampling the "best" of a universe (if, indeed, the insertion of the affective term in the description of the end sought had not made him immune to further shock). The resultant list, it will be apparent to students in the field, leaves out on one ground or the other much of value. It omits on grounds of insufficient generality such first-rate treatises as Alexander Dallin's *The Soviet Union at the United Nations*,[13] Jan F. Triska and Robert M. Slusser's *The Theory, Law, and Policy of Soviet Treaties*,[14] the works on military strategy of Herbert Dinerstein, Raymond Garthoff, and Thomas Wolfe,[15] and studies of Soviet relations with bloc, East Europe, China, etc., too numerous to mention.[16] It excludes on grounds of length such excellent documentaries *cum* commentary as Xenia Eudin and Robert Slusser's *Soviet Foreign Policy 1928–1934,* and Alvin Rubinstein's *The Foreign Policy of the Soviet Union.*[17] It passes over, also on grounds of length, many excellent articles, of which generous examples are to be found in such collections as Alexander Dallin's *Soviet Conduct in World Affairs* and Robert Goldwin's *Readings in Russian Foreign Policy,*[18] Ivo Lederer's *Russian Foreign Policy,* and Philip Mosely's *The Soviet Union 1922–62: A Foreign Affairs Reader.*[19] Also not to be found on the list—although for reason now of

13. New York: Praeger, 1962.

14. Stanford, Cal.: Stanford University Press, 1962.

15. For instance, Herbert Dinerstein, *War and the Soviet Union,* rev. ed. (New York: Praeger, 1962); Raymond Garthoff, *Soviet Strategy in the Nuclear Age,* rev. ed. (New York: Praeger, 1962); and Thomas Wolfe, *Soviet Strategy at the Crossroads* (Cambridge: Harvard University Press, 1964). Also deserving mention in this connection is Arnold L. Horelick and Myron Rush, *Strategic Power and Soviet Foreign Policy* (Chicago: University of Chicago Press, 1966).

16. For bibliography on relations with World Communist system see Triska and Finley, *Soviet Foreign Policy,* pp. 457–60.

17. Eudin and Slusser (2 vols.) was published in 1966 (University Park: Pennsylvania State University Press), Rubinstein (2nd ed.) in 1966 (New York: Random House).

18. Respectively, New York: Columbia University Press, 1960, and New York: Oxford University Press, 1959.

19. Respectively, New Haven: Yale University Press, 1962, and New York: Praeger, 1963 (published for the Council on Foreign Relations).

the imponderables shaping Mr. Hammond's and my choices rather than for lack of comprehensiveness and length—are a few (however, a very few) works of unquestioned merit that others might quite as reasonably include.[20] And excluded too, of course, because of the constraints of time, are certain post-1968 publications of substance.[21] Finally, the roster of authors lacks a number of names highly regarded, and rightly so, for their labors in the vineyard—names like Aspaturian, Barghoorn, Brzezinski, and Roberts.

Yet one is not looking for the rigor of mathematician or statistician in these matters, as indeed one cannot. And when all the above is granted, one can still claim for the 22 works in question that they would probably overlap appreciably with another 22 independently selected, the segments of entries not repeated differing little in quality from one another. And one can therefore further claim that they *fairly* approximate a true microcosm of the best, and that inferences based upon them are *fairly* generalizable to the whole of that best. At the least, the underlying method minimizes such influences as any bias of this analyst might exert.

THE SCOPE OF THE SAMPLE

Examination of the larger, more formal characteristics of the constituents of our sample yields a number of interesting observations. Whether it be addressed to scope and orientation, to approach, or to findings, scrutiny has some rather surprising results. Table 2 presents schematically the relevant data.

Examination discloses first the dearth of works that are on target, if one takes the target to be the dispassionate discussion of Soviet external conduct from 1917 to recent times. One is initially struck in this connection by how few of the titles confine themselves to such conduct, how many discuss it not in convenient isolation but within

20. I would cite only Robert D. Warth's *Soviet Russia in World Politics* (New York: Twayne Publishers, 1963), Herbert S. Dinerstein's monograph, *Fifty Years of Soviet Foreign Policy* (Baltimore: Johns Hopkins Press, 1968), and perhaps one or two more of the volumes on the Cold War, such as Walter LaFeber's *America, Russia, and the Cold War, 1945–1966* (New York: John Wiley, 1967). All of these are histories, Dinerstein's a treatment of only 73 pages.

21. See n. 29 below.

TABLE 2

Soviet External Conduct: Major Formal Characteristics of Sample of Leading Works

Author[a]	Short Title[b]	Year[c]	Subject[d]	Scope Time[e]	Approach[f]
(1)	(2)	(3)	(4)	(5)	(6)
Bouscaren	Soviet Foreign Policy	1962	PR	ABCD	AH
Dallin	Soviet Foreign Policy after Stalin	1961	PR	CD	H
Fleming	The Cold War and Its Origins	1961	ex	ABCD	H
Gehlen	The Politics of Coexistence	1967	PR	D	A
Goodman	The Soviet Design for a World State	1960	PR	ABCD	AH
Halle	The Cold War as History	1967	ex	BCD	H
Kennan	Russia and the West	1961	ex	AB	H
Kintner	The New Frontier of War	1962	ex	ABCD	A
Kulski	Peaceful Coexistence	1959	PR	ABCD	A
Librach	The Rise of the Soviet Empire	1965	PR	ABCD	AH
Lukacs	A New History of the Cold War	1966	ex	CD	AH
Mosely	The Kremlin and World Politics	1960	PR	BCD	C
Overstreet	The War Called Peace	1961	in	D	A
Schuman	The Cold War	1967	ex	ABCD	AH
Schwartz	The Red Phoenix	1961	in	CD	C
Shulman	Beyond the Cold War	1966	ex	CD	AH
Shulman	Stalin's Foreign Policy Reappraised	1963	PR	C	AH
Strausz-Hupé	Protracted Conflict	1963	ex	ABCD	A
Triska	Soviet Foreign Policy	1968	PR	ABCD	A
Tucker	The Soviet Political Mind	1963	in	CD	C
Ulam	Expansion and Coexistence	1968	PR	ABCD	H
Wolfe	Communist Totalitarianism	1961	in	BCD	C

a. For first names, those of colleagues if any, see Table 1 above.
b. For full titles, see Table 1 above.
c. Of publication.
d. Scope of subject matter covered; ex = focus external to USSR (usually relations between it and West); in = focus beyond foreign policy proper (usually the whole of the internal society); PR = focus on USSR foreign policy proper.

e. Scope of time period covered in some depth; A = 1917–39, or pre-World War II; B = 1939–45 or War; C = 1945–53, or Stalinist postwar; D = 1953 and on, or post-Stalinist.
f. A = analytical and H = historical, with italics indicating major emphasis where both are found; C = collection (of articles or essays).

the context of material of broader reference. Metaphorically speaking, the metal we are looking for occurs, more often than not, not in pure form but embedded in various ores, from which it can be extracted only with effort. Twelve, or about 55 percent, of the sample center on other though related topics (Table 2, Column 4). Eight of these center on broader topics external to the Soviet Union: on the Cold War or relations with the West (Fleming, Halle, Kennan, Lukacs, Schuman, and Shulman–CW)[22] or on the behavior of international communism (Kintner and Strausz-Hupé). Four center on broader topics internal to the Soviet Union, namely, Soviet society in its totalitarian totality (Overstreet, Schwartz, and Wolfe) or, in Tucker's case, its political mentality and outlook. These 12, in somewhat different words, concentrate on matters in which Soviet external conduct is properly speaking one element and one only, making treatment of that conduct incidental to the treatment of something more inclusive. Conversely, these works give to other elements like Western or American conduct, or internal economic or cultural policy, equal attention. Only 10 works, in contrast, focus sharply on Soviet foreign policy proper, these being Bouscaren, Dallin, Gehlen, Goodman, Kulski, Librach, Mosely (with certain reservations), Shulman-FP, Triska, and Ulam.

One is further struck by how few of the works deal with their subject matter over the full span of Soviet rule (Table 2, Column 5). While one or two points involved in the overall judgment are disputable, it is nevertheless by and large true that 12 of the 22 titles— again, about 55 percent—have nothing or very little to say on one or more of the four large periods into which one might provisionally divide Soviet diplomatic history: pre-1939, 1939–45, 1945–53, and 1953 on. Kennan virtually ends his story at 1945, treating the postwar era in a single, very general chapter. Halle, Mosely, and Wolfe start their stories, generally speaking, with 1939. Six works concentrate almost exclusively on the postwar era (Dallin, Lukacs, Schwartz, both Shulmans, and Tucker), having little to say on earlier periods; while of these Shulman-FP virtually ends its account with 1953. Two works

22. As a shorthand method of distinguishing the two Shulmans, I shall refer to *Beyond the Cold War* as "Shulman-CW" and *Stalin's Foreign Policy Reappraised* as "Shulman-FP."

(Gehlen and Overstreet) are concerned only with the post-Stalin times. Only 10, therefore, can be said to treat in reasonable depth all periods to the time of writing: Bouscaren, Fleming, Goodman, Kintner, Kulski, Librach, Schuman, Strausz-Hupé, Triska, and Ulam. In consequence of the foregoing distributions in combination, only six of the sample both center on the topic of central concern and cover it in its temporal entirety, namely, Bouscaren, Goodman, Kulski, Librach, Triska, and Ulam. Only one in about four of the representative list, in other words, deals squarely with Soviet foreign policy from 1917 to the present. One could with reason increase this number by two, for Kintner and Strausz-Hupé consider the subject on which formally they focus, the behavior of international communism, as in effect synonymous with Soviet behavior. But even as reconstituted the number is scarcely one-third the total.

Though this result is less surprising, one is struck last in this connection by how few of the works are strictly dispassionate in tone and orientation. To be sure, whether one looks at avowed purpose or execution, in this reader's judgment—and the determination has to be in large part subjective—the constituents of the sample are more concerned on balance with information and instruction than with moving the reader to action in one direction or another. By and large they evidence a contemplative rather than a manipulative intent (Lasswell's terms), they are (Bentham's terms) expositorial rather than censorial, they are bent on description rather than prescription. They are therefore all, in this reader's judgment, to be classified on balance as serious studies as against political tracts or polemics. However this may be too generous an estimate: Triska, for one, notes a high polemical content.[23] And in any event, in all but a few cases the emotive strain, if not predominating, at least lies always close to the surface.

With several of the works, a practical aim is almost as important as the aim of understanding. Fleming, for instance, baldly describes his treatise on the Cold War as an effort to forestall the end of the American dream and of Western civilization. Goodman proposes to make Soviet objectives clearer to the understanding, and then to inquire what they imply by way of appropriate Western responses.

23. Triska and Finley, *Soviet Foreign Policy*, p. xiii.

Kennan allows as part of his concern correcting the misinterpreta-
tions of the historical record which he believes his Soviet counterparts have been guilty of purveying. Kintner wants to disseminate an
improved understanding of Communist strategy and technique in the
further interest of strengthening our ways of coping with them.
Wolfe wants to help produce a more informed and intelligent citi-
zenry.[24]

Insofar as execution in the large is concerned, a number of works
have significant chapters or sections of a prescriptive character. Goodman's concluding chapter for instance gives his ideas on what the
Western response should be to the kind of Soviet behavior delineation
of which is set forth in the first 13 chapters. Kennan's final chapter, "Keeping a World Intact," exhorts the public to learn to take a
less *simpliste* view of the world, which is to him the lesson to be
learned from his analysis of Soviet-Western relations of the past.
Kintner, in his Part Three, "Counterattack"; the Overstreets, in their
Chapter 17, on "Too Late for Credulity"; Wolfe, in his last chapter,
"Communist Vulnerability and United States Foreign Policy"—all try
to draw the conclusions in terms of what American policy should or
should not be, how it should or should not react, in the light of the
findings on Soviet behavior earlier revealed.

Some works, moreover, allow an emotive strain to creep into chapter titles. One might cite in this connection Fleming's chapter on the
Korean War called "The Crucifixion of Korea," Kulski's chapter on
Soviet relations with the Communist countries of East Europe, which
he calls "Soviet Colonial Protectorates," Librach's chapter on Soviet
relations with underdeveloped countries, which he entitles "New
Worlds to Conquer," and a chapter subdivision of Strausz-Hupé
named "The Communist 'Scavengers of Revolution.'" In two cases
the emotive strain may be said to reach even into the book's title: I

24. Denna F. Fleming, *The Cold War and Its Origins: 1917–1960*, 2 vols.
(Garden City, N.Y.: Doubleday, 1961), p. xi; Elliot R. Goodman, *The Soviet
Design for a World State* (New York: Columbia University Press, 1960), p.
xvi; George F. Kennan, *Russia and the West under Lenin and Stalin* (Boston:
Little, Brown, 1961), pp. vii–viii; William R. Kintner and Joseph Z. Korn-
feder, *The New Frontier of War* (Chicago: Regnery, 1962), p. viii; Bertram
D. Wolfe, *Communist Totalitarianism*, rev. ed. (Boston: Beacon Press, 1961),
p. xv.

refer to the Overstreets' *The War Called Peace: Khrushchev's Communism*, and Librach's *The Rise of the Soviet Empire*.

As far as detail of execution is concerned, and here I anticipate somewhat, most of the works exchange occasionally, and some exchange frequently, language neutral in tone for affective description or polemics against advocates of contrary view. These divide according to the direction of movement in which they seek to impel. On the one hand lie those whose concern is alerting the reader to the full magnitude of the Soviet threat as they see it, and warning him against heeding the siren call of "wishful thinkers" who hold a less bleak view of the enemy and his intentions. In this category belong in varying degree Bouscaren, Dallin, Goodman, Kintner, Kulski, Librach, the Overstreets, Strausz-Hupé, and Wolfe. On the other side lie the works of Fleming and, despite his abjuration of advocacy or defense, Schuman. These tend to excuse Soviet misdemeanors, chide American cold warriors, and plead for understanding and restraint toward the Soviets—or, in Schuman's case, for joining with the Soviets in world government. Halle, Kennan, and Lukacs are also liberal with affective language, though applying it more evenly to the two parties to the Cold War. Somewhat more restrained than these three, Ulam is equally even in his application.

The number of works which meet even the modest degree of unruffledness of expression that one can reasonably expect of a social scientist is accordingly small. I would cite only seven, although the judgment must be in high degree subjective, and others might justly find more. These seven are Gehlen, Mosely, Schwartz, the two Shulmans, Triska, and Tucker.

THE APPROACHES OF THE SAMPLE

Examination of the works of the sample shows, second, a dearth of analyses. Classified on the basis of the approach to or mode of handling the subject matter, the 22 works fall into three categories (Table 2, Column 6)—namely, collections, histories, and analyses. Four of them fall into the first group. Eleven are wholly or primarily histories. Only the residual seven belong to the final, or most sophisticated, category of analysis.

The four collections are the works of Mosely, Schwartz, Tucker, and Wolfe. These four, comprised of articles or book chapters written at various times over spans of from six (Tucker) to 21 (Mosely) years, were structured at the time of writing by no single principle. They form integrated wholes (to the extent, indeed, that they do) by virtue of the retrospective application, separately or in combination, of three techniques: provision of an introduction and/or conclusion to serve as summary; provision of section headings and a pattern of organization to lend at least the appearance of structure; and provision of running commentary to act as a sort of glue joining together disparate parts in the interest of continuity and flow. Mosely, which alone of the four deals predominantly with Soviet foreign policy, is probably the least satisfactory in mounting an integrated attack; though the 25 essays, covering the 21 years 1938–59, are grouped sensibly, largely on a chronological principle, he lacks any truly summary section. Schwartz's self-characterization is "essentially one observer's journalistic history of the Soviet Union since World War II," the constituent articles (originally out of the *New York Times)* having been "knit together by what this writer hopes is enough additional connecting material to provide a coherent whole."[25] IIis opening and concluding chapters, written for the occasion, frame intervening sections which are organized topically. Tucker, about two-fifths of whose book deals with Soviet foreign policy, organizes his 10 essays reasonably into three sections treating in order change in the Soviet system and certain internal and external relations respectively (my terms), prefacing the whole with an introduction sounding a common theme. Wolfe, about one-third of whose 25 subdivisions deal with Soviet foreign policy proper, organizes these essays from a span of nearly 20 years under the concept "Key," each group purporting to deal with one of the distinguishing facets of Soviet totalitarianism like "The Struggle for Power" and "The Coordination of Culture." Like Mosely, Wolfe's book lacks any truly unifying section.

All in all, none of the four can fairly be called integrated, as manifesting an integral approach. Structure is mechanical; in only one case (Schwartz) is a true summary attempted—and that with indifferent success; and save possibly in the cases of Tucker and Wolfe, global

25. Harry E. Schwartz, *The Red Phoenix* (New York: Praeger, 1961), pp. xi–xii.

theorems or leitmotivs are conspicuous for their absence. The remark
of one of the reviewers of Tucker—namely, that the 10 essays "bear
the marks of different origins and purposes"[26]—can be extended to
the others as well, as can the criticism of one of Schwartz's reviewers
to the effect that for all its informativeness and astuteness of observation, it " . . . falls far short of the mark of a 'history' of Russia's
rise from the ashes of war, for it lacks the scope, synthesis, documentation, and perspective that a genuine historical account should
contain."[27]

The 11 histories of the sample divide almost equally between those
which are purely that (five) and those which contain a slight amount
—usually a chapter or two—of analysis. The former group consists
of Dallin, Fleming, Halle, Kennan, and Ulam. The primary (chronological) division may run in terms of supposed periods of years or
lesser units down to a year or less (Fleming), the time unit being
labeled by the principal event or series thereof or development
(Fleming—"After Roosevelt, April–August 1945"; "After Hiroshima,
August–November 1945"; "Rising Tension, November 1945–July
1946").Or it may run in terms of a leading actor or event (Kennan
and Halle), as instanced by Kennan's "The Provisional Government,"
"Brest-Litovsk," "Unofficial Allied Agents," The North Russian Intervention," "Collapse in the North," etc. The chronological principle
usually is at some point supplemented with a geographical one. Chapters may be left ungrouped, without any further attempt made to
bring order into the narrative—as with Kennan's 25, Halle's 39, and
Ulam's 12. Or they may be grouped into parts, as Fleming's 25
("Enemies and Allies, 1917–1945," "The Cold War in Europe, 1945–
1950," "The Cold War in East Asia, 1945–1955," and "The Second
Cold War, 1955–1959") and Dallin's 25 ("The International Situation of the Soviet Union at the End of the Stalin Era," "The Malenkov-
Molotov Era," "The First Khrushchev Era," "The New Course in the
Middle and Far East," and "Khrushchev in Command"). In any case,
what analysis there is (and in Halle's and especially Kennan's case
there is an appreciable amount) is confined to the interstices of a
primarily chronological account. Narrative is king.

26. *Times Literary Supplement,* March 26, 1964, p. 247.
27. *American Historical Review,* 67, no. 2 (January 1962): 492.

The six histories containing some formally heralded attempt at analysis are Bouscaren, Librach, Lukacs, Schuman, Shulman-*CW* and Shulman-*FP*. In Bouscaren and Librach this takes the form of two chapters which preface the historical narrative—"Ideology and Protracted Conflict" and "Strategy and Tactics" in Bouscaren's case; "Communist Doctrine and Soviet Foreign Policy" and "Peaceful Coexistence" in Librach's. In Shulman-*FP* the analysis is found in the initial and final chapters, on "Introduction to the Argument" and "The Evolution of Soviet Policy," which bracket the chronological story they interpret. Schuman and Shulman-*CW* bring analysis into the history of the Cold War (before, during, and after) which essentially they are telling by inserting chapters on the internal Soviet order and, in Shulman's case, on the changing international environment, that are related in a causal way to evolution in external conduct. Lukacs offers the most extended analysis, in the form of the entire second part of the book. Following Part I, which deals with the "Main Events" in the Cold War, he turns, in Part II, to "The Main Movements" and an effort to relate to the evolution of the American-Soviet relationship, in turn, the tendencies of the two societies and of their political theories, the development of their respective national interests and national characters, and the great historical movements of the time. These analyses, interesting though they are in themselves, are indifferently articulated with the historical narratives save only in the case of Schuman and the two Shulmans.

There remain the seven works of primarily analytic character. Since most of these will be dealt with in detail further on, only a word or so need be said at this point. The seven divide about evenly in the clarity of the attack they mount. Gehlen, Overstreet, Strausz-Hupé, and Triska proceed from a simple and direct framework. Gehlen is ordered on a reasonable plan, sections taking up in turn the basis of the post-Stalin policy of peaceful coexistence in internal political maneuver and ideology, the various particular aspects of the policy (military, economic, political, and ideological, the latter used now to mean manipulation of words), and its working out in the sphere of intrabloc politics. The Overstreets take up their subject, Khrushchevian behavior as a whole, under the three major headings, "Design" or objectives, "Weapons" or means, and "Battlegrounds" or particular forums of action. Strausz-Hupé attacks its topic, Communist doctrine viewed as the science and practice of conflict management, by looking first at the international setting, then at Communist strategy and the larger vision of conflict, next at various particular methods or techniques, and last at implications and consequences for the world and especially the United States. Triska, finally, bases his attack upon conceptions of the Soviet Union as a subsystem within the international system and the formulation of Soviet foreign policy as a case of decision-making. Following a first chapter summarizing the relevant history, he devotes his next three to the "four complex variables" of decision-making (namely, institutions, personalities, doctrine, and events) and the succeeding four to the geographic arenas in which the Soviets engage the rest of the international system (respectively, the Communist world, the developing areas, the West). A ninth chapter assesses Soviet conduct along the dimension of recklessness, while the tenth and eleventh treat of participation in the institutions of a common international order (international organizations and international treaties), and a final one recapitulates the entire book.

More involved, less coherent, are the frameworks from which operate the remaining three—Goodman, Kintner, and Kulski. Goodman, treating of Soviet objectives for the world, takes up first various formulations of that objective by Marx, Engels, and the Soviet Communists, then traces the influence on the concept of such subsequent developments as Russian nationalism and the establishment of the Soviet bloc, or the relationship to the concept of such other formulations as socialism in one country, peaceful coexistence, world language, the role of war, the withering of the state, and the debate between centralism and federalism. Kintner deals with a Communist technique called political warfare, which he believes to be "The New Frontier of War," under three headings dealing respectively with the implementary machinery, the battlegrounds (China, Southeast Asia, and Latin America), and the indicated counterattack. The first or main part deals with the Party, its conquest of power, its political-warfare and ideological techniques, its targets, its utilization of the Soviet state, its operations in the free world, and the resultant condition of war and the expanding conflict of systems. Last of the three, Kulski analyzes Soviet foreign policy in 14 long chapters containing a total of 100 sections. While one can only with difficulty penetrate to the

underlying order, it appears that the first nine chapters deal mainly
with doctrine, their topics being respectively: revolution; Russian
nationalism; the residue of the faith; morality, strategy and tactics; the
two- and three-camp theses; peaceful coexistence; current objectives;
nationality doctrine; and doctrine of the underdeveloped countries. The
last five, on the other hand, treat mainly of policy and the record,
their topics being policy toward the underdeveloped countries, Pancha
Shila and the record, colonial possessions, colonial protectorates, and
the international movement.

THE FINDINGS OF THE SAMPLE

Examination reveals, finally, that the findings of the representative
sample agree only within rather narrow limits. While there are some
uniformities, the disuniformities stand out. Although it is the proper
function of later chapters, and not the present one, to make the comparisons concerned, a few preliminary comments are in order.

The 22 works agree in a rough sort of way on the major events
constituting the historical record of the relationship between the
Soviet state and other states—the most important of the raw data
from which the images are to be constructed. They would not all of
them construct a chronology of these moves or happenings exactly
like that contained in Table 3, which has been taken with minor
amendment from a recent work commemorating 50 years of Soviet
rule.[28] Bouscaren and Librach, for example, would probably add to the
entries for 1945–48 the interventions in the East European countries
that contributed to their take-over by local Communists. Fleming
and Schuman would probably include the Western interventions of
1918–20 and Soviet support of Czechoslovakia at the time of the
Munich crisis of 1938. Kennan would almost surely want to take
note of certain events of the years between Rapallo and US recognition
such as the resumption (and subsequent rupture) of ties with Britain
in 1924. Many would probably omit the fighting at Stalingrad. But,
broadly speaking, the 22 would quarrel little over the proposition that
the discussion of Soviet conduct in a given stretch of time should
begin with the events marked by this table, for example, discussion

28. Harrison Salisbury, ed., *The Soviet Union: The Fifty Years* (New
York: Harcourt, Brace & World, 1967), pp. ix–xxii.

TABLE 3

Soviet External Conduct: Major Events and Periodization, 1917–67[a]

Quinq. & Year[b]	Major Events[c]	Periodization[d]
1st: 17	Take power; face counterrevolution supported by West and Japan	1917 (Nov.)
18	Sign Brest-Litovsk Treaty c Germany	Consolidation
19	Establish Comintern	
20	War with Poland; defeat Whites	
21	Sign Peace of Riga c Poland (initiate NEP)	1921 (March)
22	Sign Rapallo Treaty c Germany; found USSR	
2nd: 23		
24	(Lenin dies)	Normalization
25		
26		
3rd: 27		
28	(Initiate First Five-Year Plan)	1928 (July)
29		Isolation
30		
31		
32		
4th: 33	Recognized by US	1934 (Sept.)
34	Join League of Nations (begin purges)	
35	Sign Treaty c France; order United Front	Cooperation
36	Support Loyalists in Spanish War	
37	(Intensify purges, which continue till 1939)	
5th: 38		
39	Sign Nazi Pact; (Germany invades Poland); invade Poland, Finland; get Baltic bases; expelled from League	1939 (Aug.)
40	Get certain Finnish territory; incorporate Estonia, Latvia, Lithuania	Expansion—I
41	Conclude neutrality pact c Japan; invaded by Germany	1941 (June)

TABLE 3 *(Continued)*

Quing. & Year[b]		Major Events[c]	Periodization[a]
			1941 (June)
6th:	42	Sign Lend-Lease accord *c* US; fight at Stalingrad	Engagement in World War II
	43	Win at Stalingrad; dissolve Comintern; concert postwar plans with West at Teheran	
	44		
	45	Concert postwar plans *c* West at Yalta and Potsdam; war on Japan; join in UN (Germany surrenders; US drops atomic bombs; Japan surrenders)	1945 (Sept.)
	46		
	47	Meet *c* West at Moscow, disagreeing on Germany; refuse Marshall Plan aid; found Cominform	Expansion—II
7th:	48	Blockade Berlin; expel Yugoslavs from Cominform	
	49	Found COMECON; end Berlin blockade; explode atom bomb (Chinese Communists come to power)	1949 (May)
			Engagement in Cold War
	50	Boycott UN; sign Treaty *c* China (Korean War erupts; UN, US organize defense of South Korea)	
	51		
8th:	52	At 19th Party Congress affirm policy of peaceful coexistence	
	53	(Stalin dies, succeeded by Malenkov and Khrushchev); propose resumption normal relations *c* Yugoslavia; hail Korean armistice; explode hydrogen bomb	1953 (March)
	54	Meet *c* West at Berlin, *c* West and China at Geneva on Vietnam; sign accord *c* China	
	55	Sign Warsaw Pact, Austrian Treaty; Khrushchev visits Yugoslavia; meet at Geneva *c* West chiefs, later foreign ministers, reaching no agreement	Relaxation—I
	56	Khrushchev denounces Stalin; dissolve Cominform; crush Hungarian revolt (Polish riots lead to more autonomy)	1956 (Oct.)
9th:	57	(Khrushchev ousts antiparty group); test ICBM; launch Sputnik	
	58	(Khrushchev replaces Bulganin, who is later denounced)	
	59	Meet *c* West at Geneva on Berlin; Khrushchev visits US, Camp David; sign Antarctic Treaty; West agrees to 1960 summit meeting	Resumption of Cold War
	60	Shoot down, denounce U-2; Khrushchev breaks up Paris summit conference; Khrushchev acts up at UN; publish Manifesto of Communist Parties	

(Continued)

TABLE 3 *(Continued)*

Quinq. & Year[b]	Major Events[c]	Periodization[a]
61	Confer c US at Vienna; (Berlin Wall erected); resume testing; sever relations c Albania; (US-backed invasion of Cuba fails)	
62	Withdraw missiles from Cuba in face of US ultimatum, attacking Chinese criticism	1962 (Oct.)
10th: 63	Sign "hot-line" agreement c US and Test-Ban Treaty; ideological conference c China fails, dispute intensifying	
64	Continue quarrel c China; (Kosygin, Brezhnev replace Khrushchev); China explodes a bomb, first welcomes and then attacks new Soviet leaders	Relaxation—II
65	(North Vietnam shoots down US plane with Soviet missile)	
66	Continue denunciation of China	
67	Sign treaty outlawing nuclear weapons in outer space; Kosygin attends UN, confers with L. B. Johnson at Glassboro	Present

a. Adapted from Harrison Salisbury, ed., *The Soviet Union: The Fifty Years*, pp. ix–xxii.

b. Quinquennium and year.

c. Where sentence lacks a subject, "the Soviets" is to be understood. Moves of other nations not immediately affecting USSR are placed in parentheses, as are Soviet internal moves. The principal abbreviations used are: "c" for "with"; "West" for governments of Britain, France, the United States.

d. On the consensus of students in the field, as assessed by the writer.

of 1948–50 with the Berlin blockade, the expulsion of Yugoslavia from the Cominform, the establishment of COMECON, the first explosion of an atom bomb, the coming to power of the Chinese Communists, the boycott of the UN Security Council over refusal to admit Communist China, the Treaty of Alliance with China, and the Korean War.

There is also appreciable agreement on the periodization of the record and the broad characterization of the time divisions thereby formed. There is unanimous agreement on setting apart the war eras of 1917–21 (Revolution to Peace of Riga with Poland) and 1941–45 (German invasion of the USSR to the Japanese surrender). There is near-unanimous agreement on dividing the between-war years at 1928 with the Sixth Congress of the Comintern in July, at 1934 with entry into the League of Nations, and at 1939 with the August pact with the Nazis. The four-division split thereby resulting is contested only by a few who, like Kulski, see no break of consequence in 1928 or, like Kennan, Shulman-*FP*, and Ulam, see an added one in 1936. There is, moreover, near-unanimous agreement that the spring of 1953, with Stalin's death, marks a noteworthy change of direction. There is less agreement on where if at all to split the 1945–53 and 1953–present parts of the postwar era. However, while a few make no division of the former (unless, by way of dating the Cold War from 1947, as do Halle and Lukacs), a number see significant modification undergone in 1949, with NATO, the end of the Berlin blockade and establishment of separate German sovereignties (e.g. Lukacs, Mosely by implication, Shulman-*FP*, and Ulam), or in 1950, with the Chinese alliance and start of the Korean War (Bouscaren, Fleming). Again, while there is some dissent, a good number divide the post-Stalin era in 1955 with Khrushchev's accession to power, in 1956 with the ferment in Poland and Hungary, or in 1957 with Sputnik. For those who carry the story into the '60s, the fall of 1962 and the Grand Confrontation over Cuba (Halle and Lukacs), or the same in conjunction with the deepening of the split with China in 1963 (Ulam), mark a shift of considerable importance. Indeed, so substantial is the agreement on periodization as a whole that Table 3's schedule of eras, which represents my judgment of the consensus of students in the field, would evoke few objections. And the same is true in only slightly less degree, I believe, of the estimate of an "average" characterization of the successive time divisions which I supply in the same place.

Finally, there is a measure of agreement on the conclusions as to the nature of Soviet conduct and its evolution derived from contemplating this record. There is little dissent to be found in the works of the sample from the following propositions: that Soviet conduct is hardly to be described as peaceable, that its aims include the spread of communism and expansion of Soviet influence, that in pursuit of these aims it is active, militant, and not too moral, that it employs military force and the threat thereof cautiously, and that it treats its own, namely, other Communist states, no more considerately than the rest of the world. So, too, is there little dissent from these propositions: that Soviet conduct issues from motives other than altruistic, that it represents a disturbing influence in the world, and that it fluctuates over time, between more and less militant modes.

However, beyond all this lies only difference, divergence, dissent. The leading works may agree on the major events of the historical record. But they disagree often and strenuously on their relative weights, the relationship between them, the interpretation to be laid on them. Some see the Nazi Pact as a Soviet initiative, the outcome of a long and settled plan on Stalin's part to turn the Hitlerite threat west. Others see that Pact as a response, specifically a response to Western appeasement at Munich, and the Soviet reading of that appeasement as a Western attempt to turn the Hitlerite threat east. The leading works may also agree on the grouping of these events and the summary characterization of the periods so formed. But they disagree long and loud over further assessment and explanation. For some the expansionism of 1939–41 and 1945–49 is defensive, motivated by fear, while for others it is offensive, motivated by ambition. Finally, while they may agree on the nature of conduct as qualitatively conceived, in its totality and over the entire stretch of time investigated, and unite in seeing it as something less than peace-loving, they disagree sharply and acridly over the degree to which it exhibits this hostility, over the precise character of its causes and magnitude of its consequences, and over the extent and significance of the changes marked therein over time. It is these disagreements that make for the differences of image presently to be explored and evaluated.

For all its many excellent points, recent American academic literature on Soviet external conduct, taken in its broad characteristics, is deficient. It is deficient in full-span treatments centering on the topic proper, especially so in those of purely contemplative orientation. It is deficient in analyses. Within certain broad limits, it reaches radically diverse findings. These are the conclusions to which this chapter's survey ineluctably leads. Provided only that the sample selected is a reasonably accurate representation of the universe of the best works on the subject, this is where a review of the constituent titles takes one.

Of the 22 works scrutinized, on a general construction only eight can claim to center on the subject in its temporal entirety. Only seven of the 22 can claim on the whole to be analyses. Only five can do both (Goodman, Kintner, Kulski, Strausz-Hupé, and Triska). And, while analyzing conduct over the entire period from 1917 to date of writing, three of these (the first three) attack their subject from a conceptual framework of indifferent sophistication, four of them (the first four) betraying strong tendencies to exchange the role of expositor for that of censor and advocate. In short, with the notable exception of Triska, there exists no thoughtful, dispassionate analysis of the subject in its temporal entirety. True, the trend may be called moderately favorable, the most recent of the works (Triska and Ulam) being, as shall presently be documented, works of unusual merit. Yet the judgment remains substantially as rendered, and updating (to early 1970) the review on which it rests would mitigate its severity only slightly.[29]

29. As the most important of the publications which have appeared since 1968 I would list Richard F. Rosser's *An Introduction to Soviet Foreign Policy* (Englewood Cliffs, N.J.: Prentice-Hall, 1969), and Robert G. Wesson's *Soviet Foreign Policy in Perspective* (Homewood, Ill.: Dorsey Press, 1969). Both are dispassionate studies of the subject in its temporal entirety down to and including the 1968 invasion of Czechoslovakia, hence works of some merit, which is the reason for my agreeing in the text to some mitigation of the severity of my general judgment. But they are primarily histories rather than analyses, as such largely eschewing general characterization. And in the chapters in which they do turn to analysis (the first three in Rosser, the next to last in Wesson), they confine their attention almost wholly to the single issue of the role of ideology in conduct.

The 22 works agree generally that Soviet conduct on the whole hardly merits the adjective "peace-loving," which the Soviets use to describe themselves. They agree generally that the components of conduct, such as its aims and adherence to moral norms, likewise scarcely merit the plaudits of the civilized world, as the Soviets themselves think they do. But on the degree to which these summary judgments apply; on the precise character and magnitude of the causes and consequences of conduct so described; on the extent and significance of conduct's evolution over time—on these points there is not only disagreement, but often serious, deep-seated disagreement. To quote Triska again, "The scholarly consensus about Soviet foreign policy includes agreement upon most of the historical detail of what the Soviet Union has done in the international system, and very little more."[30]

These conclusions need to be accompanied by certain caveats. The very variety noted in respect to formal characteristics—the disparateness of scope, orientation, and attack; the presence of some works, notably among the histories, which resist the explicit drawing of general inferences that appear warranted by the data they present; the sheer complexity of a topic like state conduct, relevant categories for the consideration of which may be differently perceived and articulated by different observers, if indeed perceived and articulated at all above the subconscious level—these considerations necessarily impart to any summary judgment on findings a certain provisionality that the reader should always keep in mind. Also to be borne in mind is the fact that the extension of the conclusions to the entire universe— conclusions on both formal characteristics and findings—is no stronger than the sampling procedure, which is to say no stronger than the assumptions that the 22 works selected by Hammond, by the bibliographical sections of the two periodicals and especially *Foreign Affairs,* and by myself from the totality of general publications for 1959–68 are indeed fairly representative of the best that has been done.

Finally, fairness to the authors of the works of the sample compels the reminder that the adverse judgments here rendered say nothing about their merits measured on their own standards. That Mosely produced no integrated account of Soviet foreign policy in this context

30. *Soviet Foreign Policy,* p. xiii.

means nothing: he did not intend to. That Lukacs produced no systematic analysis in this connection has no significance: he intended only a history, and at that a history mainly of Soviet Russia's role in the Cold War. That Dallin covers only the postwar period is neither here nor there: he intended no more. And so with many others.

These points taken under advisement, however, the conclusions still stand. On the whole, in their larger figures, the academic output of the sort defined leaves much to be desired. Whether this applies also to the best of the sample and their correlative "images," individually differentiated and assessed in the fullness of their substantiating data and reasoning is the point to which, logically, inquiry next addresses itself.

CHAPTER 2

Major Types

As suggested in the preceding chapter, the most cursory review of the literature on Soviet external conduct turns up important differences of findings on the nature of that conduct. "Images" vary. One observer finds one shape or configuration as the result of his investigation. Another reports a second quite separate and distinct. This is hardly surprising. Indeed, arguing a priori, one would be quite surprised if some 20 students, coming from backgrounds uniform only in respect to membership in the academic fraternity, and setting out to treat a subject matter of enormous complexity and high controversiality, did *not* come up with different results.

If, however, the qualitative matter of the existence of a divergence of images may be taken as settled, being a point visible on casual inspection, this is not the case with such matters as the nature and extent of the differences. Nor is it the case with a matter such as the character of a sensible classification pointing up differences. To these further matters the instant chapter addresses itself, beginning with some definitions and a survey of suggestive existing schemes.

EXISTING CLASSIFICATIONS SURVEYED

A classification is an arrangement of a set of phenomena according to selected values of a given dimension or trait. Types are the subgroups thus formed. Instancing a classification of phenomena from the realm of social phenomena is Aristotle's breakdown of states according to the number of rulers.[1] The values he discriminated were rule by one, by few, and by many, and the names he gave the types thus formed were monarchy, aristocracy, and, for government of the many, state.

There is no inherent superiority of one system of classifying a given

1. *Politics*, 3.7.

30

set of phenomena over another. Arrangement according to values of one dimension is quite as valid as arrangements according to values of another. Pretensions to the contrary—the claims that System A is "natural," but System B "artificial"[2]—are error. What makes one system superior to another, apart from greater clarity of definition, are such matters as the greater ease with which the phenomena in question can be matched against the dimensions and values so defined, the greater relevance of the dimensions and values to the end for the sake of which inquiry has been instituted, etc. These are matters the determination of which may well take a certain amount of experimentation in the form of trial applications to the group involved. The division of living creatures according to habitat—sea, land, and air—though quite valid in itself, was superseded by the division according to internal structure because, through experience, the latter proved superior in achieving the end in view, namely, the efficient systemization of knowledge in the biological field.[3] Perhaps another way of putting the same thing is to say that a classification vindicates itself to the extent that it points to types of things radically distinguished from one another, that is, distinguished from one another in respect to not only one but many separate traits.

Existing classifications of behavior which may be helpful in establishing a scheme for the differentiation of images of Soviet conduct are to be found in the literature of students of individual conduct marching under the banner of psychology and ethics as well as literature of the students of international affairs. Classifications from the former which illuminate the problem are numerous. Erich Fromm in his *Man for Himself,* for example, develops a fivefold breakdown of human "characters" marked by a primary division into Nonproductive and Productive Orientations and a secondary division of the former into Receptive, Exploitative, Hoarding, and Marketing.[4] Receptives and Exploitatives alike see the goods of life (persons, things, ideas) as outside themselves. While the former, however, are dependent, relying on others to seize the goods for them, and are cheerful and optimistic, the latter are independent, grabbing for themselves, and are suspicious and cynical. Hoarders, having little faith

2. Morris R. Cohen and Ernest Nagel, *An Introduction to Logic and the Scientific Method* (New York: Harcourt, Brace, 1934), p. 223.

3. Ibid., pp. 223–24.

4. New York: Rinehart, 1947, pp. 62–107.

in getting goods they do not now possess, center on saving what they have, valuing security and order above all, and are clean, neat, and punctual. Marketers, seeing their personalities only as commodities, with an exchange value, change these to match the prevailing "image" and meet the demand of the day. Productive, finally, is the name Fromm gives to the "good man" of the classics of philosophy, the man Fromm would have all men be: reasonable, loving, imaginative, creative. Others have offered simpler breakdowns: Jung his introverts and extroverts, James his tough- and tender-minded, contemporary popularizers their self- and other-directed. Students of ethics have used a threefold scheme made up of types whose guiding principles are, respectively: "Mine is Mine, and Thine is Mine" (the Sinner); "Mine is Mine, and Thine is Thine" (perhaps Everyman); and, finally, "Mine is Thine, and Thine is Thine" (the Saint). These three correspond fairly well, in the order given, to Fromm's Exploitative, Hoarding, and Productive orientations.

Schemes from psychology and ethics, of which the above are probably a fair sample, are helpful in stimulating the imagination and encouraging recognition of logical possibilities on a very abstract plane. But beyond this they offer little. Fromm's, for instance, is unduly complex, is founded on a mélange of principles inadequately articulated and systematized, mixes categories derived directly from experience with one (the Productive character) concededly not so derived, and uses concepts ("cheerful," "clean," changing personalities) that scarcely could be usefully applied to national actors. Jung's and James's refer to mental states hard to get at and deal with even when those to whom they belong are individual human beings.

Classifications from the literature of state as opposed to personal conduct have been less numerous, more primitive, less elaborate. As early as 1660, Harrington drew a distinction in the behavior of "empires" which adumbrated a line of thought that has been with us ever since. Empires, he said, could be either empires of increase, interested in enlarging their dominion, or empires of preservation, interested only in preserving what they already had.[5] Nearly 300 years later, an American scholar, Charles O. Lerche, Jr., addressing himself to the

5. James Harrington, *The Commonwealth of Oceana,* reprinted in Francis W. Coker, *Readings in Political Philosophy,* rev. and enl. ed. (New York: Macmillan, 1938), pp. 517–18.

same point, had nothing to add. Said Lerche, there is a "basic principle in international politics: there are only two major types of strategic purpose" a nation can adopt in its dealings with other nations, and these are the strategies of either the promotion or the protection of common values.[6] Writing several years before Lerche, in the most celebrated textbook on international relations of its day, Hans Morgenthau extended somewhat the classification. Morgenthau distinguishes "three typical international policies," corresponding to three typical or basic patterns of politics, whether domestic or international. These are policies tending to keep power, called "status quo," policies aimed at acquiring more power through a reversal of existing power relations, called "imperialism," and a policy of demonstrating power, called "prestige."[7] Proceeding more cleanly and elegantly, Arnold Wolfers distinguishes policies by reference to three objectives of "self-extension," "self-preservation," and "self-abnegation."[8] Self-extension implies the acquisition of values (territory, domination, redress of grievances, emancipation from foreign control, etc.) not already enjoyed. Self-preservation means the maintenance, protection, or defense of the existing distribution of values, usually called the status quo. Self-abnegation means the quest for goals transcending the national interest narrowly conceived, like international solidarity, lawfulness, rectitude, or peace. The promotion/protection dichotomy is echoed, with differences of terminology and emphasis, by a number of other contemporary authors as, for instance, Frederick Schuman.[9] So too is the extension/preservation/abnegation triad, which Haas and Whiting, for instance, have taken over.[10]

These efforts at typing leave something to be desired. The Lerche dyad, good as far as it goes, is incomplete. It is conceptually stunted.

6. *The Cold War and After* (Englewood Cliffs, N.J.: Prentice-Hall, 1965), pp. 23–24. See also, for somewhat more extended discussion, Charles O. Lerche, Jr., *Concepts of International Relations* (Englewood Cliffs, N.J.: Prentice-Hall, 1963), pp. 18–22.

7. *Politics among Nations,* 3rd ed. (New York: Knopf, 1960), p. 39.

8. *Discord and Collaboration* (Baltimore: Johns Hopkins Press, 1962), p. 91.

9. *International Politics,* 2nd ed. (New York: McGraw-Hill, 1937), pp. 498–500.

10. Ernst B. Haas and Allen S. Whiting, *Dynamics of International Relations* (New York: McGraw-Hill, 1956), p. 59.

The mind cries out for recognition of the remaining logical possibility, call it contraction, retraction, liquidation, or what you will. Nor does Morgenthau's third term provide what is needed: either a quest for prestige is a form of the quest for maintaining power, in which case it is a spurious and not a genuine third possibility, or it is a possibility arrived at by adding a new principle to the one which distinguishes status quo from imperialism, in which case it renders the complete schema quite impure. Wolfers' triad, because it does fill the logical lacuna, and provides what is missing, is the best of the three. Yet some of his elaboration raises questions, as his discussion of the limits of "self" and his suggestion that the quest for self-preservation may, under the banner of security, often be practically indistinguishable from the quest for self-extension.[11]

To these meager pickings from the standard texts on international politics, the more recent, more recondite literatures of foreign policy analysis and of comparative foreign policy have little to add. The list of works constituting the former is not a long one.[12] The "systems" approach to the study of relations between nations has tended to preempt thoughtful analytic effort bent in the general direction. George Modelski's *A Theory of Foreign Policy*, which appeared in 1962, may be taken as representative.[13] In this provocative little book Modelski argues for the following mode of dissecting and visualizing the process of formulating foreign policy: certain individuals called (1) policy-makers, pursuing a set of (2) aims (which are composed of the interests of groups within and the desired favorable behavior on the part of other states and groups without), and following a set of (3) principles (being ends worthy in themselves), take a set of means called (4a) power inputs (roughly, the resources of the nation) and transform them into another set called (4b) power outputs (roughly, the policy or conduct proper), doing so within the context of (5) the international environment.[14] Modelski describes and exemplifies each of the terms and phases of the process thus visualized, ending with a discussion of the conditions for maintaining

11. Wolfers, *Discord and Collaboration*, p. 92.
12. For a review of this literature, see James N. Rosenau, "Comparative Foreign Policy: Fad, Fantasy, or Field?" *International Studies Quarterly* 12, no. 3 (September 1968): esp. 298–300.
13. Princeton Studies in World Politics Number 2. (New York: Praeger).
14. Ibid., pp. 1–11.

the necessary equilibrium among them. He does not, however, distinguish different modes of behavior beyond noting that there are two types of power output, the maintenance of existing resources and the creation of new ones. Since these two correspond generally to the staple increase/preservation alternatives of the texts, he gives us little beyond what we already have. The literature on comparative foreign policy, still newer and still smaller, does no better.[15]

Taken as a whole, the classifications above resumed make a beginning. Whether the terms used are increase/preservation, promotion/protection, or the more complete extension/preservation/abnegation, it is apparent that those who have applied themselves to the question of differences in the conduct of states are getting at much the same sort of distinction, namely, a distinction running in terms of the expansionism of ends and/or means. Moreover, what they are getting at are distinctions that are real and important. The differences are real inasmuch as history provides us with examples of each of the possibilities. Tsarist expansion into Siberia, Napoleon's into central Europe, and our own into the western part of the North American continent instance behavior falling in the first or positive category of the set of three. The Holy Alliance, the network of arrangements entered into by France following the first World War in the interests of containing Germany, or the network of arrangements entered into by the West following the Second World War in the interests of containing Russia, instance behavior of the second or neutral sort. Britain's liquidation of empire following the Second World War instances the third or negative sort. The differences are important inasmuch as, from the point of view of the American (or other national) observer or policy-maker, the choices which other nations make among the three have an immediate and direct bearing on the possibilities of realizing American goals and so on American choices.

In a still broader context, the suggestions of international-affairs experts and psychologists alike point to a good way to start in the search for fruitful typologies that apply across the human domain. For everyday living brings us into contact with differences in the behavior of individuals as well as nations answering to differences along an expansion-contraction scale. There are those bent on increasing the stock of money, goods, etc., in their possession. There

15. Rosenau, "Comparative Foreign Policy," passim.

are those bent on preserving such stock of money, goods, etc., as they may already have. And there are those, though more rare, that are bent on divesting themselves of the money, goods, etc., they may have, usually in the interest of helping others. To advance, hold or retreat; to increase, hold, or decrease: these are purpose-, attitude-, and action-alternatives open in any human context.

On the other hand, existing classifications run only in terms of the expansionist dimension, and there are other dimensions in terms of which one would like to assess and compare the behavior of states. One would, for instance, like to know more about the conduct of a state than whether it aims to increase or merely maintain its power. Assuming the former, one wants to know also how much of an increase it may seek, and how quickly, whether the kind of power it seeks to increase is control or influence only, how the increase is sought, whether by persuasion or force, through candor or guile. Existing classifications do not speak to these points, and thus provide no ready means for distinguishing the conduct of two states in the respects involved.

Exemplifying this last point is the fact that existing classifications provide no ready means for distinguishing Soviet conduct from American in the immediate postwar period. As far as these classifications are concerned, the conduct of both the nations in the period named must qualify as expansionist, self-extensionist, or what, inasmuch as both in the period named aimed at increasing the weight of their power in the councils of mankind, the one through such moves as the take-overs in East Europe, the other through such moves as the supplanting of British power in Greece and Turkey, the establishment of a far-flung system of air bases, remobilization, etc. Conversely, the classificatory system ignores such distinctions as these: that one, but not the other, sought a substantial enlargement of the more complete kind of power called rule or control; that one, but not the other, acted frequently in a coercive manner, and in disregard of its treaty obligations; perhaps most important—though the last word has yet to be said on this point[16]—that for one the expansion was a

16. For introduction to debate on the point prompted by new, "revisionist" school of historians see Arthur N. Schlesinger, Jr., "The Origins of the Cold War," *Foreign Affairs* 46, no. 1 (October 1967): 22–52.

matter of initiative, for the other a matter of response. And these distinctions, it is submitted, are matters of concern to any observer attempting an intelligent appraisal of the events of those days.

Existing classificatory schemes, while they do constitute a beginning for the analyst of Soviet conduct and the images thereof, therefore constitute a bare beginning. While they do advance us beyond the aggressive/peace-loving dyad by means of which the layman differentiates actors on the international scene, they leave us a considerable distance yet to go. And although it would be quixotic, in a field so complex as this, to expect a scheme as satisfactory all-around as that of the botanist or zoologist, still we should be able to do better than we have.

A CLASSIFICATORY SCHEME PROPOSED

The discussion of the preceding section, if it did not uncover adequate classifications among those presently in existence, at least suggests criteria for the adequacy sought. These criteria are: (1) that the dimensions or characteristics in terms of which conduct is to be analyzed be chosen with the end clearly in mind for which the scheme is to be established; (2) that the values assigned to each dimension be logically exhaustive; and (3) that these dimensions and their respective values be carefully defined and distinguished. Present these criteria, and one has the means of accurately and meaningfully identifying the conduct of a given historical state, of contrasting *this* sort of conduct with *that,* of comparing usefully; absent these criteria, and one can proceed only impressionistically. Application of such a scheme will at least produce classes or types in the loose sense of ranges of values along a spectrum, and it may point to a further, more deeply grounded classification, made up of types distinct from each other in respect to a number of different dimensions, each being defined by possession of a certain cluster of traits.

Now, characterizing and differentiating carefully the full array of images of Soviet conduct constituting the sample of Chapter 1 shares, with other efforts in pure science, the purposes first of enabling us to see more clearly each image in its fullness, and second of enabling us to compare them to a meaningful norm and to one another. But the images themselves, despite disclaimers to the contrary in some cases, have come into being largely for practical reasons; they have been developed as part of an effort to gauge the implications, for the kind of world we want, of the nature of the leading power among the other nations, this effort in turn being part of an effort best to plot our own course toward the goal desired. And the end of the present effort to describe and analyze these images, which as earlier stated is the end of enabling imagists better to serve their practical aim, is perforce itself also practical. Accordingly, the classificatory scheme to be sought is one that would be set up to determine how much of a threat Soviet conduct poses for the achievement of the goal of American policy—a peaceful world of free and equal nation-states.

The scheme I propose to fulfill this objective is that set forth in Table 4. It is made up of two main continua: one for hardness of conduct in the aggregate, the second for constancy in such conduct over time. The first continuum is broken into five ranges of values—in descending order, Ultra-Hard, Hard, Mixed (neither Hard nor Soft), Soft, and Ultra-Soft. The continuum for constancy or invariance in conduct over time is broken only into the three values of high, medium, and low (or, alternately, little changing, moderately changing, and significantly changing). A scale of numbers along the top is provided as a means for converting these and other qualitative values into quantitative equivalents.

The continuum for hardness of conduct in the aggregate—this behavioral equivalent of Mohs' scale of hardness for minerals—is a synthesis of nine lesser continua or scales, referring each continuum to a dimension into which conduct as a whole has provisionally been analyzed. The first five of these continua are descriptive of dimensions of conduct proper. These five are, respectively: (1) expansionism of ends; and in the realm of means: (2) expansiveness; (3) militancy, or addiction to force in the general sense; (4) militariness, or addiction to the military instrument and violence; and (5) turpitude or immorality.

Conduct is expansionist with respect to ends in the degree to which it views the long-run objective as an increase in, retention of, or decrease in what power it enjoys: high, medium, and low values are respectively expansion-minded, protection-minded, and contraction-minded. Conduct is expansionist in respect to means in the degree its actual day-to-day, year-by-year moves tend to increase, hold, or decrease the power it enjoys: high, medium, and low values are, re-

TABLE 4

External Conduct and Its Images: A Proposed Classificatory Scheme.[a]

Conduct and Its Elements	Continua of Values[b]										
	10	9	8	7	6	5	4	3	2	1	0
In the Aggregate[c]											
A. Hardness or Egotism		Ultra-Hard		Hard		Mixed		Soft		Ultra-Soft	
B. Invariance (Constancy)			High-Little Changing		Medium - Moderately Changing				Low - Significantly Changing		
Basic Dimensions											
1. Expansionism of Ends			Expansion-Minded		Protection-Minded			Contraction-Minded			
2. Expansiveness of Means			Expansive			Protective			Contractive		
3. Militancy (Addiction to Force in General)			Coercive						Incentive		
4. Militariness (Addiction to Violence)			Militarist						Non-militarist		
5. Turpitude (Immorality)			Immoral		Mixedly Immoral				Moral		
Contextual Dimensions											
6. Addiction to Initiative			Initiatory						Responsive		
7. Offensiveness of Motive			Ambition						Fear		
8. Malignancy of Impact			High-Threat			Medium-Threat			Low-Threat		
Special Component											
9. Hardness Toward Own[d]			Domineering			Cooperative			Subservient		

a. For explanation of terms and rules for use, see text.

b. Numerical equivalents are to be understood only in the most approximate of senses; their sole function, as explained in the text, is that of aids to the aggregation process.

c. Toward the sum total of other states. See note d.

d. Toward states of one's own kind, defined by internal structure—in the Soviet case, toward other Communist states.

spectively, expansive, protective, and contractive. (These facets I sometimes further differentiate by degree of power, separating out the extreme degree of rule or control or the decisive voice in larger affairs from mere influence or a voice in larger affairs short of decisive.) Conduct is militant in the degree to which it uses coercively as against incentively the various instrumentalities of policy (economic, political, psychological, and military) taken collectively. Conduct is militarist to the extent that it resorts to the military instrument, that is, the instrument of violence par excellence, polar values being militarist and nonmilitarist. Conduct, finally, is depraved to the extent that it ignores moral rules, high, medium, and low values being highly immoral, mixedly immoral, and highly moral in that order. (This facet I break sometimes into the two subfacets of deceptiveness, or disregard for truth, and faithlessness, or disregard for promises.)

The residual four components of the synthetic hardness continuum are dimensions in looser senses. The first three are dimensions in a relational or contextual sense. They are: the addiction of conduct to the initiative, whether initiatory or responsive; the offensiveness of the motivating force, whether ambition or fear; and the malignancy of the impact on the world outside, contrasting values of which are high-, medium-, and low-threat. The final component is hardness or egotism of conduct toward the special group of other nations whose internal structure is like one's own (in the Soviet case, other Communist states), values of descending magnitude being domineering, cooperative, and subservient.

The procedure for applying the scheme to a particular image, for assessing a given image in terms of the scheme, comprises a number of steps in the case of conduct in the aggregate. These are, for each dimension: (1) arraying all statements relating thereto, (2) estimating mean position on the continuum of qualitative values, (3) converting to numerical equivalents, and then (4) taking the unweighted average of all, finally, (5) converting back to the qualitative equivalent on the aggregate continuum. An image describing Soviet conduct as having objectives of unlimited power, as being highly expansive in fact, highly militant, militarist, and immoral; an image visualizing conduct as highly charged with initiative, motivated by the lust for power, posing mortal danger for the future of mankind, and tyrannical toward other states of its kind—such an image would be rated either

9 or 10 with respect to each dimension, the average of 9+ putting its view of conduct in the aggregate in the uppermost or Ultra-Hard range of the overall continuum. On the other hand, an image visualizing Soviet conduct as being expansion-minded and expansive in moderate degree (7), highly militant in general (9) but loath to resort to the military instrument (3), indifferently immoral (5); an image which describes conduct as broadly charged with initiative (7), which ascribes this conduct to a mixture of ambition and fear (5), characterizes it as a disturbing influence in the world (6), and finds it moderately hegemonic toward its own (7):—such an image would, in respect to the various dimensions, be numerically rated approximately as indicated, the average of 6+ converting to a qualitative designation of Hard in the aggregate.

In the case of constancy or invariance of conduct in the aggregate the procedure is somewhat different. In this case, the determination or rating of constancy as high, medium, or low, and change as virtually null, moderate, or significant, rests mainly on how the imagist views one or more of the generally recognized shifts of emphasis or direction in Soviet foreign policy noted in Chapter 1: that is, those of 1921, 1928, 1934, 1939, 1941, 1945, and 1953, with the last given particularly great weight. Viewing the 1953 shift, for example, as a mere change of tactics rates an 8 or 9; viewing it as of some long-range importance rates a 4–6; while viewing it as of considerable long-range significance rates a 2 or 3.

The various dimensions of the scheme have been derived by a mixed process. They have been derived partly by the logical device of abstracting from the totality of conduct those aspects which seem to be factors in an overall judgment of hardness, as commonly understood. They have been derived partly by ascertaining what aspects the sample of images under scrutiny actually pay attention to. They may claim to meet the criteria of a good classificatory scheme because they are relevant to the end in view: that is, they imply distinctions of importance to American determination of its course. For clearly whether the USSR means to expand or not and does expand, and, if so, whether it means to expand its control or only its influence—these things make a difference to what sort of a posture we take, what sort of policy we devise. Clearly, too, do the militancy of means the USSR employs, the amount of violence to which habitually the USSR resorts, the degree to which the USSR observes rules of honesty and fidelity. So, too, does the frequency of initiatives within the sum total of Soviet actions. Also, though less directly, it makes a difference to our decisions, to the kind of world we want, and what we do to get that world, whether Soviet ends and means are what they are for offensive or for defensive reasons—whether out of ambition or fear—since which of these they may be bears heavily on what we do in response. And it makes a difference how much adverse impact Soviet conduct so described presently has on the peace of nations and the independence and welfare of other nations. Finally, it makes quite a difference to us whether this conduct has changed materially over the years. For if conduct has changed (and especially if it has changed in a direction more compatible with our ends) there is more hope for the future we want.

The scheme under discussion and the rules for its application are shockingly imperfect from the purist's point of view. There is no doubt a fair amount of double-counting emboweled within it: hardness toward other states of similar structure is accounted for in 1–6 as well as 7, military coerciveness in 3 as well as 4, etc. There is a question as to the propriety of considering expansionism of aim and offensiveness of motivation—the pull from ahead and the force from behind—as separate phenomena. There are other important dimensions than those listed—for instance, the rationality of conduct. Conversion of phrases descriptive of qualitative values into numerical equivalents is necessarily a risky business. Aggregation by equal weighting is of course open to challenge.

I am aware of these objections. I think most of them are valid. I would point out, however, that there are answers to some of them. Conversion into numerical equivalents and averaging, for instance, is simply the most convenient method available for performing the aggregative function and is to be taken for no more than this. Translation back into phrases descriptive of qualitative values (Ultra-Hard, Hard, etc.) provides, and is intended to provide, protection against the dangers to which quantification often leads—viz., the danger of pretending to a spurious precision. As for other deficiencies, I would remind the reader that the objective is not a perfect scheme, which is obviously out of reach, but a scheme less imperfect than what is presently at hand. And for the scheme under advisement one can at least claim the virtue of bringing out into the open, for critical examination, assumptions heretofore tacitly held only, without full realization as to purport and impact.

THE IMAGES OF THE SAMPLE RATED

Applying the descriptive scheme to the images of the 22 works of the sample, or, rather, measuring them against the scheme, according to the rules set forth, produces the results summarized in Table 5. As therein disclosed, all images fall in the upper three ranges of the continuum for conduct in the aggregate. In fact (although this the table does not disclose), all save possibly Fleming fall in the upper half of that continuum. Nine fall in the Ultra-Hard category, 7 in the Hard, 6 in the Mixed or Middling. As further disclosed by the table, 13 images see high invariance or little change in Soviet conduct over the years, 5 finding moderate change therein, 4 significant change. Detailed inspection of works yielding representative images in the three categories will make clearer the process by which the ratings have been derived and allow the reader to judge for himself their validity.

Representative of works yielding an Ultra-Hard image is the *Protracted Conflict* of Robert Strausz-Hupé and others, which first appeared in 1959.[17] Centering upon Communist and Soviet conduct, which it views as interchangeable, this work develops its thought in sections dealing in order with the international setting within which communism operates, with Communist strategy and strategic "vision," with the operational principles guiding implementation of strategy, and with present and future implications of the above for the world at large and for the United States in particular. Its thesis is that communism is a revolutionary movement which sees its conflict with the older, democratic regimes of the West as boundless, which seeks total victory in that conflict, which acknowledges no limitations to the means to be employed in service to the objective, and which coordinates in an amazingly skillful manner the wide range of instrumentalities at hand for carrying on the battle. The operational principles which *Protracted Conflict* identifies are the following: (1)

17. Robert Strausz-Hupé, William R. Kintner, James E. Dougherty, and Alvin J. Cottrell, *Protracted Conflict,* Harper Colophon ed. (New York: Harper & Row, 1963).

TABLE 5

Soviet External Conduct: Images of the Sample of Leading Works
Assessed Against the Classificatory Scheme of Table 4[a]

Author	Short Title	Conduct in the Aggregate	
		Hardness	Invariance
Bouscaren	Soviet Foreign Policy	Ultra-Hard	Little Changing
Dallin	Soviet Foreign Policy after Stalin	Ultra-Hard	Little Changing
Fleming	The Cold War and Its Origins	Mixed	Little Changing
Gehlen	The Politics of Coexistence	Mixed	Moderately Changing
Goodman	The Soviet Design for a World State	Ultra-Hard	Little Changing
Halle	The Cold War as History	Mixed	Moderately Changing
Kennan	Russia and the West	Hard	Significantly Changing
Kintner	The New Frontier of War	Ultra-Hard	Little Changing
Kulski	Peaceful Coexistence	Ultra-Hard	Little Changing
Librach	The Rise of the Soviet Empire	Ultra-Hard	Little Changing
Lukacs	A New History of the Cold War	Mixed	Little Changing
Mosely	The Kremlin and World Politics	Hard	Moderately Changing
Overstreet	The War Called Peace	Ultra-Hard	Little Changing
Schuman	The Cold War	Mixed	Moderately Changing
Schwartz	The Red Phoenix	Hard	Little Changing
Shulman	Beyond the Cold War	Hard	Significantly Changing
Shulman	Stalin's Foreign Policy Reappraised	Hard	Significantly Changing
Strausz-Hupé	Protracted Conflict	Ultra-Hard	Little Changing
Triska	Soviet Foreign Policy	Mixed	Moderately Changing
Tucker	The Soviet Political Mind	Hard	Significantly Changing
Ulam	Expansion and Coexistence	Hard	Little Changing
Wolfe	Communist Totalitarianism	Ultra-Hard	Little Changing

a. For full titles see Table 1, for terms of classificatory scheme, Table 4.

indirectness, or avoidance of military showdown while the balance of forces is unfavorable; (2) deception and distraction; (3) monopoly of the initiative; and (4) attrition, or the erosion of the Western alliance system and exploitation of conflicts within same.

Relating these findings more specifically to the terms of the descriptive scheme and remembering in the course of so doing the equivalence of Soviet and Communist, one finds that Soviet conduct, according to *Protracted Conflict,* has for its objective domination of the world, or (inferentially, through an approved quote from another author) the "overthrow of all the parliamentary governments of the world and their replacement by Communist dictatorships centrally controlled in Moscow"—in short, unlimited expansionism of rule.[18] In means too it is highly expansive.[19] In respect to militancy, it stands near the extreme, as demonstrated by the vision of "protracted conflict" to which it is committed and by its embracing "attrition" as another of its four operational principles.[20] In respect to morality of means, it is grossly immoral, deception being an intrinsic part of its *modus operandi.*[21] Only in respect to militarism among the basic dimensions is conduct at all restrained. Here, while violence is not eschewed or in any way decried, as long as the main enemy (capitalism) enjoys an advantage, conduct is cautious, carrying on the conflict indirectly, through parties abroad, satellites, and national revolutionary movements.[22]

In respect to other dimensions, *Protracted Conflict*'s characterizations are also extreme. Conduct is ceaselessly initiatory, monopoly of the initiative being, as noted, one of its four operational principles.[23] Conduct is driven by an "all-consuming lust for power."[24] It has created for the open societies of the West a threat of direst malignancy, locking them in a "mortal conflict" implicating the entire future of mankind, making nonsense of the notion that coexistence is a genuine possibility.[25] It is no less hard on its own than on its capitalist

18. Ibid., pp. 7, 119.
19. Ibid., esp. Chapter 4.
20. Ibid., Chapters 3 and 7.
21. Ibid.. Chapter 5.
22. Ibid., Chapter 4.
23. Ibid., Chapter 6.
24. Ibid., p. 142.
25. Ibid., Chapter 10, esp. pp. 147, 149.

adversaries; the Soviet bosses are equally at war with the supposedly friendly comrades of the "socialist" camp and the billion people over whom they exercise "absolute domination."[26]

Conversion into numerical equivalents of these phrases descriptive of *Protracted Conflict*'s characterization of the various dimensions of Soviet conduct would on a common-sense reading, it seems to me, produce values in the range of 8 to 10. It would do so, that is, save in the case of characterization of addiction to the military instrument, which would probably rate a 7. Averaging these figures gives a result of around 9, which clearly falls in the Ultra-Hard range of the scale synthesizing all dimensions. This accounts for the summary rating for the book's image of conduct in the aggregate with which the table finally comes up.

As for invariance in aggregate behavior, *Protracted Conflict* notes no change of consequence. Goals have remained unchanged.[27] What appear now and then as signs of greater moderateness are really moves of temporary, tactical significance only in the ceaseless, contrived, almost rhythmic alternation of hot and cold, sweet and sour, hard and soft.[28] Either they are this, that is, or they are outright deceptions. The appropriate rating along this dimension would therefore seem to be "highly invariant" or "little changing."

Representative of works yielding a Hard image is Marshall Shulman's *Beyond the Cold War*, written in 1966.[29] *Beyond the Cold War* deals with the relationship named, especially the American-Soviet aspect thereof, in the years 1945–65. Successive chapters take up origins in the immediate postwar period, changes in the international environment, changes within the Soviet policy, resultant changes in Soviet policy toward the world outside, and finally the changes in American policy which seem to the author indicated in response. The work's global theme is that the policy of the Communist enemy has moderated in the last 10 years or so, and that crises other than the Cold War have come to the fore—all of this requiring of the United States a more modulated, differentiated, and balanced response.

In our terms, Soviet conduct, according to *Beyond the Cold War*, is

26. Ibid., p. 29.
27. Ibid., p. 24.
28. Ibid., p. 68.
29. New Haven: Yale University Press, 1966.

substantially expansion-minded in objective. The Soviet Union's aim is "to increase its power, influence, prestige, and security as a nation-state against the existing distribution of power in the world."[30] The aim is not, however, an unlimited one.[31] In respect to means, conduct is sometimes expansive, but sometimes not. In the immediate post-war years the Soviet Union sought "total domination" of East Europe and control of Germany.[32] But since Stalin's death it has been largely protective, generally content with the status quo in Europe vis-à-vis the West and satisfied for the moment, anyway, with denying areas in the third world to the West rather than seeking control over them.[33] In respect to addiction to force in general and violence in particular it also has varied. The immediate postwar years were years of high militancy, and resort to measures just short of war.[34] But the years since Stalin's death have been different. While in words conduct retains some of the old revolutionary ring, in deed the incentive strain seems on balance to be almost equal to the coercive.[35] Today the USSR resorts infrequently to the military instrument, and is commonly cautious. On the subject of morality, *Beyond the Cold War* has nothing to say.

In its contextual or relational dimensions, Soviet conduct is highly dynamic, active, initiatory.[36] It was largely responsible for initiating the Cold War in the late '40s, although subsequent moves have sometimes been responses to our responses in a sequence Shulman calls an "interacting spiral."[37] Conduct is motivated by an assertive national self-interest rather than a concern for the world revolution.[38] Yet this is an assertiveness not untinged with fear induced by the actions of others. Conduct poses a threat to the world outside of consider-able magnitude;[39] yet this is not a threat so total as to preclude

30. Ibid., p. 81.
31. Ibid., p. 16.
32. Ibid., p. 7.
33. Ibid., pp. 63–65.
34. Ibid., p. 7.
35. Ibid., pp. 65–70.
36. Ibid., pp. 16, 49.
37. Ibid., pp. 6, 10.
38. Ibid., pp. 52–53.
39. Ibid., pp. 80–81.

the possibility of cooperation on some issues.[40] Toward its own, conduct, domineering in the late Stalin days, today allows a limited
autonomy and preaches a concept not unlike that underlying the
British commonwealth.[41]

Conversion into numerical equivalents of the above qualitative
assessments of the various dimensions of Soviet conduct would, on a
common-sense reading, it seems to me, produce values in the range
of 6–8—in those cases in which Stalinist and post-Stalinist subdivisions of the postwar period are differentiated, nearer 8 for the former, nearer 6 for the latter. Averaging where needed and aggregating
results gives a figure of around 7 which, falling in the Hard range of
the spectrum for conduct as a whole, accounts for the summary characterization noted in the table.

In respect to the important feature of invariancy in aggregate
behavior, *Beyond the Cold War* is one of those works which see a
rather sharp break in the record, the break in question separating the
early postwar years from the later, post-Stalinist ones. As implied
above, the earlier period was rule-expansive, as the later has not been,
and the earlier was appreciably more militant and militarist than the
later has been. A measure of the overall difference is provided by
Shulman's summary characterizations of the two. Policy in the earlier
he implicitly describes as one of "militant advocacy of revolution and
the use of force."[42] On the other hand, "peaceful coexistence," the
name by which policy in the later is known, he describes as the "active,
though not unrestrained, policy of pursuing national advantage by
indirect and long-term means."[43] Shulman not only draws this sharp
contrast, but notes a "very considerable evolution" over the long run
toward the latter.[44] These considerations underlie the rating of "significantly changing" with which the table comes up on this point.

Representative, finally, of works yielding a mixed image is Frederick Schuman's *The Cold War: Retrospect and Prospect.*[45] This
work, of which the second edition appeared in 1967, deals with the

40. Ibid., p. 82.
41. Ibid., pp. 71–73.
42. Ibid., p. 54.
43. Ibid., p. 78.
44. Ibid., p. 53.
45. Second ed. Baton Rouge: Louisiana State University Press, 1967.

relationship named, especially the American-Soviet part thereof, in the context of the full 50-year span of the Soviet regime and, indeed, the even longer span which includes tsarist rule as well. Successive chapters treat the broader topic of Russian external experience of which the Soviet is seen as only the most recent phase, this retrospective segment bearing the title "Third Rome"; the Soviet internal social order; and, as prospective segment, the possibilities "Beyond the Cold War" and at the half-century point in Soviet rule. Schuman's global theorems are: that Russian conduct has since the beginning been militarily expansive; that it has been this, however, only intermittently so and in reaction to repeated invasion from abroad and to the recognition of weakness and vulnerability induced thereby; that Soviet conduct in the Cold War is simply one more instance of this general rule, having been not self-generated but originating as a response to the Western interventions of 1917–19 and 1941 and to recognition of weaknesses thereby revealed; that from present Soviet efforts to overcome these weaknesses, one can expect more moderate behavior in the future; but that avoidance of the co-annihilation that threatens mankind in this, the nuclear age, will depend also on American ability to learn the ultimate lesson of the time, the need for effective law for the international community and world government.

In our terms, according to *The Cold War,* Soviet conduct, like Russian conduct from time immemorial, is moderately expansion-minded as to objective, that objective being "protecting and promoting the interests of Muscovy in its contacts of war and peace with the other members of the modern State system."[46] Conduct emphatically does not, however, aim at taking over the world, and is only sporadically expansive in its year-by-year moves.[47] Conduct is militant enough: the doctrine rationalizing the mission is messianic and runs in universalist terms. But it is not mainly military.[48] It has resorted to force of arms rarely, and then usually for defensive reasons.[49] *The Cold War* mentions the topic of morality only to suggest that Russian actions alleged to contravene the Yalta and other major war agree-

46. Ibid., p. 12.
47. Ibid., pp. 24–25.
48. Ibid., pp. 28–29.
49. Ibid., pp. 19–20, 82.

ments might, on some reasonable interpretations of those agreements, be conceded not to be violations thereof.[50]

In respect to other than the essential or basic dimensions, Schuman's assessment is distinguished first by the low value he puts on Soviet (Russian) addiction to the initiative. Conduct is highly responsive, and the moments of rule expansion and resort to arms are traceable commonly to prior aggression from without. Conformably, conduct derives in high measure from a national self-interest of which concern for security is the major component, this concern having been born of centuries of experiencing invasions from outside.[51] Conduct poses some threat to the peace of the world,[52] but this is not a threat of overwhelming magnitude, and for much of the world's ills, and many of its crises (such as, for instance, the Cold War), the Soviets do not bear major responsibility.[53] Of the nature of conduct especially directed toward other Communist states, *The Cold War* says little.

A reasonable conversion into numerical terms of Schuman's qualitative assessments of the various dimensions of conduct would, it seems to me, produce values somewhere between 4 and 6. Their aggregation gives a figure of around 5. This figure, falling as it does in the middle of the Mixed range of the spectrum for conduct as a whole, and indeed in the middle of the entire spectrum, accounts for the summary rating noted in the table.

As for invariance of conduct over the years, Schuman notes a "drastic alteration in the age-old pattern of relationships between Russia and the West," from this drawing hope for major constructive changes in traditional behavior.[54] However, these changes lie still mainly in the future. Continuity of present with past remains the dominant relation, although a gradual softening in the post-Stalin period qualifies this somewhat. The correct description for the assessment of this feature therefore appears to be "moderately changing."

The proceedings which underlie the ratings of Table 5, and which are exemplified by the three cases just considered, are pockmarked by a number of deficiencies above and beyond those of a general nature sketched at the end of the preceding section. They involve a

50. Ibid., p. 83.
51. Ibid., pp. 15–22.
52. Ibid., p. 25.
53. Ibid., pp. 79–80.
54. Ibid., p. 25.

number of judgments of a rough-and-ready, impressionistic nature such as an athletic director has no need to rely on in gauging the age, height and weight, and other characteristics of his pool of potential football players. The works analyzed for the images contained do not all speak to all the points embraced by the descriptive scheme. Those they do speak to they do not always speak explicitly to, nor yet always consistently to. No observer can be sure he has plucked from the mass (sometimes, morass) of verbiage all the statements referring to a specific point. Nor can he be sure he has matched statements with terms of the descriptive scheme in a fashion that would win universal approval—much less statements with supposed numerical equivalents.

Yet when all this has been said, I doubt that such other observers as might undertake to "replicate" the assessments at issue would reach radically different results. In any event, the point still stands that the scheme and its application constitute one of the least imperfect ways available, within reasonable limits of time, to sketch with any degree of definiteness the outlines of the various images under scrutiny, and so take the first necessary step toward sensible classification.

IMAGE TYPES IDENTIFIED

Assessment of the works of the sample against the classificatory scheme shows a 9–7–6 distribution among the upper three values of the aggregate hardness scale, 9 falling in the top or Ultra-Hard category, 7 in the second or Hard, 6 in the third or Mixed. And this permits one to speak of types of image in the loose or casual sense of categories defined by the adjacent value ranges into which a continuum has been divided, value ranges analogous to pigeonholes labeled A–E, F–J, K–P, etc. Does the assessment, however, and do the calculations underlying it, enable one also to speak of image types in the yet more radical sense of kinds of things (1) distinguished sharply from one another and (2) so distinguished in respect to a number of different dimensions or characteristics, each of these kinds being therefore possessed of a quite distinct cluster of traits?

The answer to this latter question is a provisional yes. For close examination of the assessments and underlying calculations discloses other information bearing on the distribution of the images in question, and this information points in the direction named.

Examination reveals first that the images of each value range group
themselves fairly closely around the mean. The other eight authors of
the Ultra-Hard group join the authors of *Protracted Conflict* in commonly assigning extremely high values to all dimensions save militariness and the addiction to violence, which they rate medium-high.[55]
With *Protracted Conflict* too they affirm a high degree of constancy
over the years, conceding virtually no change of any significance.
Some exceptions there are. Dallin and Kulski, for instance, are on the
whole somewhat less harsh than the others. Their characterizations
are not quite so extreme, and they note some change of consequence
to have taken place in 1953.[56] But such exceptions are few.

The other six works in the second group—Kennan, Mosely,
Schwartz, Shulman-*FP*, Tucker, and Ulam—range moderately about
Shulman-*CW*.[57] Kennan, Shulman-*FP*, and Tucker see things much

55. See Anthony Bouscaren, *Soviet Foreign Policy: A Pattern of Persistence*
(New York: Fordham University Press, 1962), esp. Chapters 1 and 2; David
J. Dallin, *Soviet Foreign Policy after Stalin* (Philadelphia: Lippincott, 1961),
esp. Preface, Part One–Chapter 1, Part Three–Chapter 5, and Conclusion;
Elliot R. Goodman, *The Soviet Design for a World State* (New York:
Columbia University Press, 1960), esp. Introduction, pp. 63–65, 125–28,
471–73; William R. Kintner, and others, *The New Frontier of War: Political
Warfare Present and Future* (Chicago: Regnery, 1962), esp. Introduction,
Chapters VII–X and p. 295; Wladyslaw W. Kulski, *Peaceful Coexistence: An
Analysis of Soviet Foreign Policy* (Chicago: Regnery, 1959), esp. Introduc-
tion; Jan Librach, *The Rise of the Soviet Empire: A Study of Soviet Foreign
Policy*, rev. ed. (New York: Praeger, 1965), esp. Introduction, Chapters 1–3;
Harry and Bonaro Overstreet, *The War Called Peace: Khrushchev's Com-
munism* (New York: Norton, 1961), esp. Foreword and Part One; Bertram
D. Wolfe, *Communist Totalitarianism: Keys to the Soviet System*, rev. ed.
(Boston: Beacon Press, 1961), esp. pp. 214–19, 247–58, 270–93, 294–305.
56. Dallin, *Soviet Foreign Policy after Stalin*, p. 223; Kulski, *Peaceful
Coexistence*, p. 149.
57. George F. Kennan, *Russia and the West under Lenin and Stalin*
(Boston: Little, Brown, 1961), esp. pp. 183–93, 248–59, and Chapter 25;
Philip E. Mosely, *The Kremlin and World Politics: Studies in Soviet Policy
and Action* (New York: Vintage Press, 1960), esp. Chapters 11, 12, 20, and
25; Harry E. Schwartz, *The Red Phoenix: Russia Since World War II*
(New York: Praeger, 1961), esp. Introduction, Chapters 1 and 9; Marshall
D. Shulman, *Stalin's Foreign Policy Reappraised* (Cambridge: Harvard Uni-
versity Press, 1963), esp. Chapters I and XI; and Robert C. Tucker, *The
Soviet Political Mind: Studies in Stalinism and Post-Stalin Change* (New

in the same light as Shulman-*CW*. Differences among them center
on such points as the precise timing of the important changes perceived to have occurred, and the leading determinants of behavior
and variation therein—whether pressures from outside (Shulman) or
from inside (Kennan, Tucker). Mosely, Schwartz, and Ulam ascribe
appreciably more continuity, less change, the first two at a somewhat
harder level on balance, Ulam at one a trifle softer.[58] Mosely and
Schwartz see conduct in a light, one might add, that at times seems
almost as dim as that in which Kulski and Dallin see it. Yet there
remains a perceptible difference in the overall images of these two
sets with views near the common border of the Ultra-Hard and Hard
categories. Mosely and Schwartz see ends and means as appreciably
less total than Kulski and Dallin, and see conduct prior to 1945 as of
a kind not incompatible with Western objectives.[59] They thus stand
on balance appreciably closer to their nearest neighbors in the Hard
group than to their nearest neighbors in the Ultra-Hard.

The other five works of the third group—namely, Fleming, Gehlen,
Halle, Lukacs, and Triska—stand close to Schuman's, Fleming somewhat to his soft side, the other four to his hard.[60] Halle and Lukacs
see conduct in a somewhat harsher light than the others, finding the
Soviets mainly responsible for the Cold War, Halle in addition find-

York: Praeger, 1963), esp. Chapters 7, 8, and 10. Meaty passages in Adam
Ulam, *Expansion and Coexistence: The History of Soviet Foreign Policy
1917–67* (New York: Praeger, 1968), are too widely dispersed to make citation useful—but see pp. 751–52.

58. For Mosely, see *The Kremlin and World Politics*, pp. 291, 310, 403,
555; for Schwartz, *The Red Phoenix*, pp. 228, 245–46; for Ulam, *Expansion
and Coexistence*, pp. 408, 543, 570–71, 751–52.

59. For instance, Mosely, *The Kremlin and World Politics*, pp. 89, 312–
13; and Schwartz, *The Red Phoenix*, pp. 14–19.

60. Denna F. Fleming, *The Cold War and Its Origins: 1917–1960*, 2 vols.
(Garden City, N.Y.: Doubleday, 1961), esp. Chapters X, XVI, and XXXIV;
Michael Gehlen, *The Politics of Coexistence: Soviet Methods and Motives*
(Bloomington: Indiana University Press, 1967), esp. pp. 40–41, 59–60, 63–
64, 208–09, and Conclusion; Louis J. Halle, *The Cold War as History* (New
York: Harper & Row, 1967), esp. Preface and Chapters I, II, III; John
Lukacs, *A New History of the Cold War*, 3rd ed., expanded, of *A History
of the Cold War* (Garden City, N.Y.: Doubleday, 1966), esp. Preface and
Chapter XIV; and Jan Triska and David D. Finley, *Soviet Foreign Policy*
(New York: Macmillan, 1968), esp. Chapters 1 and 9, and Conclusion.

ing their conduct appreciably more fraught with substantial danger
for the world.[61] They at times see it much the same as does Shulman.
Yet there is a perceptible difference between these two sets with
views near the common border of Hard and Mixed. Halle and Lukacs
see expansiveness as purely responsive and defensive, born of fear
rather than ambition, as Shulman commonly does not. In explaining
expansiveness, moreover, they introduce (as Shulman does not) a
necessitarian element, tracing it to geopolitical forces which the
policy-maker can no more control than he can the weather.

Examination reveals, second, that there is a correlation between
position on conduct in the aggregate and position on each of the components. On the whole, an extreme position on expansionism is
matched by an extreme position on militancy, immorality, and so on
down the line; a moderate position on expansionism with a moderate
position on militancy, immorality, and so on down the line. There are
certain qualifications that must be entered to these remarks. In respect
to militarism, position is regularly more moderate than position on
other dimensions. Those of Ultra-Hard persuasion assign a medium
high value to the militarist dimension, those of Mixed persuasion a
low value. But the point holds generally. Perhaps more important, one
can say of any three works drawn respectively from the three groups
that they tend to assume the same order in respect to each individual
dimension that they assume in respect to positions in the aggregate
—although the distance between adjacent pairs may vary somewhat.

Examination reveals, finally, a correlation, indeed a surprising one,
between position on conduct in the aggregate and position on the
important matter of variation therein. The relative position of the
three views in this case does not remain the same. Rather, the 1, 2, 3
order of decreasing hardness for the aggregate becomes 1, 3, 2 in the
case of the constancy element. In other words, the Ultra-Hard imagist
commonly sees high constancy or resistance to change over time; the
Mixed imagist commonly sees some inconstancy, or some change over
time; but the Hard imagist sees considerable inconstancy, or significant change over time. Again, there are exceptions, and the exceptions need to be noted. Mosely and Schwartz, and Ulam, as already

61. Halle, *The Cold War as History*, pp. xiii, 124, 138 n.; Lukacs, *A New
History of the Cold War*, p. 348.

suggested, see the change of 1953, and change in general, as less extensive and significant than do the others of Hard persuasion. But these exceptions are few, and the point holds generally.

In sum and in short, close examination suggests that the images of the sample tend to fall into three categories rather sharply distinguished from one another in a number of ways. Of the "types" in the more radical sense of the term that are thus constituted, Table 6 sets forth the principal characteristics, retaining for them respectively the names descriptive of the range on the synthetic hardness scale to which their views of conduct in the aggregate answer. It is these groups of characteristics—"trait-clusters" in the technical jargon—that I shall have in mind when referring henceforth to the Ultra-Hard, Hard, and Mixed images or views.

One can with reason speak of three quite distinct image types where recent American academic literature on Soviet external conduct is concerned: this is the conclusion to which this chapter's efforts at differentiation lead.

There is the image of absolute egotism—egotism unlimited in end and means, egotism undifferentiated and unchanging. This type, in its utter ferocity, far exceeds the Imperialist type of the standard classification of the texts, far outreaches the Exploitative type of Fromm's classification, and surpasses even Hobbesian man with his insatiable lust for power. Indeed, it knows no recognizable equivalent in the descriptive literature of human or animal conduct. For suitable analogue one must look to the literature of the imagination—to the Great Beast of the Book of Revelations.

There is the image of egotism limited, significantly changing and changeable, answering more closely to the Imperialist type of the texts or to Fromm's Exploiter. An appropriate zoological analogue is a tiger who with the onset of maturity kills less frequently, whose peaceable and good-tempered (i.e. nonhunting) moments thus lengthen at the expense of the ferocious ones, and who may therefore be said to mellow.

There is the image of egotism intermittent and defensive, moderately changing and changeable. This type stands closer to the status quo type of the texts and Fromm's Hoarder. Naturalists record that a bear of an off-shade color who is rejected by others of his kind

TABLE 6

Soviet External Conduct: Types of Image Found in the Sample of Leading Works

Conduct and Its Elements	Types of Image and Their Content		
	A. Ultra-Hard	B. Hard	C. Mixed (Hard–Soft)
In the Aggregate	Ultra-Hard and Little Changing	Hard and Significantly Changing	Mixed and Moderately Changing
In Basic Dimensions: As to Ends	Infinitely Expansion-Minded	Highly Expansion-Minded	Moderately Expansion-Minded
As to Means	Extremely Expansive and Militant Substantially Militarist Extremely Immoral	Highly Expansive and Militant Largely Nonmilitarist Somewhat Immoral	Moderately Expansive and Militant Substantially Nonmilitarist Not Especially Immoral
In Contextual Dimensions	Relentlessly Initiatory Driven by Limitless Ambition Posing Mortal Danger to Mankind	Largely Initiatory Driven by Ambition Tinged with Fear Posing Substantial Threat to Mankind	Largely Responsive Driven by Fear Posing only Moderate Threat to Mankind
In Relation to Its own[a]	Domineering, Tyrannical	Highly Hegemonic	Moderately Hegemonic

a. I.e. other Communist states.

becomes neurotic and may, with little provocation, commit aggression, even though he is of a species habitually amiable and pacific.[62] Those holding the Mixed image of Soviet conduct may be said to conceive of the USSR as a sort of Neurotic Bear.

These three types, it is important to note, preempt the field. Recent American academic literature knows none softer. It knows no image of selfless behavior, of behavior wholeheartedly dedicated to larger cause. It knows no picturization of the USSR in the guise of Rousseau's noble savage, living and letting live, much less picturization in the form of Redeemer or Savior in which commonly the Soviet Communists see themselves.

Each of these three types, it is also important to note, has for counterpart larger images of the shape of the political world as a whole. Those who see the USSR and the Communist system it heads as the many-headed, many-horned Great Beast of the Apocalypse commonly tend to see the United States and its allies as almost diametric opposites in character, to see the in-between nations as *au fond* either basically virtuous and on our side or basically vicious and on theirs, and hence to see the world as a whole as chiaroscuro. On this view, moreover, Soviet and Nazi conduct are of a piece, Soviet radically different from its tsarist predecessor. Those of Mixed persuasion, on the other hand, see the United States and its allies and the in-between nations as pretty much of a kind—alike human, alike prone, like Fromm's Hoarder types, to look after themselves first. On this view, the Soviets, even as ourselves, are radically distinguished from the Nazis. Those, finally, who see the Soviet Union in the form of an aging predator see conduct as initially different from ours but capable of becoming alike and indeed (in many cases) so becoming already. For them, domestication of the originally feral is in the cards, if not already on the way. Chapter 8 develops these points more fully.

Finally, and almost obviously, it is important to note that each of these images carries with it an implied prescription for the appropriate Western and especially American response. For partisans of the Ultra-Hard, the appropriate response is to gird for inevitable Armageddon, to carry the ball across midfield into enemy territory (to steal

---

62. Sally Carrighar, "War is Not in Our Genes," in *Man and Aggression,* ed. M. F. Ashley Montagu (New York: Oxford University Press, 1968), p. 46.

a metaphor fancied by the group), to adopt and use to the hilt enemy political warfare and similar unconventional methods, and to do all this in the firm conviction that the only chance of avoiding slavery or nuclear holocaust is thus to stand manfully up to the Beast, determined to do or die. For partisans of the Hard, the appropriate response is firmness, but tempered and defensive firmness—containment that teaches the Tiger limits to what it can do, and by slow pressure seeks to transform it into a pussycat, and to do all this without needlessly provoking it. For partisans of the Mixed view, the appropriate response is cooperative firmness, with emphasis on the former, designed to allay the Bear's fears by showing acceptance of it as a member of the human family and gradually to elicit positive cooperation from it.

Not surprisingly, each of these views has had its close supporters among members of American officialdom. The first is so close to Secretary Dulles's and the ascendant position of the Eisenhower years as to lead some commentators to describe the Strausz-Hupé version as an apologia for that administration.[63] The second is late Achesonism, connected with the Truman administration through the person of George Kennan. The third lost its last apologist high in government with the firing of Henry Wallace in 1946.

Egotism limitless, limited, and defensive—these are the major types of pictures that the American academic community has formed for itself of Soviet conduct toward other states. The question next to be answered is how well or poorly the best representatives of each are grounded in the data and in logic.

63. Thomas T. Hammond, ed., *Soviet Foreign Relations and World Communism* (Princeton: Princeton University Press, 1965), p. 136.

PART II: EVALUATION

CHAPTER 3

The Ultra-Hard Image: The Great Beast

The presence side by side of such divergent images of Soviet conduct as those described in the preceding chapter raises a question of the adequacy of American academic effort in this direction. Where images are incongruent there is a strong presumption that some, at least, have been poorly developed. This imparts added urgency to the task of evaluating individual studies, which is the concern of this part of the inquiry.

Evaluation implies norms, rules for separating "good" from "bad." For these I take certain simple criteria—some essential, some secondary—to which I believe few would take exception. So, I take "good" to mean "scholarly," in the most approbative sense, and "scholarly" (following *Webster's New International Dictionary*) to imply "accurate and well-disciplined learning." The essential marks of "well-disciplined learning" I take to be clear-cut general characterization substantiated by the historical record.[1] Secondary marks to which occasionally I shall refer are the enrichment of characterization by comparison, by awareness and criticism of alternative interpretation, by moderately neutral reporting. To the extent a work exhibits these attributes I shall call it "good," to the extent it fails to do so, "bad." An exhaustive critique on these criteria of the full sample being out of the question, I further proceed by confining extended comment to three of the leading delineations of each image, detailed analysis to one or two central propositions of each of these nine.

Such a *modus operandi* is concededly not perfect. The choice of criteria may be open to some challenge. So too may be the selections

---

1. For a similar reading of scholarship see Merle Curti, ed., *American Scholarship in the Twentieth Century* (Cambridge: Harvard University Press, 1953), pp. 1–2.

entailed by the further sampling. Yet the criteria collectively serve as a fair model of the kind of work and product most of us who aspire to being called scholars expect to have to meet in order to deserve the title; and the further sampling is not drastic.

LEADING EXPRESSIONS

Works developing the Ultra-Hard image of Soviet conduct, and visualizing the USSR as the Great Beast, are, as earlier recorded, the following: Bouscaren, Dallin, Goodman, Kintner, Kulski, Librach, Overstreet, Strausz-Hupé, and Wolfe. Of these nine I take Goodman, Strausz-Hupé, and Wolfe as representative of the best, on the standards given, and shall presently treat them, accordingly, in some detail.

Bouscaren, Dallin, and Librach, being primarily histories, are light on general characterization, and what there is they do not build up systematically from the data. The image is there, but dimly, and definition requires something of the reader. This is less true of Bouscaren than the others. But where Bouscaren does seek to analyze, he depends, and describes himself as depending, upon others, notably Strausz-Hupé.[2]

Kintner, Kulski, and Overstreet, who do attempt some systematic analysis, I exclude for different reasons. Kintner and Kulski mount their attack on the subject from a conceptual framework that lacks the coherence and orderliness of Strausz-Hupé or even Goodman. In addition, apart from brief introductions, they lack any true summary of their findings, and, Kulski in particular, they get bogged down in a plethora of detail, much of it extended quotations from Marxist-Leninist scripture, a fair amount of it repetitious. The Overstreets, of whom the above is not true, develop their themes systematically and write lucidly. But they, unlike Goodman and Strausz-Hupé, speak to a broader topic than external conduct proper (viz., Soviet society as a whole); and unlike Wolfe as well as these other two, the Overstreets confine themselves to the narrow time-span of Khrushchevian rule. Finally, the Overstreets exhibit rather less clearly than Wolfe a mode of interpreting the data—resort to the totalitarian model—of such importance to the general position as to demand special attention.

2. Anthony Bouscaren, *Soviet Foreign Policy: A Pattern of Persistence* (New York: Fordham University Press, 1962), p. 3.

But while Goodman, Strausz-Hupé, and Wolfe thus seem on balance the leaders of the group, it should be stressed that there exists a remarkable uniformity among the nine members thereof in terms of character and quality of method as in conclusions reached.

CASE 1: GOODMAN AND THE RUSSIFIED WORLD STATE

Elliot R. Goodman's *The Soviet Design for a World State*, published in 1960,[3] concentrates on Soviet external conduct, and especially the goals of that conduct, for the entire period from 1917 to 1959. Goodman's announced purposes are first to make concrete those goals (which he concludes are a world state run by the Russians) and second to question in their light the adequacy of the pattern of interstate relations presently prevailing in the non-Soviet world. Consonant with the second objective, he offers some prescriptive comment, devoting his final chapter to the sketch of a program of Western action which he believes appropriate to the challenge his findings reveal. His tone is the assured tone of one having a disagreeable duty to perform, a disturbing message to communicate.

Goodman starts out by recapitulating various formulations of the concept of a world state, notably those of Marx, Engels, Lenin, and other early Soviet leaders (Chapters I, II). He then raises the question of the bearing on the life and form of the concept of certain subsequent ideological and practical developments apparently inconsistent with it—whether abandonment or modification and, if the latter, what modification. Foremost among these subsequent developments are the revival of Russian nationalism, taken up in Chapters III and IV, and the rise of the doctrines of "socialism in one country" (Chapter V) and "peaceful coexistence" (Chapter VI). Later chapters deal with the kind of political structure the Soviets have had in mind for the projected state, whether unitary or federal (Chapters VII and VIII), its cultural affiliates, whether a set of national cultures or a single world culture (Chapter IX), and the methods sanctioned for achieving it, to what extent inclusive of war (Chapter X). A final set of chapters deals with the bearing on progress toward establishment of the World State of the interstate pattern presently prevailing in the bloc (Chapter XI, called "Way Stations to the Soviet World

3. New York: Columbia University Press.

State"), Soviet reactions to supranational plans from the non-Soviet world (Chapter XII), the bearing on the world-state concept of the classic Marxist doctrine of the withering of state power (Chapter XIII), and the response of the West appropriate to the findings revealed in the foregoing (Chapter XIV).

Goodman's findings, partly disclosed in several chapter headings, as well as his very title, are: (1) that the Soviets have today and have had from the beginning a world state as the goal of their conduct; and (2) that today and since as far back as the late '20s the form which that state assumes in their minds is that of a unit utterly Russified or subordinate to the Russian will. Goodman finds, moreover, that this is no distant objective, but one the consummation of which is set for the year 2000 and which is therefore quite "operational."[4] Other doctrinal formations or more recent developments not only do not "negate" these conclusions, but properly interpreted are quite consistent with them. The rise of Russian nationalism, for instance, means not the abandonment of the objective but its transformation from an idea originally egalitarian and universalist in nature to one inequalitarian and parochial, or, specifically, Russian-nationalist. The notions "Socialism in one country" and "peaceful coexistence" describe conditions with a definitely limited future. The present loose pattern of bloc relations is also temporary, being a "Way Station" on the road to the world state and due soon for replacement by the tighter, more integrated structure. The notion of the eventual withering of all state structures has itself withered.

Goodman's view of the objective of Soviet external conduct is thus one of near-limitless expansion of rule, and at that an expansion completion of which is set for the near future. Less fully worked out, his views of other facets of conduct are only somewhat less extreme. Conduct is expansive in implementation too, and thoroughly militant and coercive: accommodating, cooperative behavior is indulged only rarely, and then only out of recognition of necessity born of weakness.[5] Conduct is often military: the Soviet Union makes a practice of subjugating other nations by crude military force.[6] .Conduct makes

4. Ibid., pp. 127, 189.
5. Ibid., p. xvi and passim.
6. Ibid., p. xvii.

liberal use of deception.[7] Conduct is almost wholly initiatory: the Soviets pursue their goal relentlessly, continuously.[8] Conduct's motor is total ambition, revealed through Communist ideology properly interpreted;[9] and its consequences are to confront the world with grave danger.[10] Toward other Communist nations, for whose relation to the USSR "satellite" is too loose a term, conduct is a matter of a continuous tightening of control, with total subservience the objective.[11] Conduct does change from time to time; but the change is one of tactics only, goals remaining unchanged.[12] Comparatively speaking, it is a far cry even from that of the tsars; for the goal of tsarist conduct was limited rather than total, pursuit was fitful rather than persistent, and the means employed were haphazardly rather than totally repressive.[13]

The key propositions from Goodman's work which I take in subjecting it to more detailed examination are the central ones above resumed: that the Soviet aim is a world state, and a Russian-dominated world state at that. Goodman argues these propositions, I would point out, at much greater length than his colleagues of Ultra-Hard persuasion argue their near-equivalents "world domination," "world hegemony," "total control," and the like. An appraisal of his argument therefore also serves as an appraisal of the soundness of this important element in the general position.

The first of the two, that the Soviet design is a world state, Goodman develops in Chapter II. He goes about this by seeking to show continuous Bolshevik commitment from the earliest days, to this end arraying chronologically statements which he believes relevant from the Party leaders and basic Party and state documents, as well as from academic ideologues and lesser sources. And insofar as commitments in the early period are concerned, let it be said at once that he is on firm ground. His sources here are of the most authoritative. And they

7. Ibid., passim; for example, pp. 89, 176–77, 181.
8. For example, ibid., p. 473.
9. Ibid., p. 472.
10. Ibid., pp. 482–88.
11. Ibid., pp. 338, 355.
12. Ibid., p. 127.
13 Ibid., p. 128.

abound in explicit declarations of commitment to an International Soviet Republic and the like.[14]

Insofar as commitment to the objective in the later period is concerned, however, the case is different. With the data from the early 1930s and subsequent years, difficulties arise. For in the early '30s, Goodman notes, explicit references to a world state become rarer and rarer, and ultimately disappear altogether. Stalinite pronunciamentos, Party and state declarations, programs, constitutions—these fertile sources of earlier years now become barren. So, gone from the USSR Constitution of 1936 is the open assertion of the 1924 Constitution, that the USSR was to be the nucleus of a world state. Gone from the stated objectives of the Cominform, established in 1947, are such statements as those from the 1921 Statutes of its forerunner, the Comintern, counting among its aims the establishment of an international socialist republic. Stalin now speaks of the USSR only as model for a harmonious multinational state, not nucleus of a global unit.

Goodman copes manfully with this shrinkage in evidence. He concedes that it implies a decided lowering in the level of expectation of the immediate attainment of a world state. Nevertheless, he maintains, "the goal itself remains as the polestar of Soviet policy."[15] Why? His answer, as it emerges from the second half of his second chapter, is this: that it is only the most explicit formulations of the goal that have disappeared; that other formulations, "direct and open avowals," persist, to be uncovered by the patient inquirer; that there has been a "flurry" of such formulations since the Second World War; and that, in short, the theme remains, being now sounded only "sotto voce" rather than fortissimo, as formerly.[16]

Goodman copes manfully, but his case is unconvincing. The "flurry" of formulations in question turns out to comprise only six statements, not a lot for 15 years.[17] These statements come from the works of

14. Ibid., pp. 25–41.
15. Ibid., p. 47.
16. Ibid., p. 49.
17. Ibid., pp. 47–49. Condensed, these six statements are:

   1. A 1949 statement by one Kammari of the Soviet Academy of Sciences, who in an essay on the nationality question in honor of Stalin's seventieth birthday, affirmed that the banner of proletarian internation-

academicians, from *Pravda,* and, in one case, from a speech of Khrushchev's, but in no case from the Speeches and Resolutions of Nineteenth, Twentieth, Twenty-first Party Congresses or other top documents of the period. While all six breathe an expectation of global unification, five of them speak only of the fusion of nations and economies. The sixth, which comes from an essay written in 1949 by an academician named Kammari, does refer to political fusion. But the reference is to a "commonwealth of nations" and Goodman's contention that "commonwealth of nations" is a synonym for "world state" is singularly unpersuasive.[18] Moreover, Goodman fails squarely to face, much

---

alism "had rallied around itself the great commonwealth of socialist nations of the USSR," "is rallying around the USSR the People's Democracies," "will rally around itself the whole of toiling mankind," and "will lead to the creation of a great world commonwealth of socialist nations";

2. A 1949 statement by one Dunaeva, also an Academician, who in a companion essay to Kammari's quoted (approvingly, of course) Stalin's pronouncement that the USSR "is the prototype of the future amalgamation of the toilers of all countries into a single world economic system";

3. A statement from the *Short Philosophical Dictionary,* published in 1952, holding up the USSR as "the prototype of the future unification of all the peoples of the world";

4. An approbatory reference in a 1956 issue of *Pravda* to a Leninist dictum to the effect that the "relations among the peoples of the Soviet Union . . . will have enormous significance as the model for the peoples of the whole world";

5. A 1958 statement by a Soviet ideologue, one E. Modrzhinskaia, who in the course of a gloss on the validity of Lenin's vision for the future of mankind, affirmed that "the fusion of nations remains the aim of the Communists";

6. Finally, a series of statements from Khrushchev's Leipzig speech of March 1959 which picture the future world Communist society as one marked by the disappearance of borders, the "amalgamation of nations in a single Communist family," and "the consolidation of a single world socialist economic system," in consequence of the culmination of a process now going on in the multinational Soviet Union.

18. Goodman's argument is that "beyond question" "commonwealth" specifically means world state, since elsewhere in the same work Kammari states that "J. V. Stalin appraised the creation of the USSR . . . as a new

less satisfactorily to answer, a question heavily incumbent on him to answer. That is the question of why, should the Soviets in truth have kept the objective of a world state as he claims, they have discarded the older, explicit formulations. He ascribes the reduction in forthright statements to Stalin's shift in tactics away from world revolution and toward Soviet nationalism in the late '20s, a retreat to be followed later by an advance.[19] But this only raises the further question of why, when advance was resumed, as according to the author it was in 1939 and again in 1946, the forthright statements did not reappear.[20]

Goodman's second proposition—that the world state aimed at is a Russified one—he develops in Chapters III and IV. The issue he believes he has to face here is whether the growth of Russian nationalism since the early days of the USSR means a radical shift of the role on the international scene, and substitution of the part of traditional nation state, of limited aims, for that of revolutionary state of unlimited ones. This, "all the evidence" leads him to conclude,[21] is far from the case; nationalism has not only retained the concept but invested it with an ethnocentric content earlier unknown.

His evidence comprises the almost 80 pages and 18 sections of the two chapters referred to. Chapter III sounds the theme that the Soviets, confronted upon coming to power with the dilemma of fostering Marxist internationalism from a nationalist base (Section 2), came in practice in the early '20s to prefer the Russian interest in

---

and decisive step toward the amalgamation of the working peoples of all countries into a single World Socialist Republic, as the prototype of such an amalgamation" (ibid., p. 47). But earlier mention of "world state" in the same work, in the context of Stalin's expectations for the future of the USSR at the time of the USSR's creation, is hardly a sufficient demonstration.

19. Ibid., pp. 41–42.

20. An alternative explanation suggested later in the book—namely, that the "early pattern of plain speaking . . . probably alienated more people than it attracted to the Soviet cause," the clothing of the iron hand in a silk glove being required to soothe peoples' fear—also fails to satisfy (ibid., p. 125). For, on Goodman's own showing, the dicta of Soviet leaders are full of "frank" and "candid" statements (the author's words) boding ill for the non-Communist world equal if not more ominous in portent.

21. Ibid., p. 128

cases of conflict with the interests of other elements of the international movement (Section 3); that two interpretations of the phrase "proletarian internationalism," representing two approaches to a Soviet world state, concurrently grew up (Section 5), a purist one retaining the original connotation of brotherhood and equality, the other, or Russian-nationalist one, substituting the Russo-centered meaning; and that the second one, "perverting" the original meaning of the phrase, triumphed once and for all in the late '20s and early '30s (Section 7). The measure of change Goodman finds in a comparison of a definition of "proletarian internationalism" contained in a Comintern Resolution of 1928 (Section 4), which asked sacrifice from nations first successful in throwing off the bourgeois yoke, with Stalin's "classic definition" of 1927 (Section 7), which states "bluntly" that "he is an internationalist who unreservedly, unhesitatingly, and unconditionally is prepared to defend the USSR."[22] Subsequent reespousal in 1928–34 of the original purist concept and return to a revolutionary policy of direct support for other elements in the international movement Goodman dismisses as "pseudo-leftism."[23]

Chapter IV picks up the story in 1934 and carries it on up to 1959. In documenting for this period his theme of the finality of the victory of the Russian nationalist approach to the world state over that of genuine proletarian internationalism, Goodman gives us an exhaustive catalog of instances of Soviet preference by voice or deed of the Great Russian over other interests in the national or international movement. Most of these fall in the realm of internal nationality policy and its implementation.[24] Some instances of apparently contrary tendency he also reports, notably the appeal to a "Soviet patriotism" (i.e. one transcending that of any special group within the Union), the incorporation in the 1936 Constitution of the principle of equal rights for all races and nations, and the abatement of Soviet chauvinism following Stalin's death. But the first of these he terms a "mask" behind which "stood the dominating reality of Great Russian na-

22. Quoted in ibid., p. 76.
23. Ibid., pp. 77–78.
24. For instance, whole sections deal with the rewriting of histories to extol pre-Soviet Russian conquests, the punishment in the 1940s of non-Russian peoples who had defected to the Germans in the war, and the anti-Semitism of Stalin's last years.

tionalism";[25] the second he calls a "'liberal' face" behind which lay
the ugly reality of the purge;[26] and the third he dismisses as slight
and temporary, affecting only the more absurd aspects of Stalinist
chauvinism.[27]

The third section of the chapter typifying Goodman's thinking
and presentation, I recapitulate in some detail. This section, called
"Resurgent Nationalism in the Arena of the Second World War,"
mainly resumes the following events: in 1939, denials in Comintern
writings of charges that the Soviet state had become a purely national
state, pursuing national goals, and accompanying affirmations of
nationalism as a necessary and essential means to a universal end, all
of which is exemplified by an article in the June *Communist International* of that year; in 1939–40, following the pact with the Nazis,
the absorption of the western borderlands into the Soviet Union and
the defense thereof on the grounds that only through absorption did
the peoples concerned achieve "genuine national freedom and independence"; during the war, the rallying of support through the
invoking of purely Russian national heroes rather than the goals of
socialism, and the softening of hostility toward the Church, traditional exponent of Russian nationalism; at the end of the war, Stalin's
victory toast to the Russian people as the "Leading Force among the
Peoples of Our Country," and the hailing of the victory over Japan
as revenge for the latter's defeat of Russia in 1904.[28]

Goodman accepts all these items save the first at face value. The
exemplary article of the first item, from a June 1939 issue of *The
Communist International,* he describes further as reconciling Bolshevik internationalism with the new emphasis on national patriotism
and quotes it as calling the nation "one stage toward humanity," the
all-embracing "community which transcends all national limitations."[29] The meaning of these terms he now clarifies, aware perhaps
that he may be proving more than he wants—and that in the act of
documenting the case *against* the embourgeoisment of Soviet diplomacy he may also unwittingly be weakening his case *for* Russification

25. Ibid., p. 85.
26. Ibid., p. 88.
27. Ibid., p. 103.
28. Ibid., pp. 88–93.
29. Ibid., p. 89.

of a world-state goal. The uninitiated, he notes, might be tempted to infer from the article that all the Soviet leaders had in mind as future goal was absorption of all nations into a single, Communist world system, power relations among existing nation states not to be modified. However, such a premise, he goes on to point out, though "superficially attractive, does not seem to penetrate behind the Soviet manipulation of nationalist terminology nor grasp the connection between this nationalist terminology and the cause of socialism." Properly interpreted, the quote is an exercise "in Aesopian language," and for "humanity" one should read "world-state." Moreover, he continues, "the manner in which the peoples of the world are to achieve their fulfillment, as nations, specifically require that they be incorporated into an ever-expanded Soviet state, the ultimate and logical extension of which is a Soviet world-state."[30] Nothing further is said to substantiate this gloss on the passage, which inverts its meaning. The identifications—"world-state" for "humanity," and "expanded Soviet state" for "world-state," are apparently self-evident.

As further illustration of Goodman's thinking, I add from the fifth section of Chapter IV a statement from an editorial of a 1948 issue of *Voprosy Filosofii* lauding "Soviet patriotism" as a "patriotism of a new kind," which "blends harmoniously with proletarian internationalism."[31] The reader who is tempted to construe "proletarian internationalism" literally in this statement Goodman quickly sets straight. "Proletarian internationalism," he tells us, really equals Soviet patriotism, and behind Soviet patriotism, on Goodman's rendering, stands the "leading role of the Russian nation." Properly to interpret the statement, one is to discard the "empty" phrase "Soviet patriotism" and thus derive the formula, " 'Proletarian internationalism equals Soviet Russian nationalism,' an aggressive nationalism with unlimited aims." This in turn is called a "frank" equation, which amounts to saying, "We will pursue the goal of a world state, but only in such a way as exalts the position of the Russian people." Again, nothing further is said to substantiate the substitutions constituting this gloss.

Goodman seems to be arguing, in the nearly 80 pages above summarized, the following: that the growth of Russian nationalism has

30. Ibid.
31. Ibid., p. 101.

meant not the abandonment but the retention and Russification of the world-state concept because the developments normally understood by nationalism have included: (1) in the realm of theory, a reinterpretation or "perversion" of the phrase "proletarian internationalism" to connote Russian hegemony; and (2) in the realm of practice, the elevation to dominance of the Russian element in a state, the Soviet state, that logically extended would become the nucleus of a world state.[32] But this is the thesis on the fairest construction I can supply. And the first criticism I have of Goodman's second proposition is that he himself supplies no comparably clear-cut summary of his reasoning. He fails to articulate the intermediate steps in the argument—to show how the wealth of data he provides adds up to the conclusion he thinks it adds up to. At times, indeed, he writes as if this wealth of data, instead of performing the critical function of determining the conclusion, performs the subsidiary one of providing support for a conclusion already determined on other grounds. For as early as the fourteenth of his 79 pages, he speaks of a Russian-nationalist approach to a world state which presumes as already resolved the issue of the inquiry hardly begun.[33]

Assuming Goodman's argument to be what I take it to be, it is open, second, to serious objection in its theoretical component. That the phrase "proletarian internationalism" has been drained of its egalitarian and refilled with Russo-centered content Goodman poorly documents. His one citation directly to the point—Stalin's characterization of an internationalist as one who unreservedly defends the Soviet state—dates from 1927. Subsequent statements cited either carry an egalitarian connotation uncontested by the author or have the Russo-centered connotation on an interpretation by the author that involves undefended word-substitutions begging the very question at issue. The citation from *Voprosy Filosifii* mentioned above (p. 71) is a case in point. These statements are, again, few in number and, again, come from periodicals rather than the highest sources. Finally, Goodman makes no attempt to connect "proletarian internationalism" to any of the later formulations of the world-state concept he cites in

32. Ibid., pp. 126–27.
33. Ibid., p. 63.

Chapter II. He leaves the connection generally unexplained, contenting himself with the bare assertion that it exists.[34]

Assuming Goodman's argument to be what I take it to be, on fairest construction, it is open, third, to serious objection in its practical component. The validity of the tens of historical instances Goodman presents of Soviet elevation of Russian and debasement of non-Russian interests within the USSR and bloc are not here in dispute. The objection lies partly in Goodman's tendency to exaggerate the implications of phrases indicating preference for the Great Russians, for example, taking as an example of Great Russian chauvinism a reference to the "great Russian people" as "elder brother" among the nations of the USSR joined in "indissoluble fraternal friendship."[35] The objection lies partly in the playing down of moves of contrary tendency, as, for instance, downgrading the Comintern's antinationalist emphasis of the 1928–34 period as "pseudo-leftism" and as mask for Stalin's drive for power within the USSR;[36] calling the reduction in Great Russian nationalist appeals subsequent to 1953 a mere pushing into the background of the "more absurd aspects of Stalinist chauvinism";[37] and dismissing Soviet rapprochement with Tito in 1955 as simply a "reversal of Stalin's futile policy."[38] The objection lies mainly to the procedure of treating present practice as indicative of desire for the future—of deriving objectives from behavior, ends from means. The coupling of an ideal of equity with inequity of practice is not rare in human experience; it is, indeed, quite common. Commitment to the holding of such opposites may be a matter of plain, unrationalized inconsistency; or it may be recognized and rationalized—the holder may genuinely believe self-preference today to be indispensable to the achievement tomorrow of a general condition of equality.[39] But common it is, and of this Goodman has taken no account.

34. Ibid., p. 101.
35. Ibid., p. 104.
36. Ibid., pp. 77–79.
37. Ibid., p. 103.
38. Ibid., p. 104.
39. Moreover, such rationalization may, objectively, be correct, that is, a neutral observer may agree to the validity of the asserted causal relationship.

The influence of Russian nationalism on Soviet objectives is a matter of importance, and Goodman adduces a vast body of data in trying to settle it. But he has not framed carefully enough the argument the data are meant to support, nor on the likeliest construction of that argument (viz., that nationalism has meant the Russification of the world-state concept) has he spelled out clearly how his data tender their support. He spends much time arraying instances of Russian nationalism—entirely too much, since he could legitimately take this phenomenon for granted, referring for details to a number of solid earlier treatises.[40] Contrarily, he spends little time—much too little —on what is really important: critically assessing these data and demonstrating just why they have the significance he believes they have.

As one raises one's sights once more to the Soviet Design as a whole, these same weaknesses strike one yet more forcefully. The effort and care put into first things—into definition of the issue and its terms; into the structuring of argument; into the laying out of rules for deciding whether individual events do or do not fall within the terms as defined; into the aggregating of the data—these are sparse. The effort and care put into second things—piling up the data, sourcing, and referencing—these are excessive.

Consider what Goodman is really doing in processing and making intelligible the words and deeds, the gleanings from Soviet ideology and practice, which constitute the raw data he has gathered in such quantity. These words and deeds divide on their face into the two categories belligerent and peaceful, hard and soft. What Goodman is really doing is systematically taking those of the first category at their face value, but discounting severely or dismissing those of the second. He is, moreover, engaged in his threshing operation without offering any defense of what he is doing and, perhaps, without even being aware such a defense is required of him.

So, the hard words of ideology he almost invariably refers to as "frank" or "candid," while the soft he calls "deceptive" or reinterprets to mean something quite different from what they appear to mean. Stalin's statement equating true internationalism with unconditional

---

40. For example, Frederick A. Barghoorn, *Soviet Russian Nationalism* (New York: Oxford University Press, 1956).

support of the Soviet Union is a case of "blunt" speaking (above, p. 69). The 1936 Constitution's reference to the equality of nations, on the other hand, is mere "'liberal' face" (above, p. 70). And the reference in the 1939 article from *Communist International* to "humanity" (above, p. 71) is a reference "in Aesopian language" to "world-state."[41] The criteria for deciding what is a "frank," what a "deceptive" statement; the rationale for this selective crediting—these he does not reveal.

So, again, he weighs soft deeds as transient or ephemeral, while construing those of the hard type as basic or essential. Thus the policies of collective security and the United Front in the 1930s, the abolition of the Comintern in 1943—these are tactical retreats.[42] The liberalization of policy toward the satellites and the "many roads" doctrine of the '50s are "interim" moves, calculated plays for time, to permit digestion of setbacks pending resumption of progress toward the ultimate goal of total subservience.[43] The criteria for deciding what is "basic," what "tactical" and "interim"; the rationale for this selective weighting—these, again, he does not disclose.

Nor is this all. Goodman not only sifts his data on principles unexplained and apparently capricious, building thereon a complicated, esoteric interpretation; he does so without seriously considering the less complicated interpretation that stares him in the face. That the disappearance of explicit references to a world state might simply mean that the Soviets have given up this goal; that the joining of "proletarian internationalism" and Soviet Russian nationalist symbols might, again, imply simply a belief that under the new, unexpected conditions of "socialism in one country" progress toward a still egalitarian goal required for the time being that preference be given to the interests of the Russian nation—these possibilities he fails truly to face up to, instead dismissing them in an offhand and even casual manner.

---

41. Goodman is worried by this particular substitution, and by his refusal to take this quite Marxist statement for what it says. But he offers no reasoned defense for what he has done, contenting himself with chastising those of opposite view for failing to "penetrate behind the Soviet manipulation of nationalist terminology" (*The Soviet Design for a World State*, p. 89).

42. Ibid., pp. 42–45.

43. Ibid., pp. 354–55.

In short, Goodman proffers a complicated solution to his problem, and a tortuous way of reaching it, when a much simpler solution and more acceptable method lie ready at hand. And this is a pity. For the problem he has raised is an important one; he has raised many of the right questions, if not always in clear-cut fashion; and in ferreting out his data he has displayed an indefatigability virtually without parallel.

CASE 2: *Protracted Conflict* AND SHORT-OF-WAR MILITARISM

The second of the leading expressions of an Ultra-Hard image of Soviet conduct is the *Protracted Conflict* of Robert Strausz-Hupé and others, already noted in some detail in Chapter 2. Published in 1959, this work was reissued in 1963, enlarged to include a second preface and an epilogue.[44] Described by its publisher as "A Challenging Study of Communist Strategy," it can legitimately be considered a study of Soviet as well as Communist behavior for, as will be documented in the criticism below, it conceives of the Soviet leaders as controlling and directing the entire movement, and a preponderance of its data come directly from the Soviet experience, most from the postwar period.

As stated in its preface, the purpose of *Protracted Conflict* is analysis and, beyond analysis, the establishment of a common conceptual consensus among policy-makers and opinion elites.[45] True to this purpose it does not contain a detailed prescription for future American policy, this to await a second study for which the one at hand is to provide the base. Nonetheless, as the preface also notes, it does arrive at certain broad judgments on proper American response to Soviet behavior as revealed, and there is about it an urgency of tone that conveys even more by indirection. The proclaimed method is the "scientific" one of developing a theory—and the theory of "protracted conflict" is that theory—to which the facts of global crisis, however repugnant they may be, can yield their meaning.[46]

Protracted Conflict, as mentioned above, mounts its attack from a well-thought-out conceptual framework. It breaks down its topic on

44. Harper Colophon ed. (New York: Harper & Row).
45. Ibid., p. xiv.
46. Ibid., p. 6.

rational principles and relates these to one another in a coherent fashion. Successive sections deal with the setting or international environment in which the Communists live and act; their strategy in broad outline; the doctrine underlying that strategy; the "operational principles" which govern the implementation of strategy (four chapters); and the implications of the strategy and implemental efforts in terms of their effectiveness, the problems confronting the West, and likely future developments. In the case of each subtopic, it looks to what both Communist literature and the historical record have to say, proceeding systematically and generally in sober fashion.

From the above, Strausz-Hupé and associates fashion a number of reasonably clear-cut generalizations about their subject. Communism, they find, aims at "total victory" over the rest of the world. Communists are guided by a highly rational way of looking at the world and plotting action within the world to gain this end. The relationship to the rest of the world they look upon as one of almost boundless conflict—conflict occurring in not one but in many dimensions, conflict ebbing and flowing in an indefinite number of phases, hence "protracted." Doctrine teaches this way of conceiving the situation. It also teaches how conflict is to be managed. Specifically, doctrine dictates four operational principles for the making of strategic and tactical choices. These are the indirect approach—fighting the enemy through third parties; deception and distraction; monopolizing the initiative; and attrition, or exploiting conflicts in the enemy's camp. Following these principles, the Communists have achieved considerable success and are confronting their enemies, the West, with a crisis implicating the future of humanity.

Since Communist and Soviet are interchangeable, Soviet conduct is equally hard. Spelled out more fully in the preceding chapter, its objectives are unlimited and unchanging, its methods of pursuit virtually unrestrained. Driven by a lust for power, it is responsible for most of the crises that have afflicted the world since the Second World War. As closed society differs from open, so Soviet conduct differs from that of the United States and other democratic states.

The key proposition I select from *Protracted Conflict* in subjecting the work to closer examination is the proposition that Soviet conduct is distinguished *inter alia* by the indirect approach. Chapter 4, which develops this proposition, defines the indirect approach as one of avoiding a military showdown until such time as a balance of power shifts from the enemy's favor to one's own, reliance for the meantime to be placed upon indirect, irregular, and unconventional strategies.[47] The definition and subsequent variations thereon put a certain amount of stress on the negative element, of avoiding general war and proceeding obliquely. At the same time, the behavior referred to is presented as an approach, a mode of implementing a strategy of protracted conflict, a directive of doctrine calling in general for total, relentless hostility, the vocabulary and examples subsequently used running in terms mainly of the use or threatened use of military force. In other words, read carefully and in context the proposition makes a conditional or qualified affirmation, in which stress belongs on the positive element of the use of military means. Specifically it affirms a substantial resort to the military instrument, resort qualified only by stopping short of the point where general showdown threatens, resort qualified only by the reliance upon indirection which makes more feasible this stopping-short. More precisely, it either affirms this, or it affirms something inconsistent with the major themes of the work. I therefore assess it on this construction, affixing to it, as more apt, the substitute label "short-of-war militarism."

The data Strausz-Hupé and associates adduce in support of this general characterization fall into two categories: certain pronouncements of the Party and its leaders, and certain specific events from the year 1939 on. The latter again divide into events manifesting the behavior without being related to any particular implemental technique and, on the other hand, events that are so related. The particular implemental techniques in question, introduced into the exposition at half-point and discussed generally as they arise, are those of the graduated and ambiguous challenge, and the use of proxies, controlled and ad hoc.

The general statements comprise mainly pronouncements from Lenin in 1920, from the Comintern's Third World Congress in 1921, and from an article by Karl Radek in a 1934 issue of the American periodical *Foreign Affairs*. The Radek citation reads:

47. Ibid., p. 42.

The object of the Soviet Government is to save the soil of the
first proletarian state from the criminal folly of a new war. . . .
The defense of peace and of the neutrality of the Soviet Union
against all attempts to drag it into the whirlwind of a world war
is the central problem of Soviet foreign policy.[48]

The earlier two citations, which appear only in footnotes, speak
about avoiding battle under disadvantageous conditions.[49]

The principal historical events unrelated to any specific techniques
presented in evidence are, from Stalinist days: in the late '30s, Soviet
encouragement of an intra-West split and pursuit of the role of *tertius
gaudens,* culminating in the Non-Aggression and Neutrality pacts with
the Nazis in 1939 and the Japanese in 1941; in 1946, the maintenance
of Soviet troops in Iran past the agreed-on deadline, but subsequent
withdrawal under American pressure; in 1948–49, the Soviet blockade
of West Berlin, yet eschewal of interference with the American airlift;
and, in 1950, the Communists' attack on South Korea, with its reliance
on proxies.[50] To these are added three episodes from Khrushchevian
days which ultimately ended in Soviet retreat on a show of Western
firmness: in the spring of 1957, pro-Communist elements' precipitation
of crisis in Jordan following King Hussein's firing of pro-Soviet
Premier Nabulsi; in the fall of 1957, a Soviet attempt to reduce Syria
to satellite status; and, in the summer of 1958, ominous Soviet warnings aimed at forestalling Western military intervention in the Near
East in the wake of disorders in Lebanon and the anti-Western coup in
Iraq.[51]

The specific techniques of indirection to which the demonstration
now comes are first defined and then exemplified. The tactic of the
gradual challenge is the tactic of confronting the opponent with a
move so ambiguous, and so similar to a legitimate move like na-

48. "The Bases of Soviet Foreign Policy," *Foreign Affairs* 13, no. 2
(January 1934): 206.
49. Lenin's reads in part: "to accept battle at a time when it is obviously
advantageous to the enemy and not to us is a crime." The Comintern's reads:
"The Communist Party must develop into a militant organization capable
of avoiding a fight in the open against overwhelming forces of the enemy."
(Both are quoted in *Protracted Conflict,* p. 42 n.)
50. Ibid., pp. 43–50.
51. Ibid., pp. 50–52.

tionalism, that the opponent is uncertain about a proper response and temporizes till too late.[52] Exemplifying this tactic, said to be well adapted to the "gray areas" of the world, is the Indo-Chinese War.[53] In this war the Communists, by disguising their challenge as a national liberation movement (the Viet Minh), and by following a strategy of cultivating or compelling widespread community support, so deceived and confused the French that the latter failed to take decisive action until the situation was lost.

The tactic of fighting by proxy is the almost self-explanatory one of using others' forces to do one's dirty work. It carries the obvious advantage of enabling one to disown legal responsibility and so provide a safeguard against retaliation. Proxies used by the Communists may be controlled, a category which embraces the governments, parties, etc., directly under the Communist writ. Or they may be ad hoc, a category which includes governments, parties, etc., which, wittingly or not, further Communist objectives—neutral elites and governments, fellow-traveling parties, ethnic minorities and indigenous rebel groups in the free world or, indeed, "anybody who is prepared to undercut Western policies."[54] Specifically instancing use of controlled proxies are the use of the East European satellites in shipping arms to Guatemala in 1954 and Egypt in 1955 and the use of volunteers—actual, as by Mao in Korea in 1950–51, or threatened, as by Moscow in the Suez crisis of 1956.[55] Instancing the use of ad hoc proxies are: the use of the Algerian National Liberation Front in the late '50s, the Front being a group, say the authors, who, though probably led by Arab patriots who were not Communists, were shrewdly exploited by the latter; and the use of the Egyptians in 1956, who were "for all practical purposes" acting in the proxy capacity whether the decision to nationalize the Suez Canal was made on Moscow's suggestion or their own.[56]

The evidence for the principle of the indirect approach, so summarized, has a certain persuasiveness on first glance. However, on closer security, it loses much of this quality. Neither the general pro-

52. Ibid., pp. 52–53.
53. Ibid., p. 54.
54. Ibid., p. 57.
55. Ibid., pp. 59–62.
56. Ibid., pp. 63–64.

nouncements nor the historical data quite bear the load they are intended to.

Of the three general pronouncements—from Lenin, the Comintern, and Karl Radek—the last one is beside the point, while the other two must confront the challenge of being mere revolutionary rhetoric, and out-of-date rhetoric at that. Radek's statement, about the Soviet government's object of saving the USSR from being dragged into the whirlwind of a new world war, says only part of what it is supposed to. The principle of the indirect approach calls for the avoidance of war. But it does so within the context of pursuit of a policy of militant initiative only, and under the conditions only of an unfavorable power balance. Radek's statement calls for much more—for the avoidance of war within even the broader context of a policy of response, and under broader conditions unqualified as to time and power balance.

The appeal to statements from Lenin and the Comintern presumes a continued relevance to operational thinking that requires defense. That statements of this sort are faithful indicators of the operational thinking of those that utter them is far from self-evident. They may be this. But, again, they may be merely the brave effusions of the crusader. It is incumbent on those who rely on them to say something to substantiate that they are the first rather than the second. This is particularly so in the case of the authors of *Protracted Conflict*, who on the page preceding the two that contain the statements write that "Communists . . . never render candid accounts of the rationale of their actions."[57] The particular statements at issue, moreover, date back to a time of abnormalcy at the dawn of the Soviet era—a time since which much has happened, including the dissolution of the Comintern.

The historical data also are in a number of cases off the point or at least not unambiguously on it. The 14 specific cases cited, from Nazi Pact to Nasser's nationalization of Suez, alike are presented as centrally, that is, Soviet directed, militant Communist initiatives cautiously pursued, that is, pursued to a point short of embroiling the central power in direct military confrontation with superior force. But although the second part of the characterization is beyond chal-

57. Ibid., p. 41.

lenge, for Communist actions in all cases were indeed cautiously pursued so as to avoid major confrontation, the first part is not. The Algerian revolt and Suez affairs are cases not of Communist initiative, as the term "proxy" implies, but of indigenous nationalist initiative subsequently exploited by the Communists: points which parts of the text in effect concede.[58] So, too, are the events which sparked the three Middle East crises of 1957–58.[59] The Indo-Chinese War, while classifiable as a Communist initiative, is not a case of one centrally (i.e. Soviet) instigated and directed.[60] The dispatch of Chinese "volunteers" to North Korea in the late fall of 1950 is almost certainly a case of Chinese rather than Soviet initiative.[61] The Nazi Pact, the Iranian overstay, the Berlin blockade, the North Korean attack on South Korea, and the arms shipments to Guatemala and Egypt are thus the only reasonably certain cases of Soviet initiative.[62] And so instances supporting the generalization shrink from the original 14 to six. The six, moreover, while including some initiatives, like Berlin and Korea, that brought the Soviets to the brink of a major showdown, also include some like the Nazi Pact and arms shipments that did nothing of the kind and that are quite unexceptional in the behavior of nation states, offering slender documentation indeed for the theorem at issue.

58. Ibid., pp. 63–64.
59. Principal initiators were anti-Western, pro-Nasser forces. See G. Barraclough, *Survey of International Affairs 1956–1958* (London: Oxford University Press, 1962), pp. 161–82.
60. For the view, if anything, the Soviets disapproved of Ho's "liberation movement," at least in the early days, see Bernard Fall, *The Two Vietnams* (New York: Praeger, 1963), esp. pp. 195–200.
61. Although the Russians are likely to have been consulted. On this point see Peter Calvocoressi, *Survey of International Affairs 1949–1950,* (London: Oxford University Press, 1953), pp. 509–10; and Allen Whiting, *China Crosses the Yalu* (New York: Macmillan, 1960), pp. 152–60.
62. I put in the qualifier partly because the Nazi Pact may legitimately be viewed also as a Soviet response, partly because the Korean attack, though almost beyond challenge a move that without Moscow approval would not have been made, and in high probability a Moscow initiative, has still not conclusively been demonstrated to have been the latter. See, for example, Richard W. Leopold, *The Growth of American Foreign Policy* (New York: Knopf, 1962), p. 680; also P. Calvocoressi, *Survey of International Affairs 1949–1950,* pp. 473–75.

In sum, much of the evidence for the indirect approach on close analysis melts away. Corollary to this is the fact that the data adduced lend themselves as readily, if not more readily, to quite another interpretation of Soviet behavior—one quite foreign to the general theme of *Protracted Conflict*. For to the extent that initiation of the great crises of the era turns out to be traceable to sources other than the Soviet Union, the cautiousness of conduct documented by the book—the determination to avoid general, direct confrontation—is no longer the mere qualification of a posture of general militarism, but, as it were, a posture in its own right—the posture of unqualified defensiveness suggested by the Radek statement. And such an interpretation is incompatible with the general theme of *Protracted Conflict*.

As the above suggests, *Protracted Conflict*—to return to the book as a whole—suffers from certain procedural weaknesses, and these go far to offset its structural strength. These weaknesses I call habits of casual ascription and loose association. The attempts occasionally made to break them have the effect of blurring the overall picture.

Casual ascription is the habit of tracing to one source, without explanation, moves formally tracing to another. In *Protracted Conflict* it and its correlative, the casual identification of authors, initially take the form, exemplified by the treatment of the indirect approach above resumed, of picturing all Communist moves, with whatever party or state they may originate, as manifestations of a single strategy, a single will—ultimately Soviet strategy, a Soviet will. I call the ascriptions and identifications casual because nowhere in the volume are they, and the premises on which they rest, systematically faced up to, as sound procedure requires.

So the volume constantly speaks of Communist strategy as an integrated whole, confronting the West with a single, unified challenge and crisis. So it shifts facilely and nimbly in successive paragraphs, and even within a single paragraph, from "Communist" to "Soviet" or "Sino-Soviet" and back again.[63] It speaks of the bloc as directed by a "central intelligence"[64] and likens it to "an organism seeking to respond to individual situations on behalf of the entire organism

63. For example, Strausz-Hupé, and others, *Protracted Conflict,* pp. 45–46.
64. Ibid., p. 1.

rather than of its individual parts and capable of speaking with a single voice."[65] It finds, as "power center" of the international Communist movement, the Soviet Union, which "disposes over a formidable array of forces globally deployed and ready at any given moment to do Moscow's bidding."[66] Yet the validity of this organismic premise, so vital to the entire argument, it fails to confront directly and examine critically. It takes the monolithic character of the movement for granted, as above and beyond challenge. And more than this is to be expected of a serious work written in 1959—with the experience before it of the Yugoslav defection, the 1956 revolts and their sequelae, and the first rumblings of Sino-Soviet discord.

Less satisfactory yet is the extension of the procedure to cover non-Communist moves. The concept of the ad hoc proxy is indefensible. To see events like the Algerian revolt and nationalization of Suez as manifestations of Soviet strategy because they further Moscow and Peking objectives, or undercut Western policies, is to reason illegitimately from an identity of result to an identity of cause. This is not to say that indigenous nationalist movements do not have a place in a discussion of Communist strategy. They do. But their place is that of favoring conditions, or independent occurrences taken advantage of, rather than events initiated and directed.

The second procedural weakness I refer to, loose association, is another kind of offhand grouping of ideas, that of ranging under a single term a number of disparate, even discordant notions. When the catchall label that results is then applied to the conduct of a particular nation, the effect is to invest that conduct with a quite unwarranted intensity and distinctiveness—in the case of a pejorative catchall, to clothe conduct with menace of unwarranted dimensions and unusualness. The authors of *Protracted Conflict* exemplify this weakness by ranging the Nazi Pact and the provision of arms to Guatemala and Egypt alongside the Berlin blockade and Korean War as instances of their indirect approach, their short-of-war militarism, unmindful of any important distinction among them, unmindful too of the fact that the first two are matters of universal practice. Other exemplifications, from other portions of their work, include the

65. Ibid., p. 145.
66. Ibid., p. 56.

ranging, as examples of deception alongside deliberate falsification, of such disparate items as ambiguous statistics and exaggerated claims of operational ICBMs and other items of strength, unmindful of any important distinction, unmindful of the fact that misleading and exaggerated statements (and even, at times, prevarication) are not unknown to non-Communist and Western powers.[67] The net effect is an exaggeration of Soviet conduct and its uniqueness along these dimensions.

The authors of *Protracted Conflict,* it should be said, are not entirely unaware of the procedural weaknesses revealed in their work. A discussion of the Sino-Soviet rift in the epilogue added in 1963 represents belated if oblique deference to the obligation of saying something about the organismic premise.[68] The corpus of the Communists' operational principles, on the whole presented as matters of singular, unparalleled cunning, at times are represented as matters of quite pedestrian common sense.[69] But evidences of this awareness are sporadic and dim. And in expressing the awareness—in conceding a Sino-Soviet rift, in conceding the existence of authentic, anti-Western nationalism in the third world, in conceding the commonplace quality of much of what the Communists do—the authors introduce an element of ambiguity. Validity is gained, but only at a price. And that price is a loss of clarity and consistency.

This review must therefore also end on a negative note. Strausz-Hupé and associates have, like Goodman, striven honestly and industriously to fulfill their aims—in their case, the aims of establishing a common conceptual framework for the analysis of Communist (Soviet) conduct and of constructing a theory of that conduct to which the repugnant facts of global crisis would yield their meaning. And to a degree they have been successful. They have come up with a usable framework. They have produced a set of reasonably clear-cut generalizations to serve, under the name Theory of Protracted Conflict, as explanation for "the facts which matter," properly assessed.[70]

67. Ibid., Chapter 5. For comparison see deceptive American statements in the U-2 crisis, and the statements of the Johnson administration on Vietnam that gave rise to the so-called "credibility gap."
68. Ibid., pp. 173–78.
69. Ibid., pp. 40, 42.
70. Ibid., p. 6.

Yet it turns out on careful examination, as in Goodman's case, that if the theory fits the facts, it is only because the facts have first been culled and given meaning on principles of assessment not sufficiently recognized as such, let alone defended. If the theory fits the facts, in other words, it is only because the facts have first, quite unconsciously no doubt, been fitted to the theory.

CASE 3: WOLFE AND THE TOTALITARIAN KEY

Bertram D. Wolfe's *Communist Totalitarianism: Keys to the Soviet System,*[71] the last of the three leading works of Ultra-Hard persuasion, is a 1961 version and slight enlargement of a work entitled *Six Keys to the Soviet System,* which was originally published in 1956. Its scope is Soviet society in its entirety, its coverage the full span of the Soviet period, with emphasis on the war and postwar years. Its purposes are in the first instance to describe the nature of the Soviet animal, especially the scope and limits of change therein; in the second instance to contribute some of the elements of a general theory of totalitarianism; in the third instance to make easier the planning of policy in a land where "every citizen is, or should be, in some measure a maker of policy."[72] Its declared approach is "analytical" and "predictive," the author pridefully affirming his willingness to put to the test of conformity to the facts of the future any of the major propositions presently set forth.[73] Its tone is assured, urgent, in spots polemical.

Communist Totalitarianism is a collection of essays written over a period of 19 years, from 1941 to 1960, each dealing with a given aspect or element of the Soviet system. Related essays are grouped together under the heading "key." There are 23 of these essays in all, including minor ones called "postscripts," and seven "keys." The seven keys are, in order, "The Struggle for Power," "The Coordination of Culture," "The Worker in the Workers' State," "The Two Types of Soviet Election," "The Kremlin as Ally and Neighbor," "The Nature of Totalitarianism" (called the "master key"), and "The Soviet System and Foreign Policy." The last three most concerning this paper, most of the commentary and criticism below will refer to them.

71. Boston: Beacon Press.
72. Ibid , pp. xiv, xv.
73. Ibid., p. vii.

Wolfe's global theorem is that the Soviet system, as the species "totalitarianism" which it exemplifies,[74] is an autocracy of limitless power, seeking absolute control over its people within and the world without. It is, moreover, a regime of extraordinary durability. In consequence, according to Wolfe, we on the other side are in a war to the death, and it is incumbent on us, if we are to win that war, to devise an effective counterrevolutionary strategy. Such a strategy would include the lifting of self-imposed inhibitions against the use of force, the insistence that treaties entered into be self-enforcing, and the mounting of a propaganda campaign which would broadcast the truth that our side, not theirs, is the true friend of the freedoms and justice for which all yearn.

Consonant with this overall view, Wolfe's version of Ultra-Hard conduct glows with diamantine brilliance, eclipsing even that of Goodman or Strausz-Hupé. The aim is "total conquest of the world" and may become conquest of whatever other planets men may reach.[75] The means are: an unceasing expansiveness and a militancy that marks as enemy all other nations, especially the United States; an addiction to the military that stops just short of provoking all-out war; and an amorality marked by addiction to deception and "poisoned semantics," peace being looked upon as a maneuver rather than a principle.[76] Conduct is relentlessly dynamic, pressing on regardless of victories or concessions won from the other side.[77] Born of an ideology-produced lust for power, it is utterly intractable; nothing we do makes a difference, and attempts to counter it by any means short of force are doomed.[78] It has been successful to a degree few appreciate,[79] and it confronts us in the free world with "mortal danger," with "a universal, unitary, unending war to the finish."[80] Toward its own, conduct is tyrannical, exercising "ultimate control" over the billion-plus in the

---

74. Or "modern" or "communist totalitarianism": Wolfe uses the three interchangeably.
75. Ibid., pp. 76, 252.
76. Ibid., pp. 257, 295, 296, 299, 301.
77. Ibid., pp. 294–95.
78. Ibid., pp. 295–98.
79. Ibid., p. 252.
80. Ibid., pp. 298–99, 305.

Communist world.[81] It is unchanging and apparently unchangeable: goals, at least, are unshakable.[82]

Wolfe ties his concept of Soviet foreign policy to his concept of the kind of polity to which the Soviet system belongs. The Seventh Key to the Soviet system (Foreign Policy) cannot be understood, he tells us, without the Sixth or master key (The Nature of Totalitarianism).[83] The connection is cardinal to Wolfe's thinking. It is, moreover, a connection asserted or assumed by other students holding the same general position, not to mention the many leaders from outside the academic community who hold that totalitarian nations are inherently aggressive. Accordingly, to it I direct attention in examining more closely the adequacy of *Communist Totalitarianism*.

The central notions in Wolfe's argument, the nature of totalitarianism and the Soviet system, are worked out in the two essays comprising the Sixth or master key, of which the essay called "The Durability of Despotism in the Soviet System" is the later and more complete. Totalitarianism, according to the first four sections of this essay, is an extreme species of a genus called "total-power system."[84] A total-power system is one in which state power preponderates and is exemplified historically, *inter alia,* by Rome, Byzantium, tsarist Russia, and the oriental despotisms such as the Chinese empire. What differentiates totalitarianism from earlier species is its revolutionary aim and, consonant with that, the scope of the power aspired to. Earlier species were bent only on preserving the status quo; they were content to be stronger than society but not coextensive with it. Totalitarianism, on the other hand, has the revolutionary aim of fashioning a new man, a new society, a new world. In accordance with this it seeks more than undivided and unchallenged power: it seeks all-embracing power, aspiring to convert the state-stronger-than-society into the state-coextensive-with-society. Human nature being refractory, the total state is as a result "perpetually at war with its own people and with the rest of the world."[85] The weapons in this war are mass propaganda, terror, isolation, indoctrination, total organization, and

81. Ibid., p. 253.
82. Ibid., pp. 2, 255.
83. Ibid., p. 294.
84. Ibid., pp. 270–76 for the core of the development of the concept.
85. Ibid., p. 294.

total regulation.[86] Totalitarianism thus stands at the opposite pole from democracy, the other major contemporary type of social system. As a member of the larger class of total-power systems, totalitarianism is a closed system, a self-preserving as against a self-transforming system. It has a powerful "self-perpetuating institutional framework," which is "calculated to assimilate the changes which it intends and those which are forced upon it, in such a fashion that—barring explosion from within or battering down from without—the changes tend to be either inhibited or shaped and assimilated as within-system changes in a persistent system with built-in staying powers."[87] Substantiating this generalization are the cases of Rome, Byzantium, and many others. Wolfe does not attempt to spell out for us what he would consider a "change in the system," what a "within-system" change.[88] But the context makes clear that he considers the elements of autocratic control and reliance on terror, at least, to belong in the category "fundamental";[89] for he points out that in closed systems disturbances like the death of a dictator are, by some inexorable dynamic, soon resolved by the dissolution of collective leadership and the appearance of a new dictator.[90] And, in similar vein, he suggests that there is a like built-in drive toward maintenance of a high level of suppression and terror, these commodities tending to perpetuate themselves.[91]

That the Soviet system fits the type to a "T" seems to be Wolfe's message in the last eight sections of the "Durability" essay, where he turns from general to particular. The Soviet system is a "closed, single-centered, modern totalitarian society," he says in summary, its state seeking to be coextensive with the whole of society and the whole of life.[92] Its revolutionary aims are to transform the Russian into the "new Communist man," and win the world for communism.[93] Con-

---

86. Ibid., p. 268.
87. Ibid., p. 275.
88. In fact, he states (ibid., p. 281) that it would take a separate study to attempt the inquiry necessary to make the prior and basic distinction on which the above distinction rests, namely, the distinction between "what is fundamental to totalitarianism," and what is superficial.
89. Ibid., p. 281.
90. Ibid., p. 23; see also p. 282.
91. Ibid., pp. 9, 126, 251.
92. Ibid., p. 294.
93. Ibid. p. 278.

sonant with these aims, Lenin and Stalin set up, and Khrushchev and the other epigones inherited, a society "totally fragmented or atomized," dominated by a durable political system, "a regime of absolute force," itself controlled by "a centralized, monolithic, monopolistic party."[94] As a result, the Soviet system is "perpetually at war with its own people and the rest of the world."[95] If given a chance, its people would "vote with their feet" by the millions in favor of our system and cross over to our side, as demonstrated by the refusal of Chinese taken prisoner in the Korean War to return to their native land.[96] Comparatively speaking, the Soviets far more perfectly realize the type than their Fascist and Nazi competitors.[97]

The Soviet system also is highly change-resistant. The Bolshevik power-machine is the same today as when first established. It proceeds by zigzags to "basically unchanging goals."[98] It possesses a dynamic, a momentum, that keeps changes to the "within-system" category.[99] It has a built-in mechanism such that, faced with the death of the dictator, drives it inexorably toward the setting up of a new one, making collective leadership a transitory affair only—a process manifested by the ultimate success of Khrushchev's consolidation of power in 1957.[100] Again, when faced with a relaxation of purge and terror, its built-in tendency drives it inexorably toward reinstitution of these measures. The operation of this tendency is also manifested by developments in post-Stalin Russia. For, as Wolfe sees it, although there has been relaxation along this line, this does not mean the "moderate" purge has been dispensed with, nor even the blood purge (*vide* Beria and at least 25 of his friends), but only that they have been "held in reserve in case of need."[101] And, although reduced, the use of terror

94. Ibid., pp. 280–81.
95. Ibid., p. 294.
96. Ibid., pp. 289, 297.
97. "The Soviet state has existed longer, is more total, the power of Stalin and his successors more absolute, the purges bloodier and more sweeping and more continuous, the concentration camps larger and more 'useful' than anything Mussolini dreamed of or Hitler introduced. Only in his crematoria did Hitler's imagination exceed the deeds of Stalin" (ibid., p. 269).
98. Ibid., p. 281.
99. Ibid., p. 279.
100. Ibid., pp. 281–82.
101. Ibid., pp. 283–84.

toward the society, the concentration camps, etc., are still there.[102] Finally, the ideas at the very core of Leninism—ideas about organization, the dictatorship of an infallible elite, etc.—far from eroding have grown and expanded.[103] Wolfe concludes his "Durability" essay by urging that the main danger faced by the West is a too-ready self-deception marked by taking each shift in tactics (collective security, the Grand Alliance, peaceful coexistence) as a fundamental transformation.[104]

Such are the considerations Wolfe advances in affirming the association between Soviet external conduct and totalitarianism and in asserting that the Soviet enemy "can only be understood properly with the help of certain theoretical criteria of a socio-historical nature."[105] Like so much of Wolfe, they carry a certain conviction at first look, a conviction enhanced by the forcefulness and readability of the prose in which they are clothed.

However, the more closely one looks at them, the less adequate they seem to their purpose. In the first place, the argument is not clearly articulated. Wolfe nowhere says precisely just how he believes totalitarianism helps one understand the hardness of Soviet foreign policy. In the second place, on the fairest assessment, the argument, although provocative, suffers from three major defects. On this assessment, Wolfe seems to be urging this upon us: that Soviet foreign policy is Ultra-Hard and change-resistant because it is the outer extension or shell (my term) of a kind of system that is in essence Ultra-Hard and change-resistant. The questionable points here are the validity of the correspondence between shell and essence, the fit between the Soviet system and the absolutes defining the totalitarian type, and the attribution to particular and type of change-resistance.

The correspondence between shell and core, presumed only by the treatment of the Sixth Key, is clearly affirmed elsewhere. Only when Russia is democratic once more, Wolfe writes earlier in the book, will the outside world be safe and regain its hope of a genuine, just, and enduring peace.[106] And subsequently he says (italics his), *"When*

102. Ibid.
103. Ibid., p. 288.
104. Ibid., p. 292.
105. Ibid., p. 294.
106. Ibid., p. 19.

they are ready to make peace with their own people then we will know—and only then—that they are ready for real peace with their neighbours and with us."[107] But this is the closest he comes to recognizing this assumption cardinal to his argument. He does not confront it directly, much less examine it and weigh it. And this he needs to do. Though the theorem has an elegance and symmetry that are very persuasive—for what is more clear than that hard exterior and hard interior go together, soft and soft?—and although it deserves serious attention, still enough instances of contrary tendency come to mind, and come readily enough, to deprive the theorem of the claim to self-evidence. One thinks, for instance, of British or French imperialism of the late nineteenth century or the relatively peaceful policy of Franco's Spain or Tito's Yugoslavia today.[108]

The fit between the Soviet system and the absolutes defining totalitarianism Wolfe treats, in the argument resumed above, as perfect. The Soviet state, like the type, rules over a society "totally fragmented and atomized," with which it is unendingly at war; it, like the type, is a regime of "absolute force," "a total and absolute State, under total and absolute rulers."[109] But surely this is going overboard: Wolfe has let an infatuation with extreme terms carry him away. The Soviet Union is not *that* perfect, and Wolfe recognizes this indirectly. He sometimes speaks of the Soviet power as totalist in aspiration.[110] Soviet history knows more than a few instances of refusals to conform to the dictates of the supposedly all-powerful, and Wolfe cites some in his section "The Secret Places of the Heart."[111] A regime of absolute force poorly describes the post-Stalin system, and Wolfe documents this too.[112] To describe the condition between rulers and people as war, and Wolfe stresses he means war in a literal sense,[113]

107. Ibid., p. 296.
108. Cf. R. Barry Farrell, "Foreign Policies of Open and Closed Political Societies," in *Approaches to Comparative and International Politics,* ed. R. Barry Farrell (Evanston, Ill.: Northwestern University Press, 1966), pp. 167–208.
109. Wolfe, *Communist Totalitarianism,* p. 267.
110. Ibid., p. 279.
111. Ibid., pp. 289–90.
112. Ibid., pp. 284–85. Wolfe contends, however, that the more relaxed situation is only temporary.
113. Ibid., p. 314.

is false on any common-sense construction of terms. Surely one would place the Soviet Union near the upper end of a scale in these matters. But not at the absolute top.

The attribution of change-resistance to type and particular is intriguing. So is the allied typology of a "self-preserving," as distinguished from a "self-transforming" system, the former with its built-in propensities to absorb shocks and to shape them as "within-system" changes. The reasons for affirming these things are, however, tenuous. At times Wolfe appeals to us on the grounds that "the whole dynamics of dictatorship calls for a personal dictator, authoritarianism for an authority," etc.[114] Yet this is at bottom another way of saying, "what is will continue to be," and ultimately of presenting as a matter of predication what is really a matter of definition. He offers a more serious argument in urging, at the beginning of the "Durability" essay, that the total-power systems of which totalitarian systems are a species are change-resistant, and in citing the longevity of the Chinese, Roman, and tsarist empires by way of example. But the question at once arises whether a relative changelessness shown to attach to the conservative species of the genus can reasonably be supposed to carry over to the more dynamic, revolutionary species. The history of certain other members of the revolutionary species, notably Nazi Germany and Fascist Italy, hardly inspires confidence that the answer to this question would turn out to be affirmative.

To establish a proposition about built-in propensities and self-correcting or self-regulating mechanisms requires considerable investigation. The validity of affirmations about homeostasis in the human body, for instance, rests on hundreds of observations to the effect that a break in the circulatory system is indeed corrected by the clotting of blood, etc.[115] We lack such data for totalitarian systems, since they are relatively recent phenomena, and Wolfe is therefore to be forgiven for not supplying them. But precisely for this reason he is not entitled to consider the self-corrective nature he affirms about them as more than hypothetical.

As for attributing changelessness to the Soviet system, Wolfe would again seem to have yielded to the temptation of ascribing undue per-

114. Ibid., p. 282.
115. Cf. Walter B. Cannon, *The Wisdom of the Body*, rev. and enl. ed. (New York: Norton, 1939), Chapter II and passim.

fection. Judged by the record up to the time *Communist Totalitarianism* appeared (1961), the post-Stalin collective leadership and liberalization had persisted long enough to make "temporary" hardly an apt term. And if the record up to today (1969) is used as a test—and this predictive test is the test Wolfe invites us to use[116]—the term would seem singularly inapt. For post-Stalin moderation has now persisted quite a long time, long enough, in fact, to lead some highly competent observers to refer to the system today as "post-revolutionary" and "post-totalitarian."[117]

Wolfe has, in short—I think it fair to say—performed the task of tying his Ultra-Hard concept of Soviet external conduct to the totalitarian model not so much by rigid demonstration as by a certain loose and impressionistic procedure of juxtaposing like ideas. Outer matches inner, particular general, general is Ultra-Hard by definition, and there we are: the chain is complete, encumbered by a minimum of references to the record. Hence what he presents with conviction as self-evident truth or truth well substantiated—and most of what he writes exudes this conviction—is in reality entitled to the status only of hypothesis.

Wolfe aspires to give us the beginning of a theory of totalitarianism, and he does that. But he believes he is much further along with the job than he is. For it is a bare beginning he gives us. In constructing his theory he hardly gets beyond the stage of definition, and confusions beset even these initial efforts. The usefulness he claims for his "keys" in providing an understanding of the Soviet Union is, accordingly, overstated.[118]

116. Wolfe, *Communist Totalitarianism*, p. vii.
117. For instance, Richard Lowenthal, "The Soviet Union in the Post-Revolutionary Era: An Overview," in *Soviet Politics Since Khrushchev*, ed. Alexander Dallin and Thomas B. Larson (Englewood Cliffs, N.J.: Prentice-Hall, 1968). The general point stands despite recent indications of change in a Stalinist direction.
118. A good theory about a species of polity first defines the species, doing so in clear, unambiguous terms; then predicates certain things as true of the species so defined; then guides the submission of these affirmations to empirical test. The strength of the understanding of a particular of the species to which the results are applied, and about which predictions are made based on the results, depends on how carefully these preliminary steps have been carried out, not to mention also, of course, on how carefully the particular in question is shown to bear the features defining the type.

As one turns back to *Communist Totalitarianism* as a whole, from the Totalitarian Key to the more direct supports Wolfe offers his Ultra-Hard characterization, one finds the situation hardly more satisfactory. Like Goodman, Wolfe resorts at times to the capricious devices of selective crediting and selective weighting in sifting his data. Like Strausz-Hupé, he indulges the practice of casual ascription. Like both, he lapses into an imprecision of terms. For instance, the reader is told implicitly that he is deluding himself if he does not take at face value the proclaimed aim of world revolution, but, on the other hand, deluding himself if he does take "peaceful coexistence" at face value, no criterion being offered for distinguishing a true from a false statement.[119] China is as late as 1960 treated as part of the Soviet Union, the dictates of its rulers Soviet dictates, the resistance of its people resistance to Soviet rule.[120] That the Soviet aim is "total world conquest," nowhere directly documented, apparently rests on nothing stronger than an assertion that Lenin meant world conquest when he said "world revolution."[121]

Wolfe does essay systematically to document his proposition that

---

In saying that Wolfe's theory barely gets beyond the definition stage and is beset with confusions, I have a number of criticisms in mind. While his concept of totalitarianism is in a general way apprehendable, there is a disturbing inconsistency in its formulation. At one point the concept is defined in terms of actuality, of all-embracing power actualized, while at another point it is defined in terms of aspiration, of all-embracing power aspired to (Wolfe, *Communist Totalitarianism*, p. 279). At one point "single-centeredness" seems clearly part of the definition, at another not so (cf. ibid., p. 275 with p. 294). As already noted, a variety of names are supplied—"totalitarianism," "modern totalitarianism," and "Communist totalitarianism"—with the grounds of distinction, if any, not given. Definition and predication are sometimes mixed up (see text above, page 93). Which way the inference is supposed to run between statements about type and statements about a particular is not always clear. Finally, there is throughout a paucity of empirical reference.

119. Ibid., pp. 302, 299.
120. The island of Quemoy is inferentially seen as a Soviet point of confrontation with the West (ibid., p. 296). The refusal of Chinese volunteers taken prisoner during the Korean War to choose repatriation at the war's end is presented as evidence of the pervasiveness of opposition to Soviet rulers from their own people (ibid., p. 297).
121. Ibid., p. 209 n.

Soviet conduct is ceaselessly expansive. From 1945 to 1955, he affirms in "A Note on 'Colonialism,'" the Soviet Union subjugated 13 million square kilometers of territory and 575 million people.[122] Between 1955 and 1960, in a follow-up to the above called "And One More Note on 'Colonialism' Five Years Later," he affirms a continuance of the trend, offering in support of the affirmation the subjugation of North Vietnam and Tibet, the suppression of revolt in Hungary, and the attempts on Laos, Congo, and Cuba.[123] But the figures for the 1945–55 conquests include China, which is hardly describable as a puppet even so far back as 1949–55. The six cases cited as instances of continued successful Soviet expansion of rule in 1955–60 are wide of the mark: three are cases of the expansion of influence only (Cuba, Laos, Congo), one of them (the Congo) an unsuccessful attempt; one is a case of the preservation rather than the expansion of rule (Hungary); while the remaining two (North Vietnam, Tibet) are of non-Soviet authorship. Further, his demonstration is incomplete, excluding as it does cases of contraction. If the seizures of Porkkala from Finland and Port Arthur from China in 1945 are to be noted as cases of expansion (and Wolfe does so note them), then, on careful procedure, the retrocession of the same in 1955 should be noted as cases of contraction. If China is indeed to be described as a puppet taking orders from Moscow in 1949, but a junior partner in 1960—as Wolfe claims[124]—then her change of status in the interim should be recorded as a rather tremendous contraction of the Soviet writ.

There is much to admire in Wolfe. He writes exceedingly well. He has made an honest attempt to get started in the direction he has set himself. *Communist Totalitarianism* contains many insights. His critique of Soviet authority's meddling with science and history is penetrating.[125] His understanding of democracy is profound. But he is not, I think it not unfair to say, a systematic thinker.

Wolfe criticizes, and properly so, the Soviet treatment of history as being intellectually bankrupt. He justly accuses Soviet leaders of reversing the roles of history and experience, on the one hand, and ideology or theory, on the other, forcing history to conform to theory

122. Ibid., p. 253.
123. Ibid., p. 254.
124. Ibid., pp. 217–18, 255.
125. Ibid., pp. 56–80, 95–112.

rather than the other way around.[126] He rightly calls them "terrible simplifiers," "monists" who have no tolerance for pluralism in theory or in life, for whom "doubt is intolerable."[127] He fairly indicts them of specious "reasoning by definition," saying in making this point:

> By definition, it is impossible for the Soviet Union to be imperialist; by definition, it is impossible for the United States not to be imperialist; by definition, whatever the Soviet Union does is peaceful, and by definition whatever the Soviet Union does is democratic.[128]

Yet, unhappily, he himself commits many of the same mistakes. He bends historical data of Soviet behavior to his theory rather than the other way around (the accommodating moves on the international front are deceptive, tactical maneuvers only). He presents the present international turmoil as a war to the death between the totalitarian enslaved and the democratic free world—a terrible simplification. His writing contains hardly a scrap of doubt as to the truth of what he has to say. And as for reasoning by definition, one has only to recall the grounds for his prediction that collective leadership would be transitory and a new Stalin emerge:

> . . . the whole dynamics of dictatorship cries out for a dictator, autocracy for an autocrat, . . . an authoritarian setup for an authority, a totalitarian state for a *Duce, Führer,* or *Vozhd.*[129]

Against the standards set forth at the beginning of this chapter, the leaders among the works expressing an Ultra-Hard image of Soviet external conduct fare indifferently well. Accurate in detail they are, on the whole.[130] But well disciplined, on the whole, they are not, on either of the two sets of criteria.

On the essential criteria of well disciplined, the showing is in-

126. Ibid., pp. 77–78.
127. Ibid., p. 78.
128. Ibid., p. 231.
129. Ibid., p. 23.
130. Among occasional errors: Strausz-Hupé's suggestion *(Protracted Conflict,* p. 52) that the ominous Soviet warnings directed against the West in the Lebanon crisis of 1958 occurred before the Anglo-American landings rather than after; Wolfe's placing the population of East Europe at "at least half a billion people" *(Communist Totalitarianism* p. 253), rather than about 100 million.

different. All three, it is true, issue in clear-cut general characterization, for all three make unmistakable their common conclusion that Soviet conduct stands at the Ultra-Hard end of the scale and is unchanging. And two of the three draw liberally on the historical record. Yet at the crucial juncture of the careful definition and differentiation of concepts, and their consistent application to the data, all three fall down. For all three indulge a casual association of ideas that permits them to bring the most diverse of phenomena under a single rubric, to equate with one another the most variegated conditions. For one, the global fusion of economies or nations is equivalent to political fusion, a world state. For the second, agreeing to a nonaggression treaty, selling arms, blockading a city, and waging war are alike cases of short-of-war militarism. For the third, the ruler-ruled relationship within the Soviet Union, the Soviet-Western relation in the world, and the war against Nazi Germany are alike cases of war.

All three, again, resort to another form of offhand connection, which I call casual ascription, tracing to central (i.e. Soviet) initiative hostile Communist moves from whatever element derived and sometimes, even, hostile (i.e. anti-Western) moves of non-Communist authorship. Most important, all three resort to certain sifting devices that remain unexplained and unexamined, and of which they seem quite unaware—the devices I call selective crediting and selective weighting. The net effect of the use of these devices is to put aside as false, deceptive, or tactical maneuver all accommodating moves, gestures, and doctrinal formulations, but to accept at face value all belligerent moves, gestures, and doctrinal formulations. The net effect of all the above procedures is to make the substantiation of conclusions more apparent than real.

Nor is the showing better on the additional, nonessential criteria. The exposition, while at times polemical, keeps within reasonable bounds in its occasional resort to affective language. But not many comparisons are drawn, and those that are are unduly simplistic. The claim, for instance, that for the Soviets peace is a calculated maneuver, but for the West a matter of principle;[131] or the claim that while Soviet conduct basically is a matter of a conspiratorial drive for world conquest, American conduct is basically a matter of "high-minded

---

131. Wolfe, *Communist Totalitarianism*, p. 31.

dedication to moral principle"[132]—these claims are surely excessive. Finally, no serious attention is paid to alternative constructions. Such constructions are either recognized adequately, but rejected without any true argument;[133] recognized obliquely, but dismissed as longing, wishful thinking, or self-deception;[134] or, most commonly, not even recognized.

All three of the works examined proclaim that they proceed empirically, from interrogation of the historical record to the construction of valid conclusions about Soviet behavior which would improve our understanding of and ability to predict the course of that behavior, and so permit us better to plot our own conduct toward our own goals. But the burden of the judgments rendered above on conceptualization and application to the record is that these works have mistaken for genuine empiricism a method which while appearing to be empirical remains *au fond* largely a priorist. On their own standards, too, they don't quite measure up.

The works examined have made a number of excellent contributions: in the first, an exhaustive catalog of dicta relative to goals; in the second, a coherent, well-thought-out schema for analysis; in the third, several suggestive hypotheses. But they have failed adequately to sustain the common view that Soviet conduct is Ultra-Hard. Is the Soviet objective a Russified world state? The data adduced not only do not demonstrate this, but, when the capricious sifting devices are put aside, suggest rather that this objective has been discarded. Is Soviet implementation of objectives a matter of ceaseless initiatives, militarist to the point just short of provoking general war? The data adduced not only do not demonstrate this, but, when terms are strictly defined and applied, support as readily a conclusion of rather considerable reactiveness and cautiousness. Are objectives and implementation basically unchanging? The general theorem of totalitarian changelessness offered in demonstration is provided no real support, and stands up poorly when judged on the post-Stalin experience.

If the works examined are truly representative of the leading treatments of the type, it follows that the Ultra-Hard image, picturing Soviet conduct as that of the Great Beast of the Apocalypse, has yet to be sustained.

132. Strausz-Hupé, and others, *Protracted Conflict*, p. 144.
133. For instance, Goodman, *The Soviet Design for a World State*, p. 89.
134. For instance, Wolfe, *Communist Totalitarianism*, p. 292.

CHAPTER 4

The Hard Image: The Mellowing Tiger

The second of the three major image types of Soviet conduct, the Hard image, differs from the first, it will be remembered, in two main respects. While it continues to affirm of behavior an aggressiveness menacing to peace and order among the nations, it also affirms the existence of some limits to both objective and means of pursuit, and it admits fear as an occasional motive. What is yet more important, it conceives of behavior as in significant degree flexible and mutable, capable of significant evolution.

Seven of the 22 works of the sample express views close to this image type. How well the leaders among these stand up to the criteria of scholarship set forth at the start of the preceding chapter is the concern of the present one.

LEADING EXPRESSIONS

Of the seven works in question—Kennan, Mosely, Schwartz, Shulman's two, Tucker, and Ulam—I find Kennan, Shulman's *Stalin's Foreign Policy Reappraised,* and Tucker the leaders, and I shall accordingly deal with these three in some detail.

Mosely and Schwartz I exclude partly for reasons of substance, mainly for reasons of approach. As already noted, Mosely and Schwartz vary more from the type, by virtue of attributing to Soviet behavior less changing a character and seeing, for instance, little significant change on Stalin's death. More important, both are collections, and as collections they fail to overcome (in degree considerably greater than Tucker) the disabilities which afflict this sort of work, of which a certain disjointedness or lack of integration is foremost. Finally, though Mosely and Schwartz are academicians of impeccable standing, they write largely from the perspective of the contemporary commentator, supplying little general characterization. The typical chapter from Mosely is confined to analyzing some recent development of the day or dealing with some part of the total topic; conversely, it devotes little effort to developing the overall pattern, to sorting out and applying concepts systematically. Schwartz is even more episodic, as is of course natural, given the predominantly journalistic basis of his work; and though he does provide introductions to each chapter and a summary chapter for the whole, as Mosely does not, explicit general characterization is even sparser with him.

Ulam also I exclude partly for reasons of substance, mainly for reasons of approach. Ulam too varies from the type by virtue of attributing substantial constancy to behavior. His insufficiency from the viewpoint of approach, on the other hand, is that of the history pure and simple—high on the temporal ordering and explaining of events, low on the building thereon of general characterization. Shulman's *Beyond the Cold War* I pass over in favor of the earlier *Stalin's Foreign Policy Reappraised* because the former, in line with its objectives of educating the nonspecialist, makes less attempt to document the general theses which the two together set forth.

But if Kennan, Shulman's *Stalin's Foreign Policy Reappraised,* and Tucker are the leaders among the seven works of this group, the other four make significant contributions. Mosely and Schwartz have a detachment that goes with solid, responsible commentary, and a down-to-earth respect for detail and a "feel" for events that go along with extensive personal familiarity. Shulman's *Beyond the Cold War,* resumed in Chapter 2, while repeating largely the view of *Stalin's Foreign Policy Reappraised,* does so within a broader spatial and temporal context. Ulam's work is a brilliant history, quite the equal of Kennan's or Halle's: less imaginative, perhaps, but complete in scope (as these others are not), equally thoughtful, equally well written, and more consistent in its interpretation.

CASE 1: KENNAN AND HIGH-STALIN MILITANCY

Kennan's *Russia and the West under Lenin and Stalin,* published in 1961,[1] centers on the relationship named rather than on Soviet conduct proper. Drawn from lectures delivered in 1957–58 and 1960, it covers the entire Soviet area, though giving the years from 1945 on

1. Boston: Little, Brown.

rather short shrift. Its declared objective is first to fill the void represented by the lack of a full-span treatment of the subject, and second
to counter tendentious Soviet histories by providing an account true
to Western "ideals of historical truth."[2] In the implementation of this
primarily descriptive objective, however, it does not hesitate to pass
judgments on the merits of actors or policies East or West, and its
concluding chapter in particular offers guide lines for Western and
particularly American conduct toward the Soviet Union. The tone is
moderate.

Kennan's book is chronologically ordered. An opening chapter on
the "Conflict of the Two Worlds" deals with differences in focus
between Russia and the West at the time of the revolutions, a second
chapter the failure of the provisional government. Kennan then devotes 10 chapters to Brest-Litovsk, the Western interventions, the
peace conference, and other events of the 1917–20 or so-called civil
war period, nine chapters to the 1921–39 period of first "normalcy"
and then the rise of fascism, one chapter to the period of the Nazi
Pact (1939–41), and two chapters to the anti-Hitler alliance of
the period of the Second World War. Each chapter is a discussion
centered on a key person (e.g. Stalin), a key event involving the
principals (e.g. Rapallo), or a key development on the world scene
(e.g. the rise of Hitler), as the case may be. A final chapter, "Keeping a
World Intact," treats of the postwar period.

Russia and the West does not summarize easily. It is in a sense two
books. It is both a description of the course of the conflict between
the principals named and a critique of overall Western policy in the
two world wars. Its main theme, drastically condensed, may be read
as follows: that the conflict between the two worlds originated in
a misunderstanding connected with the Western interventions of
1918–20, which the West intended as means of rebuilding eastern
pressures against Kaiser Germany, but which the Soviets saw as an
effort to strangle at birth the Glorious Revolution; that the conflict
continued (muted, of course, in 1941–45) and became intensified
largely because of the implacable hostility generated by Communist
ideology, the machinations of the Comintern, and Stalinist paranoia,
secondarily because of Western lack of perceptiveness, Western
diplomatic maladroitness, and, after the Second World War, excessive

2. Ibid., p. viii.

American moralism; that the future is nonetheless not without hope, for provided there continue the significant moderation of the Soviet attitude begun at Stalin's death, and provided the United States forgoes its simplism and addiction to moral absolutes, the chances are good that the conflict will subside, a "normal level of recalcitrance" come to prevail on both sides, and the world be kept intact. The volume's strong second theme is the failure of the West to make sensible peace with Germany in 1919 and in 1945, and to keep the peace that was made in 1919. For this the policy of unconditional surrender is to blame, inasmuch as this policy, besides paving the way for Hitler, had as its by-products bringing Soviet power into being in 1917 and bringing Soviet power into East Europe in 1945.

In the course of his historical narrative, Kennan develops his general characterization of Soviet conduct. Rather, he develops two characterizations, the work revealing a subtle, but important inconsistency. In the earlier version, found mainly in Chapter 13, conduct's objectives are the unlimited ones of world revolution and the utter extinction of capitalism, which derive from the ideology of implacable hostility and messianism already referred to.[3] In pursuit of these objectives, conduct is highly militant, exuding incessant hostility toward the West. Less clearly, it is expansive in implementation, moderately militarist, unscrupulous. Less clearly too, it is initiatory rather than responsive, driven by ambition born of revolutionary zeal, domineering in its behavior toward other elements of the Communist movement. Implementation of policy proceeds simultaneously along two paths: a more militant one leading directly to the overthrow of other governments, of which the chosen instrument is the Comintern; and a less militant, more accommodating one leading only indirectly to this end and exemplified by the quest for trade, aid, and recognition in the early '20s, and participation in traditional balance of power politics—of which the chosen instrument is the Ministry of Foreign Affairs. Of the two, the first is fundamental, the second derivative; the first high-road, the second detour. Successes have been indifferent. What have seemed to be successes of great magnitude turn out on analysis to be as much the result of Western ineptitude as Soviet skill. Conduct contrasts sharply to that of Western societies.[4]

3. Ibid., pp. 183–93.
4. Ibid., pp. 189–93.

The later version, found in Chapter 25 at the end of the volume, repeats the formulation, but with significant modification.[5] It elevates the second implemental path to a position of equality with the first and connects it to a newly discovered set of aims and motives. For in his final chapter, which contains this version, Kennan marks a true duality of motive and enshrines, along with the revolutionary, offensive, messianic one that once ruled alone, a more moderate, defensive one directed toward the protection of the national interests of the Russian state. This mix of motives, moreover, like the corresponding mix of implementary techniques, he describes as having shifted secularly in the more moderate direction, and spectacularly so since Stalin's death. The potentiality of cooperation with the capitalist world has risen correlatively, whence the final, clarion call for a commensurate moderation of response from the West. Kennan also, in this second version, comes to ascribe a low addiction only to use of military force.

While Kennan's earlier version of the Hard view differs quantitatively only from versions of the Ultra-Hard—being less extreme, less explicit, less insistent—his later version differs qualitatively, its affirmations of a national-interest motive, a decided nonmilitarism of method, and a moderating trend being elements foreign to the Ultra-Hard image.

Kennan's substantiation of the various components of his characterization of Soviet conduct is uneven. He offers virtually no demonstration at all of his last chapter's contention that the secular trend in conduct has been toward normalcy, and that post-Stalin moderation of the Soviet regime is a matter of deep and encouraging significance.[6] Moreover, his characteristic treatment of a period or episode is to sketch the setting, the details, and the denouement, to offer an explanation of the last, and then to extract a generalization about the behavior of one or both of the parties thereto, or of nations at large. Many of his generalizations appearing only in this context, the demonstration, where it is offered, is thus often tied directly to a single case only, the reader being left to uncover further evidence for himself.[7]

5. Ibid., esp. pp. 386–95.
6. Ibid., pp. 394–95.
7. His proposition about Soviet successes is an example: ". . . the standard components for a rousing Soviet diplomatic success [are]: one part Soviet

Much of *Russia and the West,* however, may be considered to serve
as substantiation of his major proposition about high Stalinist militancy, and I therefore focus upon it in subjecting the book to a closer
look. I further take, as representative of his treatment throughout, his
treatment of the middle and late '30s, that is, the so-called collective
security period of Soviet diplomatic history. Kennan, I would recall,
sees Soviet conduct at this time, particularly in his earlier version, as
uncompromisingly messianic and revolutionary, bitterly, relentlessly
inimical to the rest of the world. "Action hostile to the Western governments . . . flowed from Moscow in a single uninterrupted stream
over the course of decades," he tells us.[8] Demands for aid, trade, recognition; participation in defensive alignments—these more accommodating activities were "regrettable temporary expedients."[9] The
question I raise can thus be reformulated to ask how well his detailed
account of activity in 1934–39 fits these general descriptions.

Kennan develops his thought on the period in Chapters 20 and 21
("The Struggle against Hitler, and the Purges" and "The Non-Aggression Pact"), often in the form of a mild polemic against Western
liberals of the day. He sees the issue as whether there was a "real
possibility of an effective coalition" between Russia and the West
"for the purpose of frustrating Hitler's aggressive ambitions and preventing the catastrophe of a second world war."[10] Liberal thought of
the day, he notes, believed there was such a possibility and that the
blame for its failure to materialize lay primarily with the British and
French, whose policies of appeasement left the Soviet government no
choice but to go its own way. His own belief is that there was no such
possibility. In summarizing Chapter 20, which takes the story to 1937,
he concludes that "Russia was never really available, in the sense that
Western Liberals thought she was," as partner of West against the

---

resourcefulness and singlemindedness of purpose; two parts amateurism, com-
placency, and disunity on the part of the West" (ibid., p. 223). This proposition is tied directly to a single case only—the case of Rapallo, to discussion
of which it serves as a capstone. Further documentation of this proposition
within the book is left to the reader to ferret out for himself.
    8. Ibid., p. 192.
    9. Ibid., p. 195.
    10. Ibid., p. 312.

Nazis.[11] In summarizing Chapter 21, which deals with the years
1937–39, he concludes simply that the liberals were wrong, and that
events so proved them.[12] On this face, Kennan's summary assessments
agree with his general concept.

The considerations with prompt Kennan to say that "Russia was
never really available" in the earlier period are: that Russia was never
a "fit partner" for the West in the anti-Fascist cause; that she was at
the time the scene of "the most nightmarish, Orwellian orgies of
modern totalitarianism" (i.e. the purges); that this internal weakness
had its roots in Stalin's own character, which led him to fear an
intimacy with Hitler's opponents no less than the military enmity
of Hitler himself; and that "to the moral cause of an antifascist coalition the Soviet government of 1934 to 1937 could have added little
but hesitant, halfway measures, and a nauseating hypocrisy."[13] The
considerations which prompt Kennan to say at the end of his treatment
of the era that events had proved the liberals wrong are that a whole
series of factors had operated to keep Russia aloof from the war in its
initial stages—namely, "Stalin's personal nature, his domestic-political
predicament, the concern of his regime for the safety of Russia's Far
Eastern frontiers, the inhibitions of the Poles and Rumanians," as
well as the "indecisive, timid policies of the Western powers themselves in their response to the Nazi danger."[14]

The various considerations listed above are amply documented by
Kennan in his text. But what strikes one immediately about them is
how poorly they relate to the issue, which as Kennan himself states it
is that of the possibility of mounting an effective anti-Fascist coalition,
that is, a coalition of Russia and the West capable of frustrating
Hitler and preventing world war. The subissues immediately involved
are questions of (1) the ability of such a coalition to frustrate and prevent, and (2) the possibility of establishing such a coalition, in the
first place, which was a matter of a will to join on the part of the
respective partners. Liberal thought of the day speaks directly to these
points: such a coalition would do the job; it could be formed; it

11. Ibid., p. 313.
12. Ibid., p. 330.
13. Ibid., p. 313.
14. Ibid., p. 330.

wasn't formed primarily because though Russia was willing, the West was not. Kennan, on the other hand, speaks to considerations off the point, on it but weak, or on it but favoring the other side. That Russia wasn't a "fit" partner for the West—that is, not a true-blue anti-Fascist—is true but irrelevant. So too is the devilishness of Stalin's personal character. The internal weakness caused by the purges and the Polish and Rumanian inhibitions bear only on the contribution the Soviets could make to the joint effort, and suggest only that it was less than some thought. The indecisive, timid policies of the West are considerations to the point, but favorable to the opposite (liberal) pretensions. Stalin's concern for his Far East frontiers is to the point but weak, since as Kennan sees the matter this concern began to operate only in late 1938, with the outbreak of the undeclared Soviet-Japanese war on the Mongolian-Manchurian border.

Moreover, one is struck, as one turns now to the details of Kennan's treatment of the period as against his considerations generalized therefrom—the text of Chapters 20 and 21 as against his summaries —how much support he offers for the opposite position. His remarks on the major international crises of the time—the Rhineland in 1936, Spain in 1937, Austria and Czechoslovakia in 1938—nowhere question the adequacy of the coalition to the job. Quite to the contrary, he even suggests that as late as Munich, and the fall of 1938, the Western powers and Czechoslovakia alone could have contained Hitler.[15] And on the second and more critical of the two subissues, the existence of a will to join, his remarks support less the view he is defending than the one he is attacking, namely, that Russia was willing, but the West not, and that if Stalin ultimately turned to Hitler it was mainly the result of the rebuffs to concerted action received from the West.[16]

15. Ibid., p. 322.

16. Litvinov is described throughout as pushing strongly and sincerely the collective security line (ibid., pp. 293, 300, 314). Reoccupation of the Rhineland, according to Kennan, could have been prevented but wasn't because of lack of will on the Allied, especially British, part; and this had the effect of destroying what hope Stalin may have placed in Litvinov's efforts to stiffen effective Western resistance against the Nazis, leading the Soviet leader to wonder how these powers, unwilling to stand up to an aggression in their own backyard, could be expected to stand up to an aggression in another direction (ibid., pp. 304–05). Soviet withdrawal from participation in

Kennan's treatment of the Soviet part in the Czech crisis illustrates in its quintessence the defect to which I call attention. He notes the tragic misconception, the "desperate act of appeasement at the cost of the Czechoslovak state" that was Munich.[17] He notes that as the crisis developed, "the Soviet government reiterated, with impeccable correctness, its readiness to meet its treaty obligations to Czechoslovakia, if France would do likewise."[18] He notes that this confirmed the liberals of the West in their belief that only Russia had remained true to her engagements, and that Russia was prepared to assume the full burden of a war with Hitler over Czechoslovakia, had the Western powers played their part. He says of this position that it was "substantially accurate in the juridical sense."[19]

Yet to this favorable appraisal of the liberal view, he immediately adds and elaborates upon a rider of different tendency, and the conclusion he comes up with strikes a discordant note. "Things were not

---

the Spanish Civil War foundered "partly . . . on Stalin's extreme fear of any extensive intimacy with the liberal and socialist world of the West," but partly also on the "timidity and vacillation of the French and British whose behaviour was indeed not such as to encourage any successful collaboration in resistance to Hitler" (ibid., p. 312). From the other side, pre-1937 Western effort to come to terms with the Russians had been "pursued without enthusiasm" (ibid., p. 315). Not until 1937, according to Kennan, did Stalin start seriously to consider a deal with the Nazis (ibid., p. 315). But his doing so is explained by his deep disillusionment with the prospects of inducing the West to put up any effective opposition to Hitler, and especially to do so in East Europe, against which clearly Hitler next would move (ibid., p. 315). And he still permitted Litvinov "to continue to plug publicly the collective security line" as "after all, an anchor to windward" (ibid., p. 317). In the face of the absorption of Austria (the next crisis), the Western powers remained inactive; and from Austria's fall, says Kennan, Stalin "must have drawn . . . practically all the conclusions he was later believed to have drawn from the fall of Czechoslovakia" (namely, that the West's intent was to encourage Hitler to turn east, upon the USSR) (ibid., p. 321). So Kennan's interpretation of Soviet moves in the specific crises of the day—his treatment of the Czech crisis of 1938 is dealt with in the text proper—tend to corroborate rather than to weaken the position against which nominally he is battling.
    17. Ibid., p. 322.
    18. Ibid., p. 323.
    19. Ibid.

exactly this way in practice," he now says.[20] The Poles and Rumanians refused to allow Russian troops to cross segments of their lands to reach Czechoslovakia; the Soviet government therefore "had a ready-made excuse for delay in meeting its obligations of mutual assistance"; and even though the Rumanians were eventually to allow passage, the most appropriate route across the country was so primitive and indirect that "it would have taken the Soviet command approximately three months to move a division into Slovakia."[21] The Russian expression of readiness to assist Czechoslovakia if France did likewise (that is, Russian readiness to fulfill the terms of her treaty with the Czechs) was therefore, he concludes, "a gesture that cost Moscow very little"; and while there was a good chance that had the Czechs decided to resist they might have been saved, "it is hardly fair to say that they would have been saved by the troops of the Soviet Union."[22]

In other words, here Kennan combats the liberal position on the grounds that Rumania and Poland wouldn't allow Soviet troops to pass, that the USSR would use this as a "ready-made" excuse not to send them, that even were she allowed to send them and did send them, they wouldn't have gotten there in time, and that therefore her declaration of fidelity to obligation and readiness to help was simply a cheap gesture. And this is indeed a curious argument. For it seeks to rebut a position affirming readiness to help by demonstrating a low capacity for so doing—and at that a low capacity defined by the inhibitions and poor rail net of third parties. It is all the more curious for coming hard upon expressions favoring the target of the rebuttal.

In sum, Kennan's treatment of Soviet conduct during the middle and late '30s at the microcosmic level of initiatives and responses related to the crises of the day poorly supports his general contention for the period and his yet more general contention of high militancy. He makes well his point that the Soviet Union would be a weak and morally unfit partner within an anti-Fascist coalition. But he says nothing to refute the contention that she was ready to join such a coalition or make effective the existing one represented by the League, and that she turned toward the Nazis only after repeated

20. Ibid.
21. Ibid., p. 324.
22. Ibid.

instances in which the West showed itself not ready. He says nothing to refute the contention that Stalin, paranoiac and purge-addicted though he might be, was interested in a cooperative effort to keep the peace. He says nothing to refute the contention that, up to March 1939, at least, Stalin had a more settled design than playing the West and Germany against one another. Rather, most of what Kennan says supports these contentions. Most of what he says supports the view against which nominally he is arguing. And so for the period of the late '30s, at least, his data point to conduct appreciably less militant and more accommodating than is suggested by his phrase "hostile action" flowing "in a single uninterrupted stream."

Russia and the West is thus an ambivalent work. Along with a duality of focus and duality of versions of Soviet conduct goes a duality of findings at macroscopic and microscopic levels. There is a gap between data and conclusion, between details and general characterization built thereon, a defect generally absent from Ultra-Hard works. The general image of Stalinist conduct is one of high militancy, in which cooperative gestures are matters of briefest duration and sheerest expediency. The data point to a more moderate description: while hostile activity may still be the more weighty component, cooperative activity is at least substantial and of more than transient significance. The data point rather to the later version of conduct that appears in the last chapter. One may fairly speculate that the later version came into being because the author came to recognize this discrepancy in the support he offers for his earlier one.

One has the feeling that this ambivalence derives from an ambivalence within the mind of the inquirer—a sort of tension between two Kennans. On the one hand, on this speculation stands Kennan the statesman and loyal foreign service officer, who perhaps by the conformist pressures of the group to which he belongs, perhaps by the demands for action imposed on such a profession, perhaps by loyalty to admired superiors, is drawn to a simplified picture of the world—a picture of the outsider which emphasizes the hostile elements in the outsider's behaviour. And, on the other hand, stands Kennan the historian who, following his own precept of the need in the interests of objectivity to look at things from the other party's point of view, is drawn to a more complicated picture of reality, and a picture of the outsider which concedes the existence of some cooperative elements, reflecting some common interest with others. Not for the first time, the man of action is at odds with the man of thought, and a split commitment creates a split picture.

But, in noting the ambivalence, one should take note also of many other, more positive characteristics. Kennan is careful to look for all major data bearing on a given event, to overlook none—alternately, to avoid the temptation to sift out some of these data on unexamined and unarticulated criteria. Western attitudes and moves being at least potentially pertinent to the understanding of Soviet conduct, he takes pains to consider and report them—not to ignore them or dismiss them as inconsequential. In his use of terms, he is usually precise, not loose. While he uses the phrase "state of war" to describe the condition between the Soviet and the West brought on by the former's ingrained hostility, he takes care to distinguish it from the classic concept.[23] In his treatment of the two parties to the conflict with which he is dealing he is evenhanded. The actions of the West he describes, analyzes, evaluates on the same criteria he applies to the Soviet Union. Where he draws a direct comparison between the two, as he does in contrasting the character of the two parties' hostility toward each other, he invokes the same standards and his distinctions are well drawn.[24]

Last but not least, he is constantly attentive to the views of other students. Rather than ignoring them or dismissing them out of hand as "wishful thinking" or the like, he states them carefully, examines them point by point, only then rendering his judgment. So he does with the liberal interpretation of the Soviet collective-security period above noted. So he does with the Ultra-Hard urgings that the West seek destruction of the USSR.[25] So he does with the views that weigh heavily the impact of the 1918–19 interventions on the Soviet psyche, or weigh heavily the responsibility of Yalta for the loss of East Europe.[26] He is throughout undogmatic. "In my opinion," "in my view," are qualifiers that appear constantly. These virtues offsetting the ambivalence to which I point, he can justly claim to have lived up to his ideal of Western historical scholarship.

23. Ibid., p. 389.
24. Ibid., pp. 189–93.
25. Ibid., pp. 381–91.
26. Ibid., pp. 117–19; 361–69.

CASE 2: SHULMAN AND LATE-STALIN MODERATION

Marshall D. Shulman's *Stalin's Foreign Policy Reappraised*, the second of the leading works displaying the Hard image, appeared in 1963.[27] It centers on Soviet conduct proper and upon the years 1949–52, with some commentary upon the periods from 1917 to 1949 and 1953 to 1957. Its proclaimed objective is a deepened understanding of the evolution of Soviet policy in the last years of Stalin's life. Advice is not its concern. The tone is moderate, the language purely expositorial.

Shulman states his thesis in his first chapter, "Introduction to the Argument." He recapitulates it, and the evidence for it, in his last on "The Evolution of Soviet Policy." In between he organizes his story in a chronological fashion. The three and one-half years covered are dealt with six months to a year at a time, successive chapters being named for the principal contemporary development. "The View from Moscow in the Spring of 1949" is succeeded by "Peaceful Coexistence, Sweet and Sour" (covering later 1949), "The Peace Movement" (somewhat of an interlude), "The Effects of the Changing Power Balance" (covering late 1949 and early 1950), and two chapters on policy during the Korean War down to the moment of stalemate (June 1950 to June 1951). There follow chapters for 1951–52 on "The Diplomacy of Coexistence" and, again, "The Use of the Peace Movement," a chapter on "The Nineteenth Party Congress" leading up to the finale.

Shulman's global theorem is that the break marking the softening of Soviet conduct generally agreed to have occurred at or near the end of Stalin's life should be dated back to 1949 rather than to 1953.[28] This break he sees not merely as a softening but as a deliberate shift from one mode of conduct toward another—specifically, from a Left and more militant "syndrome" to one Right and less militant marching under the banner of "peaceful coexistence."[29] He attributes the shift less to internal than to external factors. Among important Soviet calculations leading to it he finds the following: the realization that the leftist mode taken up immediately after the war

27. Cambridge: Harvard University Press.
28. For comment on this construction, see below, p. 114.
29. Shulman, *Stalin's Foreign Policy Reappraised*, p. 4.

had, by provoking Western rearmament and America's return to the European continent, proved counterproductive and led to an adverse power-balance; the belief that this unfavorable trend would, however, soon reverse itself under the impact of expected nuclear gains; and the estimate that a time of relaxation would hasten the reversal more surely than one of continued tensions. Shulman likens the change to earlier moves to the Right in 1921, 1933, and 1941; and he finds the pattern of which it is part one of essentially oscillating character. He affirms, however, that with the projection and extension of the change beyond Stalin's death, the underlying conceptual framework of "peaceful coexistence" has come to include a longer, indeed an indefinite, time perspective, and that this has bestowed upon the change a secular and hence more significant character.

Soviet conduct, in the view which Shulman develops in the course of working out his thesis, is, as the thesis suggests, highly rational in nature, of alternately high and low militancy, secularly moderating. It is also expansion-minded in its objective: that objective, which remains fixed, is the further conversion of the world to socialism and the enhancement of Soviet power and influence.[30] In pursuit of its goal it is highly active and initiatory, though sensitive to the moves of others and hence also, at times, reactive.[31] It seems to aspire to hegemony in its relation to its own kind. It is not, on the other hand—to judge by inference on matters to which Shulman does not directly address himself—territorially expansive to any significant degree, nor addicted to the military instrument, nor particularly immoral. It is not strongly affected by the internal structure or personalities—like that of the late dictator—who may happen temporarily to be at the helm.[32] It has a profoundly disturbing effect upon the international order.[33] Yet it has not proven notably effective: Shulman in his narrative of the years 1946–53 records failures as often as successes.

Shulman thus follows the earlier Kennan and the Ultra-Hard imagists in ascribing to Soviet conduct a high degree of rationality, militancy, and addiction to initiative. But he paints the picture in

30. Ibid., pp. 9–10.
31. Ibid., pp. 3–4.
32. Ibid., pp. 7, 3–4, 260–61.
33. Ibid., p. 271.

less extreme terms; he inferentially assigns considerably lower values to other elements (territorial expansiveness, immorality); he attributes more significance to change, detecting even, as the Ultra-Hards do not, a long-run moderation. Perhaps most important, he gives to external factors, notably shifts in the power balance, greater weight as determinants, to such internal factors as personality and social structure considerably less. In this he has much in common with the later Kennan.

The proposition I take from *Stalin's Foreign Policy Reappraised* in subjecting the work to closer examination is its central theorem. This is, to repeat, the proposition that the shift toward the less militant, more moderate policy of "peaceful coexistence," which most hands agree has taken place in postwar Soviet Russia, is to be dated not from 1953, as prevailing opinion has it, but from 1949, four years earlier. I take the proposition to read "shift toward" rather than "shift to," and to imply only the initiation and not the completion or near-completion of a process, because Shulman seems on balance to intend it to read so, as he sets it forth in his key first chapter, "Introduction to the Argument." For the language of this chapter suggests only that change was beginning in the period in question, not that it had reached the critical point where quantitative becomes qualitative, and a predominantly Right syndrome replaces a predominantly Left. Shulman speaks, for instance, of outlooks "evolving" and changes "emerging."[34]

However, the text is by no means unambiguous. Shulman elsewhere uses language compatible with a second, more radical construction—namely, that change had before 1953 reached and passed the critical point, and the predominantly Right syndrome replaced the predominantly Left. His repeated comparisons of 1949 with 1921, 1935, and 1941, years which saw the virtual completion of similar changes, point in this direction.[35] So does his downgrading of changes ensuing on Stalin's death.[36] So, too, does the thrust of his remarks of his final chapter, in which he appeals for support to Soviet writings affirming qualitative change in 1950–53.[37] The reader should bear this in mind when considering the criticism which follows.

34. Ibid., pp. 1, 8.
35. Ibid., esp. pp. 7–8.
36. For example, ibid., p. 9.
37. Ibid., pp. 255–57.

An adequate demonstration of the orthodox theorem that Soviet conduct underwent a sudden Left-to-Right change on Stalin's death requires of an analyst that he define and differentiate clearly the "Left" and "Right" modes of conduct between which change is said to have occurred; array carefully the major Soviet sayings and doings in the two periods 1946–53 and 1953 on; show substantial agreement between sayings-and-doings and definitions in the order given. One who would challenge the more orthodox interpretation and argue that this change got underway in 1949 rather than in 1953 must in addition show that the sayings and doings of 1949–53 fall into an intermediate category, agreeing in some respects with those of 1946–49, in others with 1953 on. Shulman realizes all this and proceeds accordingly. He provides the necessary typology to start with and the necessary history to follow up. The question is how well he has done so.

Shulman's first and basic classification of modes of Soviet conduct and attendant distinctions is reasonably clear. The Left syndrome of Soviet conduct, as he sees it, has these characteristics, among others: it is militant, direct, "marked typically by an overhanging consciousness of the inevitability of conflict," marked too by "emphasis upon those ideological aspects which deal with the class struggle and the necessity for revolutionary advance" and by a "detachment of the Communist movement abroad from association with other elements of the national or international community."[38] The Right syndrome, associated with the label "peaceful coexistence," has these characteristics: a longer-term perspective, "flexibility of tactics, divisive exploitation of 'contradictions' abroad, and collaboration with other groups, classes, or nations."[39] It is interesting that Shulman develops these definitions by appropriation and adaptation from the Communists rather than supplying his own. For it suggests that he believes he is somehow bound to adopt their concepts in his inquiry rather than to fashion his own—and, more broadly, that the analyst is bound in confronting his human material to analyze that material in the terms in which the constituent humans analyze themselves. But whether this is true or not, the terms are reasonably clear and distinct. One can readily distinguish in the mind's eye talk breathing the imminence of war from talk arguing the possibility of peace, a re-

38. Ibid., pp. 4–5.
39. Ibid., pp. 4–5.

fusal to align oneself with any capitalist state from acceptance of alignment with some, directives to foreign Communist elements to work against all bourgeois parties from directives to work with some. One can readily agree also to call action in the first category direct, more militant, leftist, action of the second indirect, less militant, rightist.

A second "functional classification" which Shulman introduces hard on the Left-Right classification does not fare so well. This is a classification of conduct into the familiar "offensive" and "defensive." Shulman makes the introduction obliquely, observing that it "may lead to some confusion," since both Right and Left modes have "been utilized for both offensive and defensive purposes."[40] And confusion it does lead to, although not so much for the reason given as for the reason that Shulman fails adequately to spell out the distinction involved. The Left mode may, he tells us, sometimes be a mode of revolutionary advance, sometimes one of conservation of forces designed to "destabilize and undermine the *status quo*, or to force constraints upon the "bourgeoisie.'" So, too the Right mode and the "broad alliances characteristic" of it, he tells us, sometimes have been used defensively, against threats perceived from the outside world, sometimes offensively, to "open up avenues to power." In the 1949–52 period, Shulman goes on by way of illustration, the Right mode exhibited both strains: it aimed both at weakening adversaries by exploiting divisive vulnerabilities (defensive strain) and at maximizing Communist influence on the course of international politics (offensive strain). The difficulty here is that one is hard put to imagine concrete moves matching his category "defensive"—that is, aimed at undermining the status quo, exploiting vulnerabilities—which do not also contribute to the maximization of Communist influence and the opening of avenues of power, thus matching also his category "offensive." More precisely, one is hard put to differentiate here unless in terms of the directness or immediacy with which the ultimate enhancement of power is expected to ensue, which is to invoke again the principle already made use of in separating Right from Left. In any case, Shulman pursues the matter no further, leaving the reader without straightforward discrimination of the two functions, offering

40. Ibid., p. 5.

no clue as to just how one decides to which category to assign the concrete case. While he makes liberal use of the distinction, he therefore supplies no means of verifying that usage, nor of testing his additional theorem that the rightward shift of the early 1950s, unlike earlier rightward shifts, come to bear an increasingly offensive character.[41]

However, Shulman completes this preliminary section of his work by returning to his first and more important distinction, between Right and Left modes, and by sounding certain salutary warnings against reifying the terms or expecting concrete behavior at any time perfectly to reflect one or the other, and against understanding the alternation between them as "stemming from some internally generated systole and diastole of the Soviet body politic."[42] So, on balance he may be said to have shown reasonable care in defining his concepts and the rules for their use, and to have gotten his inquiry off on the right foot.

Shulman's application of his concepts to the historical record is also generally careful. Whether the object of scrutiny is the era up to the end of the Second World War, the two postwar periods 1946–49 and 1953 on that bracket the years of crucial concern, or the crucial years themselves, his readings of the data are sensible.

His reading of the era up to the end of the Second World War one has little difficulty accepting. He finds these years, as already noted, years of alternation between the two modes, 1921, 1933, and 1941 marking turns to the Right, 1928, 1936, and 1946 marking turns to the Left.[43] He doesn't adduce the factual material that led him to place one period in one category, one in the other. But on the main points involved, the shift on those dates between Left and Right as he defines them, few would disagree. The differences that do arise in this connection lie between Shulman and the imagists of the Ultra-Hard school and concern the different weights accorded the two modes rather than their definition and identification. Imagists of the Ultra-Hard school, as pointed out above, characteristically downgrade right-

41. Ibid., pp. 8–9.
42. Ibid., p. 7.
43. The periodization of the '30s is obscure. The Right period is conceived on one page to begin in 1933, on another in 1935. Treating 1936–41 as a leftist period is open to challenge. See ibid., pp. 7–8.

ward shifts to the level of the "purely tactical," the expedient or mere maneuver, or dismiss them as deceptions and distractions, leaving undefended and unexamined the grounds for distinguishing tactical from nontactical, deception from nondeception. Shulman avoids these procedures and the question-begging they contain. He makes no distinction between the two in terms of basic importance or substantiality. For him Right and Left are two syndromes or stances or approaches toward a single goal which the USSR adopts recurrently, in alternation. Neither is "more basic."

Shulman's reading of the 1946–49 and 1953 on periods is adequate, although the materials he marshals are not too extensive. The data adduced in the text which make him decide 1946–49 is a leftist period comprise consolidation of rule in East Europe, especially the reduction of Czechoslovakia to the status of a satellite, the directives to the Western European Communist parties to exchange national collaboration for struggle and strikes against the government, the promulgation in 1947 of Zhdanov's "two-camp" doctrine at the founding meeting of the Cominform, the campaign to bring Yugoslavia to heel, the call for paralyzing strikes, and the blockade of Berlin.[44] These, one can readily agree, make up a fair list of the principal Soviet moves of the time. These, one can also agree, warrant the labels "militant" and "direct." Shulman adduces in the text less of the data which make him decide 1953–57 is rightist. The stretching out in time-reference of the concept of peaceful coexistence, the invitation to accommodation to the United States, and the conversion of the two-camp into the three-camp image of the world are the main items of mention.[45] But the assertion that these years were essentially rightist is the least controversial part of his thesis.

His reading of the crucial 1949–53 years, finally, is quite adequate. He considers the following to be the important Soviet moves of this period: (1) the campaign, part conciliation part intimidation, to forestall the signing of the North Atlantic Treaty and formation of a separate West German state in 1949; (2) the conversion of the Peace Movement into an instrument for weakening the hold of Western governments on their peoples; (3) the persistence within the Soviet

44. Ibid., pp. 13–19.
45. Ibid., pp. 252, 262–63, 270.

hierarchy of both Right- and Left-oriented assessments of the impact of the change on the power balance brought about by the USSR's atomic explosion and the Chinese Communists' success in late 1949; (4) participation in the decisions launching and expanding the Korean War in the spring and fall of 1950; (5) the move toward settling that war in June 1951; (6) the 1951–52 diplomatic efforts to draw Britain and France apart from the United States, and to win acceptance for the creation of a Germany united, armed, but neutral; (7) also in 1951–52, the broadening of the Peace Movement and new appeal to nationalism, exemplified by the new directives to the French Communist Party; and (8) in the fall of 1952, promulgation through the major documents of the Nineteenth Party Congress of a more flexible, power-bloc policy based on a defensive strategic outlook and aimed at weakening the Western alliance system by harping on "nationalism, the peace issue, neutralism, trade, and other forms of collaboration with elements of the middle class."[46] These moves he sees mainly as responses to the buildup of Western power from 1947 on, this buildup in turn being seen as a response to the leftist moves of 1946–48 and, later, the Korean War.

Whether or not one agrees with Shulman's account of their origin, one can accept his judgment that the items on this list are major and deserve to be there. One can agree, too, that a number of them fall into the Right category. The efforts to split the West (item 6 above) are "divisive" and "indirect" in his or anyone's language. The Peace Movement too (items 2 and 7) clearly belongs in the category of indirect instrumentalities, aimed at the neutralization or partial neutralization of an opposing force. So, patently, does the move toward settling the Korean War (item 5) and the decisions of the Nineteenth Party Congress bespeaking adoption of a power-bloc policy (item 8). The efforts to forestall the creation of NATO (item 1) and the hierarchy's mixed assessment of new developments (item 3) point as much in a rightist as in a leftist direction.

On the whole, Shulman can therefore be said to have made his point. On sensible definitions, carefully applied, the USSR did shift "toward" a more flexible policy before Stalin died. The USSR did, starting in 1949, reintroduce tactical and ideological formulations

46. Ibid., passim; the quote is from p. 250.

associated with earlier rightist periods. To suggest, as do partisans of the more extreme form of orthodoxy, that "peaceful coexistence" sprang fully developed from the presidial forehead on March 5, 1953, having been spared the travail of ordinary birth: this is error.

But—and here I return to some earlier remarks—the critique throughout assumes the mild construction of the thesis at issue. On the other, more radical construction, Shulman is less than convincing. If he means to argue not only that the rightward shift had gotten underway by 1953 but had reached the point where a predominantly rightist supplanted a predominantly leftist orientation, the facts hardly bear him out.

For there remain many moves of leftist character in the crucial 1949–53 period, as Shulman is the first to remind us. Following the orthodox view, Shulman implies clearly that the Soviet Union was in on the planning and coordination of the Korean War and the Chinese entry therein.[47] The period around the turn of the year 1950 he describes as "A Period of Communist Toughness," of "uncompromising hardness";[48] and he describes the USSR as involved too in the coordination of the new Viet Minh attack in Indo-China in late 1950 and the Chinese invasion of Tibet.[49] The USSR throughout these years, as Shulman further notes, maintained a steady drumfire of violent and bitter criticism of the United States. And the documents associated with its Nineteenth Party Congress, although they show a lowering of the expectation of war and lay down the power-bloc policy Shulman points to (at the end of the period in question), nevertheless show no abatement in overall vituperativeness, and no change in the generally black-and-white picture of the world. Finally —what Shulman overlooks—the campaign against Yugoslavia was continuing during these years, as were the purges in the satellites. If events of this kind are to be taken as indicators of "militancy" in 1948–49, so must they be in 1951–52.

If these leftist moves are also taken into account and reasonable weights assigned to the list thus extended, it is hard to see why in the aggregate behavior in 1949–52 does not answer at least as well to the

47. Ibid., p. 141.
48. Ibid., p. 163.
49. Ibid., p. 164.

description "militant and direct" as to "manipulative, flexible, and longer-term in perspective." Certainly it is hard to see why it does not stand closer to the events of 1946–48 than to those of 1953 on. Especially is this so when one feeds into the calculation some of the moves of the later period of which Shulman barely hints: rapprochement with Yugoslavia, development of summitry, the territorial and other concessions of 1955, the disarmament offer of May 1955, etc. And accordingly, and finally, it is difficult to see why the core contention of the orthodox position with which Shulman is doing battle—namely, that the main watershed or change-over from predominantly Left to predominantly Right is to be dated March 1953—is not left essentially undisturbed.

Taken as a whole, *Stalin's Foreign Policy Reappraised* leaves a mixed impression. It is a work of considerable merit. In its sensitivity to considerations of conceptualization and method it represents an advance over the other works so far considered. In its recognition of the influence upon Soviet behavior of the environment, including the policy choices of other powers such as our own, and hence the need to take systematic account of that environment; in its successful effort to define and distinguish between the Right and Left modes of behavior in terms of which the analysis is mainly to run; in its industriousness in arraying data pertinent to the period of central concern; last but not least, in its acceptance of all data in a given class (e.g. all official dicta of the period on "peaceful coexistence"), and concomitant eschewal of the temptation to proceed selectively, taking some but discarding others, to the end of producing a tidier picture—in all these matters the work marks a clear step forward. And to these must be added an unusual sobriety of tone, a lack of dogmatism, and a fair statement and consideration of opposing points of view.[50]

Moreover, the book has made out a sound case for marking *some* distinction between the 1946–49 and 1949–53 subdivisions of Stalin's last years, and for alleging that *some* softening had set in before Stalin died. And, in so doing, it has advanced the general knowledge of the subject. The burden from now on is on those who would argue that Soviet policy remained as hard, as militant in the last four years of

50. For instance, ibid., pp. 3–4, on Kremlinology, and pp. 260–63 on the cruciality of Stalin's personality.

Stalin's life as in the preceding four. Incidentally, but very importantly, the burden from now on is on those who would argue that Soviet conduct undergoes no significant change, Soviet policy no true evolution.

Yet something clearly is lacking. The volume's characterization of the magnitude of change in Soviet conduct in the crucial period at issue (1949–53) is ambiguous. And for the thesis on the more radical of the two possible versions, it offers inadequate support. Since the version it does bear out is hardly of crashing significance, challenging orthodoxy on a less important point—for who is going to argue long and strenuously that *no* softening set in prior to Stalin's death? —one is compelled to pronounce one of two less than flattering judgments upon *Stalin's Foreign Policy Reappraised,* namely, that it either makes out a good case for a minor point, or a poor case for a major one.

CASE 3: TUCKER AND POST-STALIN MODERATION

Robert C. Tucker's *The Soviet Political Mind: Studies in Stalinism and Post-Stalin Change,*[51] the last of the leading works of Hard persuasion, is a series of essays written over a seven-year span of time (1956–63). As the title suggests and the introduction avows, the book attempts primarily to explore (i.e. describe and explain) the way the Soviet leaders look at politics internal and external, and the changes in that way brought about by Stalin's death. Treating mainly of the postwar period in Soviet history, it contains occasional flashbacks to earlier days. It attempts no evaluation, no prescription for American conduct. The tone is judicious, dispassionate.

The Soviet Political Mind is divided into three parts, dealing respectively with the Soviet system as a whole, the relation of Russian man to Soviet state, and the relation of Soviet state to the world. The essays of Part One, which bear tangentially on foreign policy, are: "On Revolutionary Mass-Movement Regimes," in which Tucker juxtaposes a concept of that name against the "totalitarian' concept of Friedrich and Brzezinski;[52] "The Stalin Heritage in Soviet Policy,"

51. New York: Praeger, 1963.

52. Carl J. Friedrich and Zbigniew Brzezinski, *Totalitarian Dictatorship and Autocracy* (New York: Praeger, 1961), esp. Chapter 1.

newly written for the book; and "The Politics of Soviet de-Staliniza-
tion." The essays of Part Three, which bear directly on foreign policy,
are "Ruling Personalities in Russian Foreign Policy," "Stalinism and
Cold War," "Russia, the West, and World Order," and—written
especially for the book—"The Dialectics of Coexistence." (The residual three essays, constituting Part Two, have virtually nothing to
say on foreign policy.)

Although as a series of essays *The Soviet Political Mind* falls short
of being a closely integrated work, there is one theme running through
it almost without break which gives it some continuity. Suggested by
the subtitle *Studies in Stalinism and Post-Stalin Change,* that theme
is that the changes in Soviet Russia brought about by Stalin's death
are substantial and significant. Indeed, they amount to a change in
form, a transmutation of one species of totalitarianism into another,
milder one.[53] In place of the "Führerist" kind of totalitarianism of
1939–53—which is defined by the presence of the elements of self-
glorification of the ruler, the terror within and expansionism without—
Soviet Russia acquired on Stalin's death in 1953 a quite different, non-
Führerist type, in which the elements just referred to are conspicuously
absent. The causes of this change lay partly with the growth of popular
pressures demanding the higher living standards which were the
promised fruit of revolution. Partly, perhaps largely, they lay with the
demise of the psychopathic personality the peculiarities of whose demands for self-realization had given the earlier form its macabre
shape.

Tucker's view of Soviet external conduct marches hand in hand
with his view of Soviet society as a whole.[54] Soviet external conduct,
too, changed radically in 1953. It retained intact the long-range goal
of victory in the contest of systems. But in other respects it underwent
a metamorphosis, and this metamorphosis amounted to a veritable
"psychological revolution."[55] In its older, Stalinist form of 1939–53,
it aimed proximately at territorial aggrandizement and the expansion
of control, ultimately at global hegemony. It was also expansive in
implementation and militant, and it placed considerable reliance on

53. Tucker, *The Soviet Political Mind,* esp. Chapter 1.
54. Ibid., Chapters 8 and 10.
55. Ibid., p. 167.

the military instrument. It accompanied a posture of uncompromising belligerence toward the non-Communist world, and like that posture it was shaped by internal forces: Stalin's paranoiac personality and an ideology which saw the world broken into two irreconcilably antagonistic camps, and which conceived of peaceful coexistence as a mere interlude between wars. Its fruits were the Cold War—for, says Tucker, "in foreign policy Stalinism means cold war."[56] Toward other Communist states it was overbearing, seeking to gain absolute control over them through a policy of *Gleichschaltung*. Its closest historical affinities are with conduct under the tsars, notably Ivan the Terrible.

Post-Stalin conduct, on the other hand, sets its proximate goals less high, and in pursuit of them employs considerably less severe measures.[57] It remains expansion-minded, but the expansion sought is now an expansion of influence rather than of control. It remains unremittingly active, but its chosen mode of attempting to realize its aims is that of persuasion rather than coercion, that of a low rather than a high degree of militancy. Its preferred instruments are those of diplomacy, trade, propaganda, and, while these are at times used competitively, they are often used cooperatively. The military instrument, *per contra*, it keeps well sheathed. It continues to be responsive to internal forces, but dominant among these now are the popular pressures and requirements of a mature industrial society, and a reformed ideology. Critical features of the latter are: a vision of the world as tripartite rather than bipolar; a vision of the triumph of socialism as no longer contingent on war; and a view of peaceful coexistence that ascribes to this policy a new and broader scope, an indefinite rather than a limited duration, and a set of components including for the first time truly cooperative as well as antagonistic elements. Conduct no longer seeks the tightening of controls over other Communist states, but rather their relaxation. Its affinities (though the similarities are not perfect) are with conduct under Lenin.

This, Tucker's version of the Hard-but-Softening image, follows Kennan's (the early Kennan's) more closely than it does Shulman's. Like Kennan, but not Shulman, Tucker describes conduct of the high-

56. Ibid., p. 167.
57. Ibid., Chapter 8.

Stalinist period in terms only slightly milder than those used by Ultra-Hard imagists. Like Kennan, but not Shulman, he sees the pattern of pre-1953 historical development as one of progressive toughening eventuating in the 1939–53 period of empire-building rather than one of the alternation between Right and Left modes every five years or so. Like Kennan accordingly, but not Shulman, he sees the primary motors of conduct and change therein as internal rather than external —factors of personality and phases of economic and social development rather than the international power-balance and perceptions thereof.

Tucker assigns a higher value to the change that took place in the early 1950s than does either Kennan or Shulman—or, for that matter, any of the other works considered by this essay. In fact, Tucker alone among the works considered conceives of the change not only as embracing a far-reaching alteration in mode and instruments, but as reaching beyond this to proximate, if not quite to final, ends themselves. Tucker alone associates change with change in the specific character of the internal structure. Tucker alone assigns to change the significance of a "decisive turn in Russian history and world politics."[58]

The proposition I take in subjecting *The Soviet Political Mind* to a closer look is affirmation of sharp contrast between Stalinist and post-Stalinist conduct: a contrast between conduct aiming at expanded control, and conduct aiming only at expanding influence; a contrast between conduct aggressive and conduct persuasive; between conduct mainly militarist in instruments chosen and conduct mainly non-militarist. Demonstration of the proposition requires clear definition and differentiation of the sets of terms, a careful arraying of Soviet sayings and doings in the two periods pre- and post-1953, and persuasive evidence that the two sets agree substantially with the respective definitions. Tucker realizes that these things are required of him, and he sets about supplying them. The question is how well he has done so.

Tucker's attention to matters of definition appears as an interpolation in Chapter 8, in which the contrast here under scrutiny is mainly drawn. "Control" and "influence" are possible "operative" aims, and Tucker starts out by distinguishing "operative" aims from aims that

58. Ibid., p. 176.

are purely formal. A formal aim, he says, is "the object one declares oneself to be seeking"; an operative aim is "the object implicit in what one actually does."[59] Of the two, which may or may not coincide, he attaches overriding importance to the second. A policy aimed operatively at control, now, is one that seeks "to get control of territory and people and to absolutize that control by every available means, the principal one being police terror."[60] A policy aimed operatively at influence is something else again. Tucker does not provide us with an elegant statement of just what that something else is, but he conveys the idea of demands drastically scaled down, of demand no longer for a controlling voice in larger affairs but merely for some voice greater than presently enjoyed.

Turning to his typology of means, Tucker tells us that a politics of persuasion "aims at influencing other governments to do or not to do certain things, such as concluding a treaty, settling a dispute, joining or not joining an alliance."[61] As such it is based upon an appeal to a mutuality of interests, and it presupposes recognition of their other government's interest in its own continued existence and security.[62] The contrasting type of politics Tucker neither defines nor names forthrightly. But he obviously has in mind a politics of forcing other governments to do or not to do, and the name he obliquely bestows on it is that of aggression.[63] Tucker affirms a fitness between respective possibilities in the realms of ends and means. So he tells us that "when the operative aim is total control, persuasion is not a fit instrument of policy," one form or another of aggression being necessitated.[64] Conversely, "when influence is the operative aim, persuasion is a logical means."[65]

Tucker's terms and concepts represent a provocative contribution to our vocabulary. They answer in a general way to differences which most observers would agree are real and significant—furthermore, to differences overlooked by many of the other works considered here. This is especially true of the control-influence distinction.

59. Ibid., p. 168.
60. Ibid., p. 169.
61. Ibid., p. 171.
62. Ibid.
63. Ibid., p. 172.
64. Ibid.
65. Ibid., p. 178.

At the same time, in his discussion of his distinctions he runs into problems. To separate out formal from operative aims is all very well and good. But to derive operative aims, or for that matter any aims, from action as distinct from words is risky. For this amounts to inferring an actor's objectives from what appears to the outsider the point toward which action is tending: inferring an end in view from an estimate of the end in fact. And this ignores the common situation in which an actor quite genuinely believes an end of one tendency best reached through means of quite another. A traveler starting out in one direction by no means necessarily signals thereby that his journey's intended end lies in that direction. The motorist heading north from New York is at least as likely to be bound for Cleveland or other points west as for Montreal. The meaning of this objection will become clearer below.[66]

Again, Tucker's contrast between a politics of aggression and one of persuasion raises questions. If persuasion is a matter of getting others to do or not to do by appealing to a mutuality of interest, that is, holding out hope of gain, then the opposing idea is a matter of invoking the threat of loss. For this opposite idea coercion rather than aggression is the more apt term. Aggression is too narrow, for it connotes armed attack and the use of armed forces; it implies invoking not any old kind of threat but invoking and indeed implementing the most drastic of all kinds; it excludes a whole range of threats less severe. A persuasion-aggression schema therefore leaves out an important range of possibilities definable roughly as nonmilitary coercion, and so common to history is this range that an attempt to interpret the record in terms of this scheme alone runs a rather considerable risk of producing a distorted picture.

Tucker's application of his terms to the Soviet postwar record also compels a mixed judgment. His findings of sharp contrast between

66. There is another, more subtle objection that perhaps should be recorded here. This is that to infer any sort of aims from action is effectively to deprive oneself of the useful means-ends schema as analytic tool. For inasmuch as the actor's means are determined also by looking at his actual conduct, this is to make ends and means rest not on different determinations but on one and the same determination. So the separateness which the different names imply becomes spurious. And so a general statement relating one sort of operative aim to one sort of politics or means—see, for instance, Tucker's "when the operative aim is total control . . . one form or another of aggression is necessitated"—becomes a redundancy (the quotation is from ibid., p. 172).

Stalinist and post-Stalinist eras attract one's assent in a general sort
of way. Yet his assertions about objectives are at times poorly sustained. And his assertions about means are extreme.

Tucker's treatment of Stalinist aims invites a number of criticisms,
some of them adumbrated in the discussion above. That the formal
aims of 1946–53 were the strengthening of peace and the encouragement of revolution is true. That these were not seriously entertained
as long-term objectives of action, which the operative aims were
intended intermediately to serve, as the wording of the text suggests,[67]
is less tenable. The inarticulate major premise here is that one cannot
conceivably be entertaining peace as the long-run aim if at the same
time one is making war or engaging in other belligerent moves. But
there is just too much evidence suggesting the contrary here. Even a
nation less entranced with the dialectic and with contradictions, such
as our own, can genuinely hold preparation for war to be indispensable
to the maintenance of peace, and the escalation of war necessary to its
recapture. Our own attitudes on Vietnam are a case in point. These
considerations compel us to grant as at least a possibility that the
Soviet's protestations of commitment to peace at the time in question
were genuine.

Again, that the operative Soviet aim of Stalin's last years was "to
get control of territory and people and to absolutize that control" may
conceivably be true, at least within certain limits. Yet the demonstration Tucker provides is not sufficient. His argument is that such control was implicit in what Stalin actually did, and especially the "whole
postwar process of Soviet *Gleichschaltung* of foreign lands," particularly the demands laid upon the Yugoslavs.[68] But not only is it faulty
as a general procedure, for reasons given above, to suppose that the
apparent tendency of an action or series thereof represents the operative aim in the eye of the actor—in the case at issue it is not even
clear that the behavior in question, Soviet *Gleichschaltung* of foreign
lands, implies the tendency Tucker believes it to.

To make clear this last point, a distinction needs be drawn between

67. The text refers to the "discrepancy" between formal and operative
aims in these years as "glaring," and to Soviet actions as "blatantly inconsistent" with the proclaimed aim of strengthening peace (see ibid., p. 168).
68. Ibid., p. 169.

the consolidation and the extension of control. On Tucker's specified method of determination, a tightening of control throughout East Europe might fairly be called the operative aim of this period, for this was what the USSR was then tending to do in this area. But the extension of control to new areas—here one is on less certain ground. The Soviets did extend their control successively to certain of the East European states in 1945–47. They tried to do so in West Berlin and Yugoslavia in 1948 but did not succeed. But this was all, Korea possibly excepted.[69] In short, the expansion of control in the sense of territorial aggrandizement can hardly be considered to have continued, on the specified method of determination, beyond 1948. As for "total control" or "global hegemony," behavior hardly justifies their being considered operative aims even during the earlier period, for the behavior in question was behavior limited both in space and in time, and limited behavior cannot support an inference of a more than limited aim. The mistake here lies in projecting tendencies unduly.

Tucker's description of means suffers from the somewhat different defect of extravagance. Were "coercion" his antonym for "persuasion," one could scarcely disagree with his negative findings on policy in the Stalinist last years. But his use of the term "aggression," and his suggestion of a substantial reliance on the military instrument, are other matters. The evidence he adduces comprises principally the following: *Gleichschaltung* of East Europe, Zhdanov's two-world pronouncement of 1947 (called a declaration of cold war by Tucker), the hate propaganda and diplomacy of invective, the Berlin blockade, the systematic shooting down of US aircraft, and the outright war by proxy in Korea.[70] These data sustain a judgment that the politics of the day were high in militancy or coercion, that is, in threats of harm. They sustain considerably less well a similar judgment in respect to reliance on the military instrument. On the above list, only the last three items represent such use of the military instrument, and each of these may be considered a special case: the blockade because

69. I say "possibly" because the extent to which the USSR was responsible for the decision to invade South Korea, and the extent to which it made its indirect contribution with a view to extending its territorial domain, are enough in doubt to make the point moot. See p. 82 n.

70. Tucker, *The Soviet Political Mind*, pp. 168–69.

use of the instrument was threatened only, the shootings because of their relative triviality and obvious defensiveness of context, Korea because of the indirection involved. Moreover, from 1948 on, the last two of these special cases excepted, the instrument was used only as a silent and inarticulate threat. Unlike 1939–41, when the Soviets used their armed forces actively, in 1948–53 they used them on the whole passively, as a deterrent. In other words, in this part of the late Stalinist period, they used them in much the same way as they have used them—and the reading here is Tucker's as well as mine—since Stalin's death.[71]

As for the application of terms to the post-Stalinist period, Tucker's main defect is, again, that of extravagance. "Persuasion" is too weak a term. The main evidence he adduces comprises the following: the slogan of détente, the meeting at the summit, the challenge to the peaceful competition of systems, the effort to break up the Western alliance with its attendant anti-Americanism, the substitution of the three-part for the two-part view of the world, the promotion of the idea of different roads to socialism, the revival of diplomacy and foreign trade, the sponsoring of cultural and technical exchange, the encouragement of official contacts with the West at many levels, the drive to normalize relations with many countries, and the participation in previously boycotted international bodies, the evacuation of Austria, the partial undoing of *Gleichschaltung* and rapprochement with Tito.[72] Now many of these moves are cases of persuasion, one would readily agree. But many are not. The effort to break up the Atlantic alliance and attendant expressions of anti-Americanism, for instance, are hardly manifestations of a persuasionist policy. And the effort to persuade middle nations to detach themselves from the Western system—a general rubric under which Tucker subsumes many of the individual moves on the above list—is persuasionist only in its relation to said middle nations. In its relation to the West such moves are hostile, militant. Moreover, as Tucker subsequently notes, the policy of persuasion broke down, temporarily, at Budapest in 1956.[73] And the ideology of coexistence developed concurrently con-

71. Ibid., p. 221.
72. Ibid., pp. 177–78.
73. Ibid., p. 179.

tinued to encompass elements of conflict along with elements of cooperation.[74]

In consequence and in sum, Tucker's contrast is overdrawn. Conduct of the Stalinist period was not so expansionist as he suggests, nor so addicted to the military instrument. Post-Stalinist conduct was not, has not been, so persuasionist. The change in 1953 accordingly was not that sharp. On Tucker's own showing, it is better described to be quantitative, not qualitative, and it is probably best described as a substantial decline in militancy.

The Soviet Political Mind, its sections on foreign policy taken as a whole, exhibits the defect of imperfect conceptualization. Tucker's conceptual apparatus and derivation of aims have not been fully thought out. Contrasting sets—control and influence; persuasion and its opposite—have not been completely defined and differentiated. Distinctions of importance—as between the militancy or coerciveness of conduct and its addiction to the military instrument—have accordingly been overlooked. And in consequence, the historical record has been pulled out of shape, and the change that took place at Stalin's death exaggerated.

Yet Tucker's concepts and vocabulary *are* a beginning, and an important one. He has, like Shulman, introduced some highly useful distinctions into the analytical baggage of the inquirer in this field, even if he has failed to work them out fully. He has, like Shulman, but more clearly, formulated a provocative hypothesis about that conduct in the postwar period. He has furnished an illuminating description of the evolution of that conduct, of change in 1953 from control-oriented to influence-oriented, greater to lesser coerciveness; and he has put forward a suggestive explanation for that evolution, tying it to the removal from the scene of the psychopathological Stalin and resultant transmutation of the character of the regime. He has, like Shulman, generally avoided the errors found to pervade the work of the Ultra-Hard imagists.[75] To cite a particularly notable example, he has, in his exposition and analysis of the development of Soviet

74. Ibid., Chapter 10.
75. I say "generally" because at one or two points, as in describing China and North Vietnam as parts of the Soviet control-sphere (ibid., pp. 167–68), Tucker ascribes a reach to the Soviet writ hardly warranted by the data.

concept of peaceful coexistence, read and taken account of *all* of what the Soviets have had to say on the subject, resisting the temptation to select some and reject others on undefended grounds.[76] Like Shulman, he has subjected Soviet conduct to careful comparisons, and has taken careful account of opposing positions.[77] He has exhibited an admirable sobriety of tone, and in clarity his style rivals Kennan's.

Tucker's concepts and hypotheses, moreover, represent a beginning which complements nicely Shulman's. The sets control-oriented and influence-oriented, aggression and persuasion, can, with proper amendment and refinement, be assimilated to Shulman's "direct" and "indirect." The basic theorems about the timing, character, and reasons for change differ more in degree and emphasis than in kind, and the narrowing of the gap between the two is certainly negotiable. On the less severe construction, Shulman's view sees the rightward shift as merely gestating in 1949–53, a point with which Tucker would find no difficulty agreeing.[78] Tucker, in affirming the importance of Stalin's personality, does not thereby deny the importance of other factors, to which he pays a Shulman-like tribute when, for example, he describes post-Stalin conduct as in one aspect "the story of official Russia's move to readjust to the real world."[79] At the very least, the two sets of theorems bracket the possibilities. And this marks a good start for working out common and generally accepted description and explanation of Soviet change in this important period.

Against the standards for judging scholarship set forth at the beginning of Chapter 3, the leaders among the works expressing the Hard image of Soviet conduct on the whole measure up well. Accurate they are. I have found no clear error of fact. And, with exceptions to be noted, they meet reasonably well the criteria of "well-disciplined." Accordingly, they show up to advantage when compared with the works portraying the Ultra-Hard image.

On the principal tests of discipline, the showing is generally satisfactory. General characterization is fairly clear-cut. True, Kennan presents two distinct versions of conduct, one of which is not far

76. Ibid., Chapter 10.
77. For instance, ibid., Chapter 1.
78. For example, ibid., p. 27.
79. Ibid., p. 176.

removed from the Ultra Hard view. Shulman fails to make clear whether the change from Left to Right syndrome he dates to the years 1949–52 was change consummated or merely change initiated. But all three make quite clear the common major conclusion that Soviet conduct, quite hard in the immediate postwar years, moderated significantly at the start of the 1950s. They also make reasonably clear their assessment of earlier periods: Kennan's, of near-uniform hardness; Shulman's, of oscillation between more- and less-hard modes; Tucker's, of a perceptible increase in hardness with the accession of Stalin to power and, later, with the events of 1939.

In the definition and differentiation of concepts, the first step in substantiation, Shulman and Tucker show measurable advance. Shulman in his distinction between Right and Left modes of conduct, which he spells out fully and explicitly; Tucker in his distinctions between formal and operative aims, operative aims of control and influence, and politics of persuasion and aggression—which he at least begins to spell out: each contributes in significant measure toward developing an adequate analytic vocabulary. And if the efforts are somewhat vitiated, in Tucker's case by a failure to complete and sharpen the emergent distinctions, and in Shulman's by a failure to spell out the offensive-defensive distinction superimposed upon the Left-Right, they still mark progress.

In the application of concepts to the data (alternately, the subsumption of the data under the concepts) there are, to be sure, weaknesses. Kennan's conclusion about Stalinist militancy in the 1930s is poorly borne out by his data: there is a gap between the two. Tucker's application of his distinctions to the pre- and post-1953 periods is at times faulty, the contrast based thereon exaggerated. But Shulman and Tucker adduce a sufficient quantity of data generally to sustain their propositions about significant change. Above all, all three resolutely reject the question-begging procedures for sifting the data found to characterize expressions of the Ultra-Hard view.

On the supplementary criteria, the three works show up uniformly well. Shulman and Tucker are strictly neutral in their reporting, their work free of affective language. Kennan, while unabashedly evaluative, passing constant judgment on the worth of Soviet or Western conduct and extracting lessons from the record for future Western guidance, nevertheless keeps these judgments from coloring his reporting.

Kennan and Tucker draw illuminating comparisons between Soviet and Western and/or pre-Soviet conduct, treating the two with an even hand. All three, but Kennan and Shulman particularly, pay careful attention to alternative interpretations, rejecting them only on reasoned analysis.

In consequence, the common image, of conduct Hard but Softening, has acquired a substantiality that the Ultra-Hard image has not, and the major proposition about change, and especially the particular proposition about post-Stalin moderation, a credibility that the Ultra-Hard affirmation of changelessness has not. One can still argue about the degree of post-Stalin moderation, its phasing in time, its causes (whether predominantly internal or external), its future. But the fact that substantial moderation of conduct, and a substantial decline in militancy, took place on or about the time of Stalin's death, is hardly arguable any longer. More important yet, it is hardly longer open to argument that the moderation in question is of secular character, and of a significance greater than earlier ones. Not least among Shulman's and Tucker's contributions is their insistence, based upon a scrupulous reading of the complete dicta and writings on "peaceful coexistence," that the phrase has a different and milder connotation than the old breathing-spell-between-wars—that it now connotes an indefinite elongation of time perspective, as Shulman would put it, or embraces cooperative as well as competitive elements, as Tucker would remind us.

To some this may appear a matter of belaboring the obvious. But the point has been anything but obvious to adherents of the Ultra-Hard point of view. And even if this were not the case, it is as truly said of scholarly as of scientific endeavor that its task is to make the obvious inescapable.

CHAPTER 5

The Mixed Image: The Neurotic Bear

The third and last of the three major types of images of Soviet conduct —the Mixed or Medium image, neither Hard nor Soft—shifts the center of attention from within to without. For what distinguishes this view most sharply from Ultra-Hard or Hard is the belief that Soviet aggression is an occasional, not a normal affair, and that it occurs not as the expression of an inherent drive or instinctive trait but as a reaction to what are or appear to be the menacing actions of environing states. A militant or coercive or expansive move which to the Ultra-Hard imagist stands as the reflection of a primary instinct, an instinct extinguishable only with the extinction of life itself, and which to the Hard imagist stands as the reflection of something on the order of a trait of adolescence that will pass with time and maturation, to those who hold the Mixed image is a simple response to a hostile environment and will disappear with the disappearance of that hostility.

Six of the 22 works of the sample express views close to this. Their assessment in terms of the criteria of scholarship set forth at the beginning of Chapter 3 is the focus of discussion in the present one.

LEADING EXPRESSIONS

Of the six works in question—Fleming, Gehlen, Halle, Lukacs, Schuman, and Triska—I find Gehlen, Halle, Schuman, and Triska the leaders and shall accordingly deal with them in some detail, the first three in this chapter, Triska in the next.

The works of Fleming, Halle, and Lukacs are in the broad sense histories. Their common concern is that particular Soviet-Western relationship known as the Cold War—as it was born, has matured, and is tapering off. Their approach, the second part of Lukacs' work aside, is chronological. Their central interest is that of providing an accurate account of the events constituting the relationship named and suggesting the causes thereof.

While it shares much with the other two, however, Halle's work is distinguished from them in two main respects, and these make it a fitter object for more extended scrutiny. Halle offers appreciably more by way of general characterization of Soviet conduct than does Lukacs, and a great deal more than does Fleming. And he offers in clearer and stronger form than Lukacs a kind of explanation for that conduct, namely, geographic determinism, that because of unusual problems raised deserves special attention.

Fleming suggests, in much the longest work of the sample, what is clearly the softest and most sympathetic view of Soviet conduct, and the only view lying on the Soft side of the scale.[1] His theme is that the Cold War was an outgrowth almost exclusively of American bellicosity; that this bellicosity derived from a refusal to accept the chief outcomes of World War II, namely, the communization of East Europe and China; and that this refusal in turn derived from a totally unreal picture of the USSR. The view that emerges from the development of this theme is one that visualizes Soviet conduct as only intermittently expansive, and then only for preemptive reasons; only intermittently military, and that largely in a defensive context; neither especially militant nor moral; largely responsive; motivated by fear for security rather than by the ambition suggested by ideology. But I use the term "emerges" advisedly. For in Fleming, more than in any of the other works, characterization is particularist, the general image latent and implicit. On the analogy of a fist fight, Fleming gives a blow-by-blow account, while leaving it to others to draw implications and generalize about the postures, strategy, and tactics of the two opponents. Fleming is not, I would add, insensitive to problems of careful procedure.[2] But his follow-through is imperfect. The occasional promise of extended careful analysis is not fulfilled. And his

1. *The Cold War and Its Origins: 1917–1960,* 2 vols. (Garden City, N.Y.: Doubleday, 1961). For the closest thing to a summary of findings and view of Soviet conduct, see Chapter XXXIV, "Why the West Lost the Cold War."

2. For example, ibid., Chapter XXXIV, and comments on pp. xiii, xix, 475–76, 311–12, 515–16.

effort to be evenhanded in his evaluation of the actions of the two opponents falls short, the Soviets commonly being treated more tenderly.

Lukacs describes the method underlying his New History of the Cold War[3] as "historical," in sharp contradistinction to "scientific." By "historical" he apparently means providing an accurate description and explanation of events aiming at "understanding," by "scientific" something else aiming at "certainty," the exact nature of which he doesn't quite make clear. He divides his study into two sections, the first or descriptive section called "The Main Events," the second, in which he searches for causes in various underlying social phenomena (peoples, societies, states, nations), called "The Main Movements." His global theorem is that by their expansion into and determination to keep East Europe the Soviets initiated the Cold War; that in their overreaction and counterexpansion the United States made a heavy contribution to its continuance; and that in so acting and reacting the two states were responding to their concepts of national interest and the peculiarities of their national characters rather than to the claims of ideology.

The view of Soviet conduct Lukacs' narrative puts forth parallels Fleming's, the major point of difference (and the one which makes Lukacs' on balance the harder of the two) being his insistence on Soviet responsibility for the Cold War. But, like Fleming's, this view is communicated in an implicit rather than an explicit manner. Only on the point of motivation does it emerge clearly, Lukacs' position here, like Fleming's, stressing the "national interest" element and reading this negatively as concern for security born of fear.[4] Further, Lukacs makes virtually no attempt to define his terms and specify the rules for their application. And there is little by way of carefully worked out conceptual framework.

But if Fleming and Lukacs are not the leaders in the group, they make their contribution. Fleming is at least aware of such problems as those of distinguishing offensive from defensive, action from reaction, of the need to view the international scene from the perspective

3. Third ed., expanded, of A History of the Cold War (Garden City, N.Y.: Doubleday, 1966). See pp. ix-xii for remarks on method.
4. See esp. ibid., Chapter XIV, "The Two States: The Development of Their National Interests."

of each actor, and or the need to examine other interpretations of the
record.[5] Lukacs is remarkably evenhanded in the judgments he makes
on the two major actors. He recognizes, for instance, that if one is to
use the concept "expansionism," and treat the moves of Stalin in
1945–48 as meeting the definition thereof, then, by the same logic,
American moves setting up bases around the world are also to be
categorized as expansionist, and Soviet moves in the mid '50s involving the relinquishment of bases, occupation rights, and privileges
as contractionist.[6]

Triska's work, besides being the sample's unique full-span analysis
of the subject proper and being ordered on a sensible scheme, like
Gehlen's work is imaginative (as modernist) in techniques used and
affirms and substantiates two or three important propositions. In this
chapter I pass it over solely because its firmest conclusion integral to
the Mixed view, namely, that of Soviet cautiousness, is the same as
the one I choose from Gehlen's work, in which this conclusion is more
clearly and simply expounded and backed up, and because this and
its other contributions are more usefully discussed in the context of
the possible lines of improvement dealt with in the following chapter,
a topic on which Triska and his colleague have more useful things
to say than any others of the sample.

Case i: Gehlen and Khrushchevian Caution

Michael Gehlen's *The Politics of Coexistence: Soviet Methods and
Motives,* published in 1967,[7] centers on Soviet foreign policy proper,
confining itself almost entirely to the post-Stalin period. Gehlen's
purpose is "to examine the assumptions behind the policy of coexistence and the methods employed by the Soviet to achieve her
foreign policy objectives."[8] Gehlen is purely expositorial: he does not
express personal opinion, nor does he seek to prescribe. His tone is
moderate.

Gehlen organizes his study analytically. He deals first with the
setting of domestic policy, attempting to identify the contending
pressures and sponsoring factions of which policy is the resultant. He
deals next with ideological roots and then with the various aspects

5. See n. 2 above.
6. Ibid., pp. 128, 160–65, 219–20.
7. Bloomington: University of Indiana Press.
8. Ibid., p. 3.

of implementation vis-à-vis the capitalist world—military, economic, political, and ideological (now taken as means). His next to last chapter is concerned with implementation vis-à-vis other Communist states. His final one is a conclusion.

According to Gehlen, peaceful coexistence is a policy of accommodation with the non-Communist world that came out of the general post-Stalin liberalization of Soviet society.[9] While retaining the goal of a world of Communist states, this policy sets the anticipated day of achievement so much further in the future as to extend indefinitely the accommodation in question. While its underlying theory is still basically Leninist, this theory contains certain new elements, such as the noninevitability of war, which, together with a shift of emphasis away from revolution and violence, signifies a genuine, if modest, ideological softening. Peaceful coexistence is a policy which, partly because of a high appreciation of the danger of nuclear holocaust, is low on risk-taking, sparing in the use of the military instrument. Conversely, it is a policy that relies heavily, though not very successfully, on trade and aid, on the personal diplomacy of summitry and traditional tactics of divide and rule, on the manipulation of foreign parties, and on propaganda. Taking into account differences among bloc nations, it is more tolerant of the autonomy of other Communist states, less insistent on Soviet dominance over them. Its day-by-day development is shaped by the shifting outcome of conflicts among the elite groups of an increasingly pluralist society. It is motivated ultimately more by perceptions of national interest than by ideology, the role of the latter being confined mainly to that of rationalizer and instrument of domestic control.

Gehlen thus sees contemporary Soviet conduct on the one hand as expansion-minded in terms of influence, and expansive and militant,[10] on the other as cautious,[11] propelled less by commitment to the cause than by concern for security,[12] tolerant of some independence on the part of other Communist states,[13] appreciably milder

9. This paragraph resumes the useful summaries at the end of the various chapters of Gehlen's work.
10. Ibid., pp. 151, 187, 208.
11. Ibid., pp. 109–27.
12. Ibid., pp. 151–52.
13. Ibid., pp. 288, 295.

than late-Stalinist and other earlier policies.[14] By implication he also
sees it as not particularly expansive in terms of rule nor particularly
successful in achieving its aims;[15] he visualizes it as conduct which,
if primarily initiatory, is on important occasions responsive;[16] and he
considers it to be, if disturbing to the international order, not cata-
strophically so.[17] In much of its implementation, it differs little, for
him, from the conduct of other states.[18]

This view is on a number of counts milder than others so far considered. For one thing, it leaves out the notion of the expansion of
rule as an element in the objectives sought. For a second, it ascribes
to conduct a degree of reluctance in the use of armed force heretofore
found only with Tucker. For a third, it sees an appreciable part of
that conduct as a response to the moves of others. In imputing motives
it shifts the stress rather strongly to fear and security considerations,
and away from ideology. Its conception of responsiveness to the pressures of competing interest groups implies a rejection of totalitarianism as causal factor. It lays a new emphasis on Soviet failures, and it
finds a new affinity between the behavior of the Soviet state and that
of other states. As for change, while Gehlen attaches a somewhat
higher value to the developments of the early '50s than do the Ultra-
Hard imagists, he attaches a lower one than do Kennan, Shulman,
and Tucker. Stalinist conduct, though harsher, more prone to violence
than later conduct, has for Gehlen a mixed character in which zeal for
the defense of the Soviet state nicely balances the compulsion toward
universality.[19]

The major proposition I take from *The Politics of Coexistence* for
closer scrutiny is the proposition that in recent years risk-taking has
been low.[20] This is one of the work's central propositions. The issue

14. Ibid., pp. 64, 202.
15. For example, ibid., pp. 189, 205, 232, 244.
16. For example, ibid., pp. 149, 186.
17. For example, ibid., pp. 63–64.
18. Ibid., p. 238.
19. Ibid., pp. 40–41.
20. Ibid., p. 127. I describe the conclusion as "Khrushchevian caution"
because the data upon which it is based, with the single exception of the
Soviet response to Vietnam, are moves that date to the years when Khrushchev was in control.

of Soviet willingness to take risks is a matter of obvious importance to outsiders seeking to understand Soviet behavior. It is also an issue others resolve quite differently. Some analysts see Khrushchev as a kind of practitioner of brinkmanship and the instigator of "rolling crises."[21] Others, such as the authors of *Protracted Conflict,* while conceding and in fact stressing the Soviets' desire to avoid military showdown, nevertheless affirm a willingness to raise the level of international tension to a point just short of such a showdown.[22]

Gehlen's treatment is found in his chapter on the military aspects of coexistence.[23] Gehlen begins by defining what he means by risk-taking. A state embarks on a policy of risk, he says, when in deciding on a given move it assesses others' probable responses to the move as a threat to its vital interests rather than certain or uncertain. An assessment is called certain if the anticipated reaction is clearly calculable and acceptable, uncertain if the anticipated reaction is not clear but "the contemplated Soviet action is not likely . . . to lead to a significant amount of tension."[24] The assessment defining the policy of risk is given no name.

Gehlen next presents a summary of the Soviet record. This is in the form of a table grading Soviet moves by level of violence in 11 selected crises of 1955–66.[25] The six gradations are respectively: (A) verbal threats; (B) provision of nonmilitary aid; (BC) physical but nonviolent provocation such as closing a border; (C) provision of military aid; (D) full or partial mobilization of armed forces; (E) deployment of forces or weapons outside the USSR; (F) actual use of military force. The 11 crises are, in the order in which Gehlen lists them: Suez (1956), Poland (1956), Hungary (1956), Middle East (1958), Algeria (1960–61), Laos (1960–61), Congo (1960–61), Vietnam (1965–66), Berlin (1958), Berlin (1961), Cuba (1962). Moves made by the Soviets in a given crisis are noted as x's at the appropriate juncture of row and column in the table.

The intermediate findings, on moves in individual crisis, Gehlen

21. Philip E. Mosely, *The Kremlin and World Politics: Studies in Soviet Policy and Action* (New York: Vintage, 1960), p. 551.
22. See above, Chapter 3, pp. 77–80.
23. Gehlen, *The Politics of Coexistence,* Chapter IV, esp. pp. 110–27.
24. Ibid., p. 110.
25. Ibid., p. 111.

now reads off the table and expatiates upon, gradation by gradation.[26] In eight of the 11 crises, he tells us, the Soviets issued verbal threats against one or another of the parties immediately concerned; in six they provided nonmilitary assistance, in four military (Suez, Laos, Congo, Vietnam); in two (the two Berlin crises) they indulged in physical but nonviolent provocations, meaning border incidents designed to force the West to deal with the East Germans and, of course, construction of the Wall. The most significant of these findings, to which he comes in due course, are that in only five of the 11 cases (Poland, Hungary, the Middle East, Berlin 1961, and Cuba) did the moves reach violence level D (mobilization), that in only three of these (Poland, Hungary, Cuba) did they reach level F, the deployment abroad of Soviet forces.

After a section taking special note of the Cuban crisis, Gehlen concludes with certain summary comments. These emphasize the care which, Cuba aside, the Soviets took to avoid steps that might lead to the use of force and a deep commitment; the heavy reliance they placed on verbal admonitions and warnings, especially in cases outside the bloc; the considerable restraint they showed in the use of force even within their system; and the curious fact that in the three situations in which their moves reached level E, they issued no threats.[27] Gehlen completes his treatment by pointing to the corroboratory findings of a more extended study.[28]

In reviewing Gehlen's development of his low-risk thesis, one is struck first by the fact that the concepts in terms of which he promises at the start to conduct his analysis he discards almost at the moment of introduction for another. Gehlen's promised scheme is one that distinguishes a policy of risk from other policies on grounds of differences in the assessment of other nations' responses. Possible assessments of these responses, as already noted, are: certain (a term used when the responses are judged clearly calculable), uncertain (when they are judged not clear, and the contemplated action not likely to lead to much tension), and risk-laden (when they are judged likely to threaten vital interests). Surely this scheme is carelessly drawn: the

26. Ibid., pp. 112–18.
27. Ibid., pp. 124–27.
28. Ibid., pp. 126–27.

logical possibilities implicit in the crossing of the two principles involved are not all recognized, and those that are indifferently defined and poorly named. But no matter. Gehlen scarcely refers to the scheme again. In what he says about Soviet attitudes and decision-making in the face of specific crises, he pays little attention to the assessment of others' likely responses, and that little is virtually unrelated to the original conceptual triad. Categorization of Soviet policy in the concrete cases as low or high risk rests on other grounds.

As the development proceeds, however, it gathers strength and one's second impression is a favorable one, for the grounds on which categorization does rest are reasonably sound, as are the other terms used, and the application to the historical record is reasonably sure. The conceptual scheme actually used to determine degree of risk incurred in the concrete case is the A to F scale of ascending severity of action reaching from verbal threat to the use of armed force. This is a reasonable scheme: choice of action along a Talk to Fight scale is a reasonable, if not perfect, indicator of one's willingness to chance another's damaging something vital. Gehlen's choice of crises for the 1955–66 period in question is also reasonable. To be sure, it can be challenged on one or two points. Some of the items included, like the Algerian crisis of 1960–61, hardly threatened the general peace as much as some excluded, like the 1958 crisis of the Formosa Straits and the Sino-Indian crisis of 1962. But a list worked out systematically, on grounds made explicit, is likely to agree fairly closely with Gehlen's. The main fault the exposition can be charged with in respect to the terms of the analysis is a paucity of supporting commentary. Finally, the historical data adduced, represented by the checkmarks in Gehlen's table and his textual comments, are with minor exceptions correct.[29] Gehlen's low-risk conclusion, on the basis of the terms actually used, may thus be considered well sustained by his data.

Yet as one ponders the completed demonstration, doubts again

29. Some exceptions: it is extravagant to call Soviet threats "ultimatums" as Gehlen does on p. 126; also, his table to the contrary notwithstanding, the Cuban crisis of 1962 was marked by a Soviet threat, same being contained in the TASS dispatch of September 11, 1962. Cf. William Welch, "The Nature of Khrushchevian Threats Against the West," *University of Colorado Studies, Series in Political Science No. 3* (Boulder: University of Colorado Press, August 1965).

intrude—though doubts of completely new character—and one's third impression resembles in tendency the first more nearly than the second. For the rather startling criticism that now occurs is that Gehlen's low-risk conclusion is better sustained than he appears to realize. He has built better than he knows. For cautiousness in responding to crises initiated by others may reasonably be weighted somewhat more than cautiousness in initiating them oneself since, events being less within one's control in the first case than in the second, there is the greater danger of being driven to sudden, spasmodic violence. And eight of Gehlen's 11 crises are crises initiated by others than the Soviets, the latter being responsible only for the two Berlin crises and the Cuban crisis. Gehlen marks the distinction between the two conditions surreptitiously in his table, obliquely in the text.[30] But he fails to draw the inference above noted. He thus gives up by default the stronger conclusion to which his materials entitle him.

All in all, Gehlen's treatment of his low-risk proposition produces a mixed reaction. To his credit, he has adopted sensible terms and applied them with reasonable care. In method, his treatment marks a clear advance over that of Strausz-Hupé and associates.[31] On the other hand, he shares with many of the school called behaviorist a preoccupation with conceptualization somewhat beyond what is needed, an addiction at times to pretentious language, and a disconcerting penchant for dropping promising ideas in early development.[32]

For *The Politics of Coexistence* as a whole, the judgment is also a mixed one. The work has much merit. It is ordered by a reasonable

30. The table recognizes the distinction by listing the crises not simply by chronology, but by chronology within the two categories, the three crises initiated by the Soviets being placed separately at the end. See Gehlen, *The Politics of Coexistence*, p. 111. For recognition in text, see ibid., p. 113.

31. See above, Chapter 3, pp. 77–83.

32. See, for instance, the last line of the risk-table referred to (Gehlen, *The Politics of Coexistence*, p. 111). On this line, in which Gehlen totals the various gradations of threat with which the USSR responded to each crisis, there appears suddenly, in the "Cuba" column, a new notation—"E_2." The explanation for this, given in a footnote to the table, is that "E is converted to E_2 in order to recognize the proximity factor as a matter affecting the level of risk." Yet in his own analysis he scarcely mentions again this undoubtedly important factor, much less deals with it at any length.

scheme of concepts, among which objectives, methods, and motives
play important parts, methods or aspects being further differentiated
into military, economic, political and ideological. It is sensitive to
the problems of proper procedure, especially those peculiar to the
Soviet field. On the critical point of the role of ideology, for instance, it recognizes explicitly the difficulty, absent interviews, of
reporting the ideas or intent in the minds of Soviet leaders, and it
warns repeatedly against confusing Soviet word with Soviet deed,
bark with bite.[33] It is free of the capricious devices for ordering the
data noted in works earlier discussed. Urging a more careful look at
actual behavior, it shows what can be done along this line with the
risk-taking analysis just reviewed. Its tone is sober throughout, and
its orientation is purely contemplative: no homiletic disgressions by
way of gratuitous exhortation to reading public or policy-maker draw
the reader's attention away from the primary business at hand, the
business of understanding.

   Withal, the work has certain defects. The treatment given the low-
risk thesis is not elsewhere repeated. The treatment given other theses
is not always satisfactory. Treatment of the role of ideology, for
instance, at many points sane, at others lacks consistency and sophistication. Ideology is defined on one page as the normative as opposed
to the cognitive part of Marxist-Leninism, while on another it is
invested with a "descriptive" nature and set apart from the "cognitive
and prescriptive" aspects of theory.[34] The point is made in the course
of the discussion that Soviet insistence on the unity of theory and
action complicates the task of the analyst—as though the analyst were
compelled in his examination of Soviet affairs to adopt the categories
of the Soviets themselves.[35] The style is often awkward and imprecise:
one misses the clarity of Kennan or Tucker, or the forcefulness of
Wolfe.

   Not least among the defects is the curiously unsatisfactory nature of
the conclusions constituting the final chapter. These affirm mainly
three things: (1) that Soviet policy-formation is today a function of
shifting coalitions among various special-interest elites in the society;

33. Ibid., pp. 21, 207, 238.
34. Ibid., pp. 22, 39.
35. Ibid., p. 22.

(2) that in determining the content of the policy ideology plays only a small role; and (3) that the only thing the West can surely expect in the future in respect to Soviet intentions and actions is change. But the third of these affirmations is vague almost to the point of meaninglessness and, in any case, indifferently related to the points made before in the bulk of the book; whereas the second, although interesting and provocative, is rather a summary of newly introduced material on the subject than a conclusion on the old. Not less curious is the absence, alongside of the conclusions on motives, of a conclusion on methods—the second term in the book's subtitle, the concern of many of the individual chapters, and the subject of many lesser conclusions well developed earlier. Gehlen might reasonably have summed up the findings of his middling chapters on the various aspects of Soviet foreign policy by affirming that Soviet post-Stalin policy has in the methods it employs been exceedingly cautious in the use of the military instrument, wide-ranging but orthodox in its employment of nonmilitary instrumentalities, and unusually unsuccessful. But he does not. Gehlen thus lays himself open to the criticism of making the least rather than the most of his materials. One might almost say of his final chapter, in fact, that it restates the weakest points of his text, and ignores the strongest. Where data and conclusions are mismatched, the weakness more commonly, as with Kennan, lies in the data. With Gehlen, however, it lies in the conclusions.

CASE 2: HALLE AND GEOGRAPHIC DETERMINISM

Louis J. Halle's *The Cold War as History,* which appeared in 1967,[36] centers on the relationship named, particularly as it involved the USSR and the United States. Apart from a brief preliminary treatment of the period 1917–39, this second of the leading expressions of the Mixed view deals exclusively with the years from 1939 to 1963. Halle's purpose, and what he believes is the proper purpose of a historian, is to record faithfully the events within his purview to the further end of uncovering the pattern underlying them.[37] A censorial mood prevails, for Halle is not reluctant to tell his readers what he thinks is good, what bad, about the performance of the major actors, American in particular.

36. New York: Harper & Row.
37. Ibid., pp. xi–xii.

Halle tells his tale in 39 chapters. The first three chapters affirm a general interpretation of the Cold War, tying Soviet and American behavior to their respective national histories. The thirty-ninth chapter, called "Epilogue," deals with future prospects, with special emphasis on the American embroilment in Asia. Intermediate chapters give a year-by-year, almost blow-by-blow, account of the waxing and waning of the conflict, picking up first the Soviet and then the American thread.

Halle's thesis is that the Cold War was a matter of historical necessity, and as such beyond the province of human will and outside the scope of moral judgment.[38] Like previous wars that threatened to upset the European balance of power, it ran a predetermined course from its beginning, which Halle dates to June 1947, to its end, which he dates to the Cuban confrontation of October 1962. The moments in that history—the Russian expansion into Europe that triggered the conflict; the American response through the Truman Doctrine, etc., which "joined" it; the misunderstanding of each other's action, which intensified it through further challenges and responses; the extension to other areas, which "generalized" it; the growing sense of the danger of nuclear disaster, which led to its defusing—all occurred because they had to. Although it mercifully stayed Cold; although its resolution in the rebuilding of the European balance was happily free of the element of unconditional surrender which made the resolutions of 1919 and 1945 the seedbed of still further strife—in the main it followed the preordained pattern that marks all strife of its kind.

Halle's version of the Mixed view of Soviet conduct, as it rises to the surface incidentally to the development of this thesis, is one of which the leitmotiv is "defensive expansion."[39] In this version, Soviet conduct aims not at world domination, nor even in any very meaningful sense at world communism, but rather at the more limited goal of enlarging and strengthening Soviet defenses.[40] It is, in its implementation too, expansive but intermittently and conditionally only, the condition being subjection to prior attack; now and again it even accepts the need to retreat.[41] Its general militancy is offset by

38. Ibid., pp. xi–xiii.
39. See ibid., Chapter II, esp. pp. 11, 17, for the bulk of the description that follows, supplementary sources being given as appropriate.
40. Ibid., p. 158.
41. Ibid., p. 16.

a sparing use of the military instrument born of considerable cautiousness.[42] While conspiratorial and secret in style, it has been not unduly
unobservant of moral norms.[43] It is in low degree rational and planned,
in high degree unplanned and improvised.[44] It is partly initiatory,
partly responsive.[45] Its prime motors are fear, concern for security,
and beyond this a compulsion generated by geopolitical location, ideology playing a small role.[46] The dangers it poses are real, but easily
exaggerated; its successes are not overwhelming. While hegemonic in
policy toward other Communist states, it is reluctantly so.[47] It is not
immutable, post-Stalin softening representing real and important
change.[48] Its affinities are not with the conduct of Japanese and Nazi
warlords, but with that of the run of great powers.[49]

The differences between Ultra-Hard, Hard, and Mixed views of
Soviet conduct are nowhere better exemplified than by the differences
respecting concepts of objectives, motivating forces, and modes of
pursuit that separate Wolfe, the later Kennan, and Halle. For Wolfe
the objective is unlimited expansion, the drive an ideology-given lust
for power, the mode of pursuit unremitting war. For Kennan the
objective is limited expansion, the drive part promotion of communism reflected in ideology, part security, the mode of pursuit active
and militant, but nonmilitarist and with marked evolution in the
more moderate direction. For Halle the objective is restricted expansion, the driving force is fear or unconscious reflex, the mode of
pursuit reactive, intermittent, and cautious.

Limited expansionism, unevenly and cautiously pursued, born of
fear and ultimately geographic necessity, hence Russian rather than
Communist—these are the key traits to Soviet conduct as Halle sees
them. And for a more detailed look at the adequacy of the support he
gives them, I now turn to each in succession.

Halle's descriptive generalizations are on the whole indifferently

42. Ibid., p. 11.
43. For example, ibid., pp. 67–75.
44. Ibid., pp. 48–49.
45. Ibid., pp. 408–09, p. 156.
46. Ibid., p. 12.
47. For example, ibid., p. 65.
48. Ibid., p. 318.
49. Ibid., p. 12.

dealt with. He leaves the articulation of data and conclusion almost entirely up to the reader, transferring to the reader's shoulders from his own the burden of close demonstration. And to this reader these demonstrations by indirection are somewhat short of convincing. For instance, although making strongly the general point of Soviet cautiousness, Halle puts an opposite construction on most of the major Soviet moves of the period. He describes as "reckless" the moves against Berlin, the 1962 intervention in Cuba, indeed, all policy from 1960 to 1962 on.[50] He calls the Korean adventure "a more violent attempt . . . than in Germany" to change the status quo.[51] He terms Moscow's threats in the Suez and Syrian crises of 1956–57 "ominous," a term hardly suggestive of caution.[52] This is not to say the moves in question cannot be validly interpreted so as to support the generalization. They can be and, witness Gehlen, they have been. It is to say only that they haven't been so interpreted by Halle.

An exception should perhaps be made of Halle's description of Soviet expansiveness as occasionally retreat-punctuated and intermittent,[53] for he buttresses this adequately by noting such developments as the following: the receding of empire that set in with the Yugoslav defection of June 1948; the contraction marked by Chinese displacement of Soviet influence in Korea and Manchuria begun, presumably, in 1950 and 1951; and the retrenchment of 1955–56 marked by the rapprochement with Yugoslavia, the retrocession of bases to China and Finland, and the withdrawal from Austria.[54] And in so doing he points to the need of refining the concept of even, uninterrupted expansiveness that lies beneath others' treatment of the subject, such, for instance, as Wolfe's. But this aside, documentation is diffuse and shaky.

Halle's contextual generalizations from the distinctive, as the more important part of his thought. This is particularly true for his propo-

50. Ibid., pp. 163, 403, 380.
51. Ibid., p. 203.
52. Ibid., pp. 342, 351; the Suez threat is also described as "gingerly" (p. 351).
53. While not completely consistent in affirming intermittence as against continuousness—see, for example, ibid., p. 17—the former is, on the whole, Halle's position.
54. Ibid., pp. 231, 227, 318.

sition about geographic determinism, which he offers as an explanation of Soviet expansiveness. These generalizations therefore deserve searching consideration, starting with an appraisal of the broader theory of international relations to which they had joined.

Halle develops his theory of international relations in his opening chapter and embellishes it in later ones, notably Chapter XVI and the epilogue.[55] He has a mechanistic view of the political universe. According to this view, the history of international relations is a history of attempts to upset and defend a certain equilibrium called a balance of power.[56] Every once in a while some single nation challenges the balance by threatening to overcome the others, and this evokes a response in the form of a protective coalition of the rest. As in all conflicts, each side now eschews a defense of what it is about in "real" terms of self-interest, and turns increasingly to defending itself in "nominal" terms, that is, to justifying its action in terms of universals like peace, justice, etc.[57] The justification becomes coarser and coarser until both come to see their conflict as a war between Good and Evil, each assigning to itself the role of Angel of Justice and to the other the role of Satan. The conceptual corruption and demonization exacerbate the basic conflict. Each now makes the kind of move called for to defend itself against the Devil, and this provokes in the other counteraction which tends to confirm the original mover's assumption, after the manner of the phenonenon called self-fulfilling prophecy.[58] Not only does the conflict thus tend to intensify, but it expands geographically, or, in Halle's words, becomes generalized, spreading from its European center to the rest of the world. The general war that ensues continues until the surrender of the challenger, conditional or less happily "unconditional," or the development of a new sense of things in common, when peace returns and the equilibrium is restored.

The Cold War is, in Halle's view, the fourth enactment of this great historical drama. In it Soviet Russia plays the role of challenger

55. Ibid., pp. 157–60, Epilogue.
56. Halle (ibid., p. 6) defines balance of power as "such a distribution of power among a number of centers as prevents the acquisition by any one of enough power to make itself master of the rest."
57. Ibid., pp. 157–60.
58. Ibid., pp. 145–49.

earlier played by Bonaparte, Wilhelm II, and Hitler, the United States the role of defender first played by England alone, later by England in conjunction with the United States. The Cold War was sparked by the 1945–47 Soviet move into the East European vacuum left by the retreating Nazis. It was joined when the United States in 1947–48 first halted, then reversed its demobilization and withdrawal from Europe. It gathered momentum as each side submerged the real reasons for its actions beneath nominal reasons associated with the attainment of worldwide peace and justice. It became intensified as each progressively coarsened the picture of the total situation, its own role, and the role of its adversary—the Soviets with their myth of the imperialist monster bent on world conquest, the Americans with their counter myth of the Great Beast also bent on world conquest.[59] It became generalized with the extension of the struggle first to the Far East, with the Korean War, and later to the Middle East, Africa, and Latin America. And it ended, in the wake of the Cuban confrontation of 1962, with de facto acceptance by both sides of the dangers to both in pursuing it further.

The Cold War, to be sure, differed in certain respects from the three earlier enactments of the drama. It stayed cold, for one thing. For another, the driving force behind the challenger's initiative was not ambition, as with Bonaparte, the kaiser, and Hitler, but fear. Specifically—and here is where the determinist account of Soviet conduct enters the picture—the Soviets moved into the area because they were driven to do so by the exposed and vulnerable nature of the space they occupy on the globe. Halle supports this determinism with two arguments. One is an explicit argument to the effect that Tocqueville in the last century had predicted the expansion of Russian power over half the world, and that what is predictable is inevitable.[60] The other, implicit, is that the expansion into East Europe is simply one more in a series of Russian expansions dating back 10 centuries, that these have all been tied to the experience of earlier beatings at the hands of the invader invited by the lack of natural frontiers, and

59. The first was exemplified by Zhdanov's celebrated speech of 1947, the second by Dulles's television speech to the American people after Eisenhower's inauguration in 1953. See ibid., pp. 233–34.

60. Ibid., pp. 10–11.

that these circumstances suggest that the overriding objective was to
drive the encircling danger back, substituting sheer space for the lack
of mountain ramparts and impassable seas.[61]

But in its major contours the Cold War followed the pattern. Above
all, it followed the pattern, as the others had done, because it had to.
The whole business was a case of "historical necessity."[62] From this
Halle draws the important corollary that in the account to be given of
it by the historian moral judgments have no part. "Fundamentally,"
the Cold War is a case not of virtue against vice but, in Herbert
Butterfield's metaphor, of scorpion against tarantula.[63]

Halle's theory is intriguing and provocative. It shows in its propositions about the genesis and intensification of conflict a sensitivity to
a key problem of political inquiry and, hence, Soviet inquiry so far
not found among the works here considered. The problem is that of
determining what is initiative, what response, among the moves of
international actors. Most other works assume each such move bears
its character as one or the other on its face. Halle finds this too simple
a view of the matter. He recognizes that what may genuinely and
understandably seem to one protagonist responsive and defensive,
may to the other as genuinely and understandably seem initiative and
offensive. In the sphere of international politics, as he puts the matter,
" . . . the process of driving . . . danger back becomes, to the eye of
the outsider, the process of imperial expansion."[64] He recognizes, too,
how this almost inevitably makes for what is—to borrow a phrase
Halle borrows from Butterfield—"irreducible dilemma,"[65] ineluctable
tragedy. For each move of this character, by virtue of its bearing a plus
sign for the mover but a minus for the one moved against, almost
inevitably generates another of the same kind. Roles and signs change
for the two parties, but the basic situation remains precisely the same,
thus insuring still further escalation. Whether Halle always correctly
applies this conceptualization of the action-reaction phenomenon to
American-Soviet relations may be debated. But his awareness that

61. Ibid., pp. 12–14.
62. Ibid., p. 12.
63. Ibid., p. xiii.
64. Ibid., p. 17.
65. Ibid., p. xiii.

something of the kind commonly goes on in the international realm cannot be.

Halle's theory is indeed intriguing, but it doesn't pass muster. The kind of demonstration needed to show "necessity" is, I would hold, the kind exemplified by the proofs of Euclidean theorems. And this kind is out of the question in the realms of the natural and social sciences, outside those of logic and mathematics. But be this as it may, Halle's support is insufficient. His arguments won't do, and his treatment of specific events betrays a belief in the possibility of different outcomes inconsistent with a true determinism.

The argument from Tocqueville won't do. To reason that Soviet expansion into East Europe was inevitable because one philosopher predicted back in 1830 that Russia would inherit half a world is to reason tenuously indeed. Tocqueville's prediction was the estimate of an astute observer—if not a wild guess, a general estimate of probabilities, an extrapolation of an existing trend as he saw it. And it proved rather spectacularly wrong. For the proportions of global area and population actually dominated by the Russians at time of maximum extension, which amount to something less than 20 percent and 15 percent (the figures are for 1948 and include satellites), fall short of the proportion forecast (50 percent) by factors of two and one-half or three times. But even had the prediction proved correct, the argument would fail. If successful predictions are taken to be indicators of necessity (even when further qualified to mean successful predictions of competent observers), then, inasmuch as even competent observers commonly disagree on forecasts, one must conclude that, in the retrospective context within which the discussion takes place, anything that happens can be shown to have been necessary— and so nothing.

Halle is on better ground when he inferentially bases the "necessity" of Soviet expansion into East Europe on a similarity to a repeated chain of events connecting expansion to fear induced by prior invasion, and the latter to geographic exposure. But not all instances of Russian expansion fit this pattern, as will be made clearer in the discussion below of Schuman. And even if they did, one would have, strictly speaking, a demonstration only of constant conjunction. That Russia habitually acts in such-and-such a way does not mean she is compelled to. Put another way, one would be unable to rebut the claims of those who, looking at the antecedents of individual events of Soviet expansion like Poland, Czechoslovakia, etc., might argue that Stalin could possibly, if not easily, have come to different, if not opposite, decisions, as he did with respect to Greece and Finland.

In any case, when he gets down to specifics, Halle tells a different story. According to this other story, the Soviets even as late as 1947 entertained the possibility of a permanent accommodation with the West.[66] June 1947 was a "point of no return"—significant phrase in itself.[67] The Soviets at that point had the option of accepting or not accepting the American response to their earlier intrusions into the middle of the continent, a response appearing to them as challenge.[68] They might, in traditional Russian fashion, have adopted at this point a policy of retrenchment, accommodation, and appeasement.[69] They might, apparently, quite easily have kept the Cold War from spreading to Asia, for the Korean War is treated as essentially accidental.[70] So Halle, through exception and qualification, so chisels away at the conceptual structure he has created as to leave the original outlines barely recognizable. So Halle, in the interstices of his narrative, assigns a substantial role to the accidental, the contingent.

Moreover, when he gets down to specifics, Halle forgets his corollary, that moral judgments are out of place. He discards the role of neutral observer, cheering on the "good guys," fulminating at the bad. The dictum about scorpion and tarantula to the contrary notwithstanding, Halle revels in normative judgments. The abdication of his proclaimed proper role is more pronounced in his treatment of the American side of the conflict. He condemns the United States for her reluctance to enter the lists against the kaiser, and for her withdrawal from Europe after the Second World War. These are all cases of a failure to see her "responsibilities"—a moral judgment, of course.[71] Conversely, he praises her to the skies for finally coming to and

66. Ibid., pp. 136–37.
67. Ibid., p. 137.
68. Ibid.
69. Ibid., p. 147.
70. Ibid., p. 204.
71. Ibid., Chapter III.

organizing the defense against the Soviets.[72] He eulogizes without stint, for their contribution to this heroic stand, Truman, Acheson, Marshall, Kennan, and Vandenberg. He condemns those, the "simplifiers," who saw the issues involved in the struggle in the crusader's terms of black and white or were beguiled by the mythos of international organization.[73] But some of these judgments on America are, on their obverse side, also judgments on Soviet Russia. So organization of the defense against the Soviets is a case of "saving the honor of humanity" by rescuing Europe from the "imminent general breakdown of civilization and obliteration of all that made life worth living, or even possible, under the Muscovite tyranny that was spreading from the East."[74] The true determinist does not curse the darkness.

The reference to myths raises a final point. Halle not only moralizes, and moralizes endlessly and understandably, but he refuses to recognize that he is doing so. He separates out sharply the realm of ideology, of the nominal—that is, of justification, myths, of virtue and vice— from the realm of the real—of hardheaded appraisal of national interest, and in urging we conduct ourselves by the latter rather than the former, he supposes he is only asking us to recognize reality. But reality so conceived is a name for certain propositions about human relationships which he believes to be true. It includes within it its own element of the theoretical or conjectural, even as do the ideologies of the simplifiers. And when, in addition, it is used affectively as something we should seek, it includes its own normative or moral element as well. This is nowhere better exemplified than in his urging that America act as guardian of the European power balance, for under the guise of asking us to accept a "fact" of power politics he is in effect asking us not only to accept the debatable existential proposition that American security is vitally affected by an overturn of that balance, but also the still more debatable moral judgment that it is good we seek to guard that balance, bad that we refrain from doing so.[75] Not for the first time has an inquirer confused his readers by passing off a value judgment as a judgment of hard, unavoidable fact.

72. For example, ibid., p. 116.
73. Ibid., pp. 232–34.
74. Ibid., pp. 116, 138 n.
75. Ibid., Chapter III, esp. pp. 25–26, 28–29.

In its conception of Soviet conduct taken as a whole, *The Cold War as History* has many admirable features. It provides a new generalization on that conduct, in its proposition about what I call intermittent expansiveness, and a new generalization on the key to that conduct— geographic determinism. It connects these generalizations with a broad theory of international relations and their evolution which is imaginative and insightful. In this theory, it exhibits a new sensitivity to the difficult problem of determining what is action, what reaction, in the affairs of nations, and along with this sensitivity it manifests a new evenhandedness in criticizing the protagonists in the global drama. And so, in the main, *The Cold War as History* lives up to its proclaimed aims of uncovering a pattern beneath the stream of events and containing the American bias of its author.

At the same time this work fails to substantiate its generalizations, its theory. It grounds a conclusion of Soviet cautiousness upon a narrative studded with actions called reckless. It rests a finding of geographic determinism on a review of moves many of which are presented individually as exercises of free will. While grand theory is determinist, the facts of the record as subsequently resumed point rather toward voluntarism. Theory and history are at odds. Although in a different way, Halle has like Kennan produced an essentially ambivalent view of Soviet (and American) behavior. Like Kennan, he has done so (again I speculate) because Halle the historian is at odds with Halle the adviser to statesmen.

Finally, and here Halle's study is inferior to Kennan's, he has at times allowed his assessments, his enthusiasm, to run away with him. The result is that at these times what he properly should present as a matter of moral judgment, he presents, misleadingly, as a matter of pure fact, a matter of accepting "reality" and the "lessons" of history. If he has contained his bias as American vis-à-vis Russian, he has failed to contain his bias as an American of one persuasion in terms of proper foreign policy vis-à-vis Americans of other persuasions. Emotional steam behind a commitment to getting the United States to discharge its responsibilities to the world, as he sees them, appears at times to override the intellect. I use the term "appears" advisedly, for the judgment implies a causal relation and, as earlier urged, proofs of such relations are outside the power of the inquirer into existential affairs.

CASE 3: SCHUMAN AND REACTIVE EXPANSIVENESS

Frederick L. Schuman's *The Cold War: Retrospect and Prospect*,[76] the last of the leading works of Mixed persuasion, is a book of lectures delivered at Louisiana State University that was published in first edition in 1961, in second edition in 1967. It deals with the subject named in the title, paying particular attention to Soviet behavior and the Russian antecedents thereof. It considers the full span of the period of Soviet rule, from 1917 to 1966. Its declared objective is "explanation and analysis, not advocacy nor defense."[77] Yet Schuman apparently believes achievement of this objective to be itself a means to the still further and ultimate objective of survival in a thermonuclear age;[78] there is occasional evaluation and a drawing of the "lessons" for both parties to the confrontation; and the tone throughout, as with Halle, is the tone of the *engagé*—of one with an urgent message to communicate.

Schuman's three lectures are entitled, respectively, "The Third Rome," "The Social Order," and "Beyond the Cold War." To these the second edition adds a postscript called "At Half Century." The three lectures present, respectively: a broad historical survey of Russian external conduct, its nature and causes; an analysis of the Soviet internal order and its development; a history of the Cold War, its causes, its evolution, and the prospects for its resolution. The postscript extends the content of Lecture Three from 1961 up to 1966.

Schuman's thesis is that the Cold War was initiated largely by the West, through its interventions and invasions of 1918–19 and those of 1941; that the Soviet actions generally believed by the other side to have initiated it—aggrandizement and resort to brute force in East Europe in 1945–48—are rather responses to prior invasion in the pattern of traditional Russian behavior; that this pattern can be expected to moderate as the Soviets overcome the weakness and sense of vulnerability at its roots; that the possibilities of winding up the Cold War and achieving a lasting peace are, from the Soviet side, therefore improving slowly; but that success in these endeavors and in avoiding nuclear disaster are dependent ultimately upon recogni-

76. Second ed. (Baton Rouge: Louisiana State University Press, 1967).
77. Ibid., p. 7.
78. Ibid., p. xiv.

tion by both sides, and especially by the United States, of the lessons of the confrontation, of which the need to avoid useless recrimination and begin the task of creating an effective world law is foremost.

Soviet conduct, in the view which emerges from the development of this thesis, is, as already expounded at some length, conduct whose main traits are a high degree of responsiveness and a moderate degree of conditional expansiveness and resort to force.[79] The Soviets do expand their rule and do resort to force. But they so do only on occasion, and commonly only in response to prior invasion or aggression against them. Conduct aims at promoting and preserving the interests of Muscovy, it is true, but it does not, as some think, aim at creating a world of Communist states, much less at world conquest. Moreover, it is, inferentially, not unduly militant, nor unduly immoral, nor unduly hegemonic toward other Communist states. It is basically Russian rather than Communist, driven by fear rather than ambition, posing danger to the world outside, but not excessive danger, growing somewhat more moderate with time. Its affinities are not at all with Nazi conduct, from which it differs greatly, but with tsarist conduct and, in fact, with that of many other units in an international order whose leading characteristic is anarchy.

Schuman agrees with Halle in characterizing Soviet conduct on the whole as conditionally expansive. But more than Halle he sees it as responsive, as internally conditioned, and as undergoing secular moderation. Unlike Halle, he finds the Soviets less responsible for the Cold War than the West, he finds that war not yet ended, and he finds the prospects of achieving long-term peace dependent, from the American side, on forbearance and restraint rather than on firmness. In contradistinction to Halle, he sees anarchy, and not equilibrium, as the normal international condition, and he sees no necessity in the unfolding of the historical drama.

The core argument of *The Cold War* is that Soviet cold-war conduct is limited and conditional military expansiveness based on fear and concern for national security, because Russian conduct historically has been this.[80] This in essence is the answer Schuman comes up with in response to the second question he puts to himself at the start of his

79. For earlier exposition, see Chapter 2.
80. Ibid., Lecture One.

first lecture, that is, why our Cold War adversary behaves the way she does. This is the result of his retrospective analysis upon which his gauge of the prospects of world peace in turn is based. And it is this to which I would direct attention as the focus of the effort to test the quality of the work, taking in turn the two premises on which the argument is based—the identification of "Soviet" and "Russian" conduct, and the characterization of the latter as conditional, fear-based expansiveness.

The argument is on its face a plausible one deserving of careful consideration. The minor premise, the identification of Soviet and Russian, has an appealing ring. There is, no doubt, much to be said in its favor. There is an a priori improbability that Russians of Communist persuasion who succeeded Russians of non-Communist persuasion would not in some measure think alike and act alike in the conduct of the state's external affairs. And Schuman is correct in pointing to similarities between tsarist imperialism and Soviet imperialism, tsarist messianism and Soviet messanism. However, there are patent dissimilarities too, of which not the least are the far-reaching, more militant character of the Communist faith and the more all-embracing character of the Communist autocracy. And whether the similarities and continuities are enough, and enough outweigh the dissimilarities to sustain a judgment of sameness in toto, and to permit a conclusion based mainly or wholly on the pre-Soviet record to control a finding on Soviet cold war conduct—this is something again. Maybe. But maybe not. In any case, this is an issue which has to be faced and discussed. And in failing to do so, as he does fail, and in treating the matter as an open-and-shut affair that need not be further considered, Schuman gets off to a shaky start.

The second strand in the argument, the major premise of the conditional, fear-based expansiveness of Russian conduct, Schuman does address himself to, and at great length. He starts off by formulating five generalizations.[81] Condensed, these are:

1. Russia has until recently been comparatively backward and weak;
2. Russia, compared to other nations, has been extremely vul-

81. Ibid., pp. 13–23.

nerable and more subjected than others to repeated, destruc-
tive attacks from abroad;

3. Russians have responded to this weakness and this aggression
by instituting political autocracy, ideological orthodoxy, territorial expansionism, messianic universalism, frantic industrialization;

4. Russia's involvement in war has, when her rulers have acted
wisely, been due not to her but to another's initiative—to
which is added a corollary: a Russia-initiated "preventive"
war against others has led to Russian defeat; an other-initiated
"preventive" war against Russia has when pursuing limited
aims been sometimes successful, but when pursuing unlimited aims never.

5. Russia's territorial aggrandizements in Europe have been the
result more often of unsuccessful military aggression against
her rather than successful military aggression by her against
others.

It is from these generalizations that Schuman in the remainder of his
first lecture derives the further conclusions that, by a certain domino
effect, a buildup of Russian strength may be reasonably expected to
reduce vulnerability and attendant fear (Proposition 2), in turn to
moderate the internal tyranny (Proposition 3) and so, eventually, to
diminish external expansiveness and aggrandizement (Proposition 5).
And these, coupled with the further finding that the Russians today
are building up their strength and moderating their tyranny, lead him
to this guardedly optimistic view of the prospects for peace.

Here is a reasonably clear set of generalizations about Russian conduct. There are, to be sure, untidy elements in the formulation. The
affirmation about territorial aggrandizement is needlessly repeated,
being found in both Propositions 3 and 5. Proposition 4, about Russia's
involvement in war, is qualified by the question-begging clause, "when
her rulers have acted wisely." The so-called corollary to this proposition is not that at all, but a proposition in its own right (in fact, two
propositions in their own right) on the new topic of not mere military
involvement but successful military involvement. But such untidiness
aside, the statements make meaningful affirmations differentiating the
subject with fair adequacy.

Schuman, moreover, presents some data in their support. Proposition 4 is buttressed by references to the embroilments with the French in 1812, the Germans in 1914 and again 1941, the French and British in 1918–19, and the Poles in 1920, with some qualification attached to the 1914 episode.[82] Proposition 5 in its turn is substantiated by connecting accretions of former Polish, Lithuanian, Swedish, and Turkish territories (presumably in the seventeenth and eighteenth centuries) to attacks on Russia made by Poles, Lithuanians, Swedes, and Turks during the period of Mongol subjugation 600 years ago and, in the Polish case, to the Polish occupation of Moscow in the early seventeenth century; by connecting advance to the West in the second decade of the nineteenth century with the Napoleonic invasion of 1812, advances in the same quarter in 1918–20 with the Allied occupation of 1918–19 and the Polish invasion of 1920, and post-World War II expansion with the Wehrmacht's onslaught; by noting that in the period 1921–39, when the West refrained from threatening, no advances at all took place; and by noting that the acquisitions of 1939–40 were motivated by a desperate need to strengthen defenses against the anticipated onslaught of the Nazis.[83]

Schuman, finally, is rigorously careful in the claim he makes for his propositions.[84] He describes them as no more than generalizations, and not statements of universal application. He disclaims completeness for the documentation he offers.

But if there is something to be said in favor of generalizations on Russian conduct, there is also something to be said in their disfavor. Propositions 4 and 5, of most immediate concern to this essay, are, carefully read, rather severely hedged. And even when account is taken of the circumscriptions, they are indifferently borne out by the historical data. Exceptions loom large, especially the exceptions from the pre-Cold War but still Soviet record, the most recent and relevant part of the whole.

Proposition 4, connecting military embroilment to prior aggression from without, is, as noted, immediately qualified by the clause "when her rulers have acted wisely." This qualification, which in the light

82. Ibid., pp. 19–20.
84. Ibid., p. 13.
83. Ibid., pp. 21–22.

of the corollary that follows appears to mean "when her rulers have not initiated preventive war," rather effectively drains the generalization of solid meaning and suggests that Schuman, on second thought, lost much of whatever confidence he started out with. If this surmise is correct, his second thought is surely the better. For taken without the qualification and tested against the most recent and relevant part of the record, the proposition does not fare too well. David Dallin, with whose detailed assessment of the topic one may usefully begin the testing operation,[85] asserts that of the six wars Russia engaged in between 1920 and 1949—with Poland in 1920, China in 1929 over the Manchurian railway, Poland in 1939, Finland in 1939–40, Germany in 1941–45, and Japan in 1945—only the first and fifth were properly speaking defensive. One can disagree with Dallin's identification of the Chinese imbroglio as offensive, for, as Dallin agrees, China's seizure of the railroad was the precipitant. One can dispute Dallin's exclusion from his list of the "incidents" between Soviet and Japanese troops on the Mongolian-Manchurian border in 1938–39, "incidents" that took many thousands of lives and (all hands agree) occurred on Japanese initiative. These considerations taken account of, the tally changes from 4–2 against Schuman's generalization to 4–3 in its favor. But a generalization resting on only four cases out of seven in the period of greatest relevance is not much of a generalization.

Proposition 5, referring territorial aggrandizements generally to the aftermath of defensive war, also starts out with a qualification, namely, confinement to Europe. Yet even with the qualification it too fares poorly. The extension of the Bolshevik writ to new European lands in 1919–20 can be reasonably related to the German and Polish invasions and Western interventions, though surely Schuman makes too much of the latter.[86] So too does the extension of the writ to parts of Finland, to East Prussia, to Ruthenia in the aftermath of the Nazi invasion. But the major permanent accretions to territory in Europe since the first days of Soviet rule took place in 1939 and 1940 with the addition of parts of Finland, the Baltic states, the eastern half of

85. *The New Soviet Empire* (New Haven: Yale University Press, 1951), Chapter V.
86. On this point, see George F. Kennan, *Russia and the West under Lenin and Stalin* (Boston: Little, Brown, 1961), Chapters 5–8.

Poland, and (from Rumania) the Bukovina and Bessarabia. And these cannot properly be related to prior aggression against the USSR, as Schuman in effect recognizes by treating them as spoils of Soviet-initiated preventive war. A case can be made for Schuman's proposition as a whole, for measured in size and population European accretions consequent upon defensive war probably exceed those consequent upon offensive war. The case is not, however, an impressive one. It would become even less so if one extended the proposition (as one should) to include Asia as well. For of the many accretions or attempted accretions in this part of the Soviet perimeter (Georgia in 1921, Mongolia in 1921, Bukhara and Khiva in 1921, Tanna Tuva in 1944, North Korea, the Chinese ports, and Sakhalin in 1945, and the attempt on Persian Azerbaijan in 1946) few if any can be reasonably related to prior aggression from without.

There is, moreover, a problem of definition and conceptualization raised by Proposition 5, proper resolution of which would probably reduce its reach even further. That is the problem of the scope to be given the terms "aftermath" and "prior." Expand sufficiently these terms, extend far enough the time interval reaching backward from a territorial accession by a given state to antecedent aggression against the state, and any aggression may be considered a reaction and hence pardonable (as can probably the antecedent aggressions as well). Confine reasonably the terms and the time interval, and positive instances supporting the generalization dwindle. In the case of Schuman's Proposition 5, reasonable definition would almost certainly lead to the exclusion from the list of supporting instances of the accessions in the seventeenth and eighteenth centuries of the Polish, Lithuanian, and Turkish and Swedish territories seized from Old Russia centuries earlier.

Returning to the work as a whole, one need say a word about Schuman's comparisons. His general position is that Russian conduct (tsarist or Soviet) is not unique, that the duality of objectives of that conduct—the egotistic (national-interest) together with the messianic element—is found in other nations as well, and that global domination is wrongly ascribed as an aim.[87] Yet in the treatment he accords specific instances of Soviet, on the one hand, and British, French, or

87. Schuman, *The Cold War*, pp. 8–9, 23–25.

American conduct, on the other, his attitude is usually more sympathetic to the first than the second. This unevenness of assessment shows up particularly in the postscript, dealing with the events of 1961–66. There he deals with American ventures in the Far East with exceeding harshness—indeed, in a fashion which suggests more rigid definitions and differentiations than he invokes in his treatment, say, of Soviet ventures in East Europe in 1939–40, or more rigorous application of common definitions and differentiations. The United States in Southeast Asia, for instance, is affirmed to be seeking hegemony,[88] though the grounds for this assertion are not given, and it is hard to see what they might be that would not justify the similar assertion about the USSR that Schuman rejects. Again, the United States in her expansion into this area is accused of many treaty violations,[89] though none such are charged to the Soviet Union in connection with her 1939–40 and 1945–48 expansions. Such unevenness is not uncommon among works on the Soviet Union, including the works of the sample. It is common, though commonly applied the other way. It is nonetheless a weakness.

Schuman has contributed much. He has contributed a fairly clear and coherent set of generalizations about Soviet conduct, prospective as well as retrospective. In these he exhibits a sense of the interaction problem—that is, the problem of deciding whether a particular move is a case of challenge and initiative, or reaction and response—that is largely subdued in the works of the Hard persuasion, completely so in the Ultra-Hard. He has shown a nice restraint in what he claims for his generalizations. He has provided supporting data, a fair amount of which is valid. He has enriched his text with comparisons, and he has attempted in these to be fair.

At the same time, the identification of Soviet and Russian, upon which the validity of the generalizations in their broader context rests, requires something by way of substantiation. And this Schuman fails to provide, treating it rather as a matter of self-evidence. Moreover, while he can and does point to some supporting data and can claim some validity for his generalizations, he overlooks other evidence pointing the other way which, if not rendering these generalizations

88. Ibid., p. 121.
89. Ibid., p. 122.

invalid, makes their reach less than impressive. This is particularly true of the Soviet era, critical for us. Finally, his work is vitiated by a tendency to subject the conduct of other nations, especially that of the United States, to more rigorous conceptual analysis and normative evaluation than that of the Soviet. On balance, *The Cold War* is accordingly a work of sensitivity somewhat marred by unevenness in comparisons, a work of provocative hypotheses only partly borne out by the data.

Against the standards for judging scholarship set forth at the beginning of Chapter 3, the leading works expressing the Mixed view of Soviet extrenal conduct fare mixedly. Accurate they too appear to be. But the tests of discipline they meet unevenly. Accordingly, although on balance they too show up to advantage when compared with the works portraying the Ultra-Hard image, compared with those portraying the Hard image the reverse is the case.

On the essential criteria of "well-disciplined," performance is varied. In respect to the first of these, clear-cut characterization, all three of the works may be said to present a reasonably vivid and coherent picture of Soviet conduct, and Schuman in particular. The single reservation that needs to be entered is that Gehlen's work, in a concluding section that promises a summary of methods and motives in post-Stalin policy, provides no concise and unambiguous description of the first and, instead, trails off into some assertions about change that are vague to the point of virtual meaninglessness.

But in respect to conceptual frameworks and substantiation, the story is different. Gehlen has a reasonably well worked out and articulated apparatus of terms—objectives, methods and their various aspects, motives; and in his conceptualization of the dimension of use of military force and its application to the historical record he substantiates an important conclusion in near-exemplary fashion. But he fails to apply his procedures as rigorously to other dimensions. Schuman does no better. Some substantiation he does offer his major propositions, both the proposition relating military embroilment to prior aggression from without and the proposition relating territorial aggrandizement to the aftermath of such embroilment. But he ignores important considerations of definition, such as the precise delimitation of the term "aftermath"; much of his data relate to pre-Soviet Russia and depend upon a presumption of continuity not adequately demonstrated; and what data he adduces from the Soviet record, while affording some support, fail to make out a strong case. Halle is least satisfactory on this score. He leaves to his reader the crucial business of matching conclusion and supporting data, and in the cases of his affirmation about cautiousness of conduct and, more important yet, in the case of his central, deterministic theorem, the match is poor, many of the details of Soviet performance in the postwar period, as he individually describes them, pointing not toward but away from the generalization. At the same time, all three, like the three Hard imagists, deserve high marks for largely eschewing the question-begging procedures of their Ultra-Hard counterparts.

On the supplementary criteria of "well-disciplined," the record is also varied. In neutrality of reporting, Gehlen measures up well, showing little emotion. With Schuman and Halle, on the other hand, this is not the case. Schuman is hardly neutral: while much of his writing at the beginning is fairly free of affective judgments, as the story unfolds and he turns from retrospect to prospect, a sense of urgency informs his writing, he takes pains in drawing from his account of the past and present what he believes to be the lessons they hold for conduct in the future (both American and Soviet), and in the end he lays about him with abandon, flaying what he finds to be the folly of the recent past, with special attention to the United States. Halle, like Kennan, is unabashedly evaluative, meting out judgments of praise or blame in generous doses—judgments, one might add (and here the parallel with Kennan ends) that fit poorly his deterministic thesis, and, worse, sometimes masquerade as judgments of fact. For the rest, Halle and Schuman (but less frequently Gehlen) draw comparisons between Soviet and Western conduct, and these help to illuminate the former, despite some unevenness in the application of common criteria. Also, Halle and Schuman (but Gehlen less frequently) take opposing views into account and submit them to some reasoned analysis.

And so the Mixed image of Soviet external conduct is only partly upheld, only fragmentarily sustained. Enough evidence has been presented, and well enough presented, to make persuasive the contentions that territorial expansion is occasional rather than constant; that engagement in military trials is infrequent rather than frequent; that when expansion and engagement occur, they usually do so in response to attack from without rather than from impulse within; and that fear is a significant motive. Enough has been shown to put virtually beyond challenge the assertion that post-Stalin conduct has been very cautious. Accordingly, enough has been presented to upset Ultra-Hard affirmations of relentless expansionism, ceaseless initiatives, and frequent resort to the military instrument. But whether responsiveness is the primary mode, fear the primary goad—these have yet to be shown. A plausible case has been made for picturing Soviet conduct as that of a Neurotic Bear. But it has yet to be made a convincing one.

PART III: MELIORATION

CHAPTER 6

Method: Some Suggestions

From description and evaluation, this investigation of images of Soviet conduct passes now to more constructive criticism. Following an effort succinctly to summarize the findings of its predecessors, and hence, among other things, to lay bare deficiencies in what we know to date or think we know about the topic of central interest, Part III turns to melioration, to improvement. Pursuing inquiry along her natural course, it turns from questions of how good (or bad) the product may currently be to questions of how it can be made better. This entails, first, suggesting lines along which, and procedures according to which, research and analysis should proceed—a job assigned to the present chapter. It entails, second, illustrating suggestions, an assignment which the following chapter seeks to discharge in the form of an analysis of one particular facet of conduct—fidelity (or infidelity) to obligation.

The discussion of method to which we are thus brought one approaches without relish. For there can be little argument on the score that insofar as such discussion is concerned, the discipline of political science has within recent years gone on a drunken spree, abandoning itself to orgies of exchange of views, or "dialogue," on such component topics as "boundaries" to the field, the virtues or vices of "quantification," various "strategies of research," diverse "models." It has too often, one is inclined to say, yielded to the temptation of discussing ways and means of doing its job at the expense of actually doing it. The complaint that "for years we have been hearing the overture, but the curtain is yet to go up," if a bit extreme, is not entirely unjustified.[1] One is reluctant to prolong the overture.

Yet, some such discussion is in order, however distasteful. It is in

---

1. The remark is ascribed to Vernon Aspaturian in Dan N. Jacobs' "Area Studies and Communist Systems," *Slavic Review* 26, no. 1 (March 1967): 21.

order because it cannot fairly be ducked. It cannot fairly be ducked because the critic who would make useful suggestions for improving academic output in a given field cannot, if he is fairly to perform the task, avoid examining and discussing the concepts and procedures upon which the validity of that output depends. Product cannot be dealt with apart from process. The proper alternative to excessive talk about method is accordingly not silence but moderate talk—talk limited to reasonable proportion, talk infused by a determination not to get sidetracked from the main business at hand. The proper alternative to unseemly worship at the shrine of "methodology"—and the spirit which I hope will seem to mark the pages that follow—is not willful disregard nor yet unseemly scorn, but seemly respect, seemly deference.

CONDITION OF KNOWLEDGE

If the works and propositions within works used in Parts I and II are representative, and if the criticism thereof is reasonable, then certain conclusions follow on the state to recent date of American academic study of Soviet external conduct—on the condition of our knowledge of that subject and on the condition of our ways of reaching it.

As to the condition of our knowledge, on demonstrations made to date two of the three image types of Soviet external conduct differentiated have some validity, but the third little if any. The view which, on the analogy of the Mellowing Tiger, sees that conduct as egotism high but limited, and significantly moderating over time—for this some good evidence has been presented. The view which, on the analogy of the Neurotic Bear, sees that conduct as egotism sporadic and defensive, somewhat moderating over time—for this too some good evidence has been presented. But the view which, on the analogy of the Great Beast of the Apocalypse, sees that conduct as egotism limitless and unrestrained, unchanging over time—for this, little solid evidence has been presented, the evidence that has been presented being unconvincing.

Correlatively, certain truths about Soviet conduct have been provisionally established. There are five of these to which particularly I would call attention. The first is that Soviet conduct has been intermittently rather than continuously rule-expansive, moments of self-extension (e.g. 1939–41) being interspersed with moments of mere preservation (e.g. 1921–39) and, once in a while, even moments of contraction (e.g. 1955–56). The second is that conduct has varied in time between high and moderate militancy, the early '20s and '50s, for instance, marking perceptible drops in the magnitude of this attribute. The third is that conduct has varied in time between substantial and low addiction to the military instrument, the periods 1946–49 and 1953 on respectively exemplifying these two values. The fourth is that conduct is not wholly initiatory, but at times responsive, and that some moments of expansiveness, high militancy, and militarism are reasonably describable as reactions to challenges from environing states rather than challenges themselves. The fifth and final, implicit in the foregoing, is that conduct is not changeless, but undergoes significant change over time, and, most especially, has moderated in the post-Stalin period. While it cannot be said that the grounds for these assertions are utterly irrefutable, it can be said they are solid enough to place the burden henceforth on those who would challenge them.

At the same time neither of the two images partly sustained has been more than partly sustained. Correlatively, there are a number of important issues yet to be resolved, much still that we don't know, much yet to learn. A number of questions already answered in crude terms need finer answers than they presently have, through more painstaking, more detailed investigation of the record. For instance, how influence-expansionist is Soviet conduct, how rule-expansionist? How militant, how militarist, how initiatory has that conduct been? Precisely when has it changed in each of the above respects, and by how much? Moreover, there are other questions that have hardly begun to be tackled systematically. Among these are the questions of morality, of motivation, of impact on the world system, of control over other Communist states. Do the Soviets on balance adhere to their given pledges? Are they motivated primarily by fear or ambition? Is the driving force to be found in ideology and the scriptures of the faith or in national interest and the unwritten imperatives of a great power —is it, that is, Communist or Russian? Is conduct seriously or only mildly threatening to the world peace? Is it primarily or only partly responsible for the international disorder of our times? Is it hegemonic or cooperative in relation to its own? To the careful answering of such queries as these the literature to date, exemplified by the 22 studies of the sample, has made scarcely a start.

The validity of alleged truths about a phenomenon is dependent upon the soundness of the method by which these truths have been reached. Soundness of method I have translated as scholarly, scholarly I have equated with well-disciplined learning, and this last I have defined essentially as providing clear-cut general characterization well substantiated by the data. The reasons for concluding that the various images have been thus far sustained, but no further, lie in the intermittence with which imagists have characterized cleanly and vigorously and followed this up with thorough substantiation in the data. While sometimes both of these conditions have been met, more often one or both have not.

Sometimes the conditions are met, or substantially so. That Soviet conduct has varied between Right and Left modes, for instance, and in the early '50s moved toward the Right—these propositions about oscillating and declining militancy (my terms) have been reasonably clearly affirmed (a certain obscurity about precise phasing aside) and then squarely and adequately documented.[2] That is, Right and Left have by the analyst in question (Shulman) been given fairly distinct meanings, and the events of 1946–49 and 1953 on then shown to accord fairly closely respectively therewith, the events of 1949–52 with a mixture of the two. That Soviet conduct has been cautious in the post-Stalin period has been affirmed with similar reasonable clarity (by Gehlen) and documented with similar adequacy, gradations along a low- to high-risk continuum being carefully distinguished and the moves of the period in question shown to fall largely at the lower end.[3] That Soviet conduct has changed from rule-expansive and aggressive in the late-Stalin days to influence-expansive and persuasionist in the post-Stalin has been clearly affirmed (by Tucker), though less adequately documented, terms being less clearly defined and the required subsumption of the data less convincingly demonstrated.[4] The same qualified judgment applies to the propositions (by Schuman) tying moments of high values of expansiveness and militarism to prior subjection to aggression from without.[5]

More often, however, one or more of the conditions have not been

2. See Chapter 4, pp. 114–20, above.
3. See Chapter 5, pp. 140–44, above.
4. See Chapter 4, pp. 125–31, above.
5. See Chapter 5, pp. 159–63, above.

met. Characterization has been less than clear and/or substantiation less than sufficient. Characterization has been sometimes dormant, or dual, or ambiguous. The characterization found in Fleming's work—of conduct little expansion-minded, of moderate to low militancy, not particularly immoral, reactive, and defensive—is not characterization which the author explicitly draws from the myriad of particular moves constituting his narrative, but rather characterization which he leaves for the reader to draw for himself, with all the risks that this necessarily entails.[6] The same is only slightly less true for others among the histories, such as Lukacs and Dallin. Again, the characterization found in the first part of Kennan—of conduct almost totally initiatory and ambition-driven, and in substantial degree militarist—is at sharp variance with the characterization of the last chapter —of conduct half responsive and fear-driven, and in low degree militarist.[7] Again, the characterization which *Protracted Conflict* calls the "Indirect Approach,"—namely, pursuit of expansionist aims through satellites and other agents, and up to a point just short of where general war threatens—has a chameleon-like nature.[8] At times —and so I have read it—the authors seem to be affirming through it something positive—unremitting expansiveness, militancy, militarism. At other times they seem to be affirming something negative—cautiousness and readiness to contract. Shulman's vacillation, over the magnitude of the shift which he affirms to have taken place in the last years of Stalin's life, is another although less important case of ambiguity.[9] In some spots he seems to be saying only that a shift toward the Right had been initiated in these years, whereas in others he seems to be saying that the shift had been not only initiated but subsequently consummated as well.

Substantiation frequently is insufficient. Whether the argument be essentially inductive, appealing for support of the generalization to the alleged facts of the historical record, or essentially deductive, appealing for support to an allegedly true generalization about a larger class to which Soviet conduct belongs, there is commonly much lack-

6. See Chapter 5, pp. 136–37, above.
7. See Chapter 4, pp. 103–04, above.
8. See Chapter 3, pp. 77–78, above.
9. See Chapter 4, p. 114, above.

ing. In the inductive case sometimes the data alleged to support the
generalization simply do not, indeed point in the opposite direction:
such is the case with Kennan's affirmation of high-Stalin militancy,
Halle's of cautiousness, Halle's of the deterministic roots of expansiveness.[10] Sometimes, again, the fit is managed only by virtue of reinterpreting the data to mean something other than what they appear
to mean, and doing so on unexamined principles: such is the case
with Goodman's affirmation of the persistence of the world state objective, and its investment with a Russified form, with *Protracted Conflict*'s affirmation of short-of-war militarism, and with Wolfe's affirmation of unremitting expansiveness.[11] In the deductive case, sometimes
assignment of Soviet conduct to the larger class is inadequately spelled
out, the fit being too loose—for instance, Schuman's to the larger
class of Russian conduct, Wolfe's to totalitarian and total-system
conduct;[12] or the generalization allegedly true of the larger class is of
questionable applicability—for instance, Wolfe and the durability of
depotism;[13] or both. Sometimes, simply too few data are supplied.[14]

Conjecturing about causes of the indifferent condition of our
knowledge, one can, I believe, with justification affirm the following:
that those who have worked in the field exhibit three different styles
or modes of demonstrating general propositions; that apparently
coupled with these they exhibit further three different casts of mind;
and that of the resulting combinations only one—and that the least
common—may fairly be said to approximate the requirements of
that kind of high discipline that defines scholarliness.

The first of the styles or modes of demonstration is that of announcing the general proposition, providing few if any clues to the meaning
of key terms, letting the data remain embedded in historical narrative,
and so, in short, leaving to the reader the task of assembling the data
and verifying the alleged fit. This I would call the historical style.

10. See above, Chapter 4, pp. 105–10, and Chapter 5, pp. 148–55,
respectively.
11. See Chapter 3, above, pp. 95–96.
12. See above, Chapter 5, p. 159, and Chapter 3, pp. 89–94, respectively.
13. See Chapter 3, pp. 89, 93, above.
14. For example, see several of Kennan's generalizations—Chapter 4,
p. 104, above.

Along with it as a rule seems to go a strong commitment to a particular overall view of the subject matter, although an inquiring spirit and a respect for and willingness rationally to engage other views; also, a mind not sensitive to questions of method, although an imaginative mind, one gifted with a felicity of self-expression. Of the authors especially studied above, Kennan and Halle have, I feel, this combination of style and mental cast. There is, second, the style or mode of announcing the generalization, providing some definition of key terms, isolating and adducing the data on which the generalization purportedly rests, but showing the fit by interpreting the data on canons unexamined and undefended. This I would call the scholastic style. Along with it as a rule seems to go a very strong commitment to a particular overall view, though one infused with admirable moral fervor, an essentially uninquiring spirit, an unwillingness soberly and rationally to engage other views, and a mind neither very imaginative nor sensitive to questions of method. Goodman and Strausz-Hupé have, I feel, this combination of style and mental cast. There is, finally, the style or mode of announcing the generalization, attending with some care to the meaning of terms, adducing the data, and showing the fit without recourse to unexamined canons of interpretation. This I would call the empirical style. There seems to go along with this as a rule a less strong commitment to a particular overall view, an inquiring spirit, a willingness soberly and rationally to engage other views, and a mind sensitive to problems of method, though a mind not too imaginative nor gifted with a felicity of self-expression. Shulman Triska, and Gehlen have, I feel, this combination.

Of these three combinations, only the third approximates the requirements of the kind of high discipline that defines scholarliness, the first, for all its merits, falling appreciably short, the second considerably so. Yet this same third combination, if our sample is any guide, shows up least frequently among students of the subject. In the sample Tucker alone with Shulman, Triska, and Gehlen exhibits it with any regularity, the other 17 writers commonly exhibiting either the first or the second. That some of those who reach Mixed or Hard conclusions exhibit it, but none of those who reach the Ultra-Hard, constitutes other grounds for affirming the superior validity of the former two as argued to date.

But whether these conjectures about causes are or are not correct, the condition of American academic inquiry into Soviet external conduct for the period in question seems clear enough. There is a plurality of images of which two, but only two, have been in any part sustained. There is a paucity of characterizations substantially confirmed, a rather high frequency of inadequate demonstration. And beneath the foregoing there is a rather extensive failure to define and differentiate concepts adequately, and to spell out and implement carefully rules for matching them to the data. While some propositions have been fairly well established, some things learned, there is a considerable distance yet to go, and much room for improvement.

EXISTING PROPOSALS FOR IMPROVEMENT

Turning from deficiencies in the state of our knowledge and their causes to the question of correctives and what can be done by way of improvement, one reasonably looks first to the suggestions of others. These take the two forms of explicit disquisitions on method in the large and specific attempts to resolve concrete problems. The former in turn divide into disquisitions (1) on Soviet conduct in general, (2) external conduct (foreign policy) in general, and (3) on Soviet external conduct in particular. I take these three up seriatim in this section, leaving to the section that follows discussion of specific attempts on concrete problems, along with suggestions of my own.

Broad disquisitions on method in the study of Soviet conduct in general may usefully be dated from the publication in 1955 of John S. Reshetar, Jr,'s *Problems of Analyzing and Predicting Soviet Behavior*.[15] Since then they have come out in modest and perhaps slightly increasing numbers, taking the forms of either chapters or sections of books or periodical articles.[16] The best of these have

15. Garden City, N.Y.: Doubleday.
16. Among the more noteworthy book chapters or sections are the following: Myron Rush, *The Rise of Khrushchev* (Washington: Public Affairs Press, 1958), esp. Appendix 2, "The Role of Esoteric Communication in Soviet Politics"; Robert Conquest, *Power and Policy in the USSR* (New York: St. Martin's Press, 1961), esp. Chapter 3; Donald Zagoria, *The Sino-Soviet Conflict 1956–1961* (Princeton: Princeton University Press, 1962), esp. preface and "A Note on Methodology"; and Alexander Dallin, ed., *Diversity in International Communism* (New York: Columbia University

recently been gathered into a single volume by Frederic J. Fleron, Jr.[17]

While ranging over a variety of issues, these disquisitions have concentrated on four in particular, the attendant discussion commonly taking the form of lively debate. These four are (1) the issue of the explanatory principle or motivating force behind Soviet behavior—whether the imperatives of industrialization, Slavic character, child-rearing habits, or whatnot; (2) the issue of the validity of Kremlinology, or the procedure of deducing the course of the leadership struggle from such indirect signs as order of listing, appearance at airports to welcome distinguished visitors, etc.; (3) the issue of the category of polity to which to assign the Soviet regime, whether totalitarian, movement-regime, or some other; (4) the issue of the validity of comparative study, or the applicability to the Soviet case of the concepts, categories, and procedures of political science in general.

The discussions on method so summarized cover a lot of ground, making many interesting observations. However, they contribute little to resolution of the concrete problem of how to proceed in order more firmly to establish the nature of the specific subject under investigation. They either fail to speak to points of method properly construed, or while so doing speak to points only indirectly related to the characterization and explanation of conduct—points which, in any case, should have been long since resolved.

The debate on explanatory principle or motivating force, so well exemplified by the Reshetar work above cited, is not strictly speaking

---

Press, 1963), esp. Dallin and Zbigniew Brzezinski's "Introduction: Issues and Methods." Among the more noteworthy periodical articles are those by a number of American and British students which, under the titles "The State of Soviet Studies" and "Kremlinology," comprise most of the January 1964 issue of *Survey* (50). Also significant are an article by Robert Tucker entitled "On the Comparative Study of Communism," which appeared in the January 1967 issue of *World Politics* (19, no. 2), and articles by John A. Armstrong and others comprising a symposium in the March 1967 issue of the *Slavic Review* (26, 1). The *Survey* articles, slightly augmented, have been published as a book, *The State of Soviet Studies,* ed. Walter Z. Laqueur and Leopold Labedz, (Cambridge: M.I.T. Press, 1965).

17. *Communist Studies and the Social Sciences: Essays on Methodology and Empirical Theory* (Chicago: Rand McNally, 1969).

a debate on method.[18] For method in its two basic senses means either a systematic arrangement of concepts or the rules for their application to the historical record.[19] Method, that is, is a way of starting investigation rather than interpreting or explaining what is found. And the question of whether Soviet conduct is to be explained by ideology, by swaddling practices, by totalitarianism, by the power struggle, or whatnot, is a question properly raised at the conclusion rather than the initiation of inquiry. This debate helps by blocking out some of the possible conclusions (and some of these will be taken up at their proper place below). But it offers no suggestions as to the procedure that will help decide between the alternatives.

The debate on the validity of Kremlinology, on the other hand, is a debate on method, properly construed, concerned as it is with procedure and the initial stage of inquiry.[20] In the writer's view, the activity of attempting to follow the power struggle through the decoding of esoteric communications and the analysis of ritual is a perfectly legitimate one, badly performed as it may be in individual instances. But its usefulness to the analyst of external conduct is limited. The most to be expected of it is help in explaining conduct at a particular moment by relating it to factional and personal struggle, and in anticipating short-run shifts.[21] It does not help to pin down the characterization of such conduct, or to relate it to deeper factors.

The remaining two debates, on the category of polity and on comparative study, also concern method, properly construed. But they relate even less directly to the analysis of conduct, being concerned with matters of conceptualization at a high level of abstraction, and they should in any case have been long since resolved.

The debate on the category of polity to which to assign the USSR

18. See also Daniel Bell, "Ten Theories in Search of Reality: The Prediction of Soviet Behaviour in the Social Sciences," in *Soviet Conduct in World Affairs,* ed. Alexander Dallin (New York: Columbia University Press, 1960), pp. 1–36.

19. Cf. *The Oxford English Dictionary,* a corrected re-issue of *A New English Dictionary on Historical Principles,* 1933.

20. See articles collectively entitled "Kremlinology" which appeared in *Survey* 50 (January 1964): 154–94.

21. Cf. Alec Nove, "Uses and Abuses of Kremlinology," *Survey* 50 (January, 1964): 175.

(and, more especially, the adequacy of the totalitarian concept), which is well exemplified by a discussion that appeared in a 1961 issue of the *Slavic Review*,[22] tends to get bogged down in irrelevancies. The objections to use of the concept of totalitarian (understood to incorporate the element of high reliance on terror) are: that with terror having disappeared from several Communist systems, the concept is out of touch with reality; that it obscures important dissimilarities between Nazi and Communist species, between Soviet polity at different stages of development; that the associated totalitarian/democratic scheme obscures important similarities between United States and USSR, etc. And these objections are beside the point, for what makes a model relevant is not whether certain historical particulars fit it perfectly, but whether it—or, more precisely, the classificatory scheme in which it is one term—points to a difference that is both important and historically realized. And the totalitarian/democratic scheme does both of these things. For the difference between high and low reliance on coercion to which, *inter alia*, it points, is a matter of importance, however "importance" may be defined, and is a difference that is historically realized. The scheme accordingly assists us in locating and meaningfully differentiating particular polities, whether or not they fit clearly the end terms. It therefore remains relevant, regardless of shifts in the location along the spectrum to which with the passage of time one may assign the USSR. Nor is it in point to observe that the totalitarian/democratic classification obscures distinctions within each half of the spectrum and similarities between states in opposite halves, or that it fails to reflect other characteristics of importance; for although these things are quite true, they are equally true of any classificatory scheme. (That many who use the scheme in question tend to abuse it, locating this or that historical particular exactly at one or the other pole of the spectrum, is of course quite true. But this is to say only that the scheme is sometimes misused, not that it is useless.)

But whether to classify the basic political structure or not, and if so, what classificatory scheme to use—these are fielders' choices. There is

22. The major articles from the *Slavic Review* in question (20, no. 3 [October 1961]) are: Zbigniew Brzezinski "The Nature of the Soviet System," pp. 351–68; Alfred G. Meyer, "USSR, Incorporated," pp. 369–76; and Robert C. Tucker, "The Question of Totalitarianism," pp. 377–82.

no compelling reason for starting one way or another. One may start with the totalitarian model. Or one may start with some other model or with no model at all beyond the generic "state." Or one may start with more than one model, letting experience decide superior serviceability. These points should have been appreciated long ago, and the discussion moved on to more practical matters, like the devising and assessing of suitable categories for describing the day-to-day functioning of structures, however they may be typed and classified.

The debate on the validity of comparative study, which is exemplified by a symposium that appeared in a 1967 issue of the Slavic Review,[23] also tends to get bogged down in irrelevancies. This last and probably most important of the four resolves itself into the question of whether the Soviet Union is to be conceived of and approached as a unique phenomenon requiring special investigative procedures, or as one among the hundred-odd other states of the world requiring no special investigative procedures. On the one side stand the particularists, who argue that the basis for Soviet studies must remain historical, who reject the militant faith of behaviorism, who speak of the Soviet regime as "sui generis," who argue the futility of measuring the Soviet regime by any standard applicable to the more conventional political systems.[24] On the other stand the generalists, who do not see the Soviet system as unique, who argue the possibility and desirability of assimilating Soviet and Communist political studies to comparative political studies generally, and who argue further the possibility and desirability of developing generalizations covering both Communist and non-Communist states.[25]

23. See Slavic Review 26, no. 1 (March 1967). The major articles comprising this symposium are John A. Armstrong, "Comparative Politics and Communist Systems: Introductory Remarks," pp. 1–2; Alfred Meyer, "The Comparative Study of Communist Political Systems," pp. 3–12; John W. Kautsky, "Communism and the Comparative Study of Development," pp. 13–17; Dan N. Jacobs, "Area Studies and Communist Systems," pp. 18–21; and Robert S. Sharlet, "Systematic Political Science and Communist Systems," pp. 22–26.

24. See the following two articles from Survey 50 (January 1964): Walter Laqueur, "In Search of Russia," pp. 41–52, and Adam Ulam, "USA: Some Critical Reflections," pp. 53–61; also Reshetar, Problems of Analyzing and Predicting Soviet Behavior, esp. pp. 2, 47–48.

25. See esp. articles of Meyer, Kautsky, and Sharlet litsed in n. 23 above.

The reason for speaking of irrelevancies in this debate, and the cardinal point to be made, is the error of contending that, the USSR being totally unique and sui generis, study thereof requires, for a starting point, a unique and peculiar conceptual apparatus. That the USSR and its foreign policy are truly unique phenomena—of this there is no question. But it by no means follows from this that investigation requires a unique conceptual framework, a unique method. Or, more to the point, it by no means follows that investigation employing a general framework, a general method, is invalidated. Let those disposed to question this take a harder look at the natural sciences, where a common framework is applied to phenomena and events which, in the fullest and strictest sense, are utterly unique.[26]

A conceptual framework, properly understood, is an ordered series of questions to be asked of the data under observation. It assumes nothing as to the values of the characteristics which the data will exhibit, nothing as to the answers that will be returned, nothing as to the overall likeness or unlikeness of the data to which applied. In a sense, the application of a framework of general concepts is unavoidable, the only genuine alternative lying between applying the framework consciously and applying it unconsciously. The historian cannot avoid the use of general concepts. Nor can the Kremlinologist. Soviet foreign policy is conceived of under general headings, however much this may be denied, and it is compared with policies of other states. For instance, "aggressive" is a general concept as is "initiative," as are "external" and "internal," "ideology" and "totalitarian." Further, Soviet policy is said to be aggressive, while American policy is not— or vice versa. At bottom, therefore, the use of such a framework is not truly at issue. The only issue is whether, as heretofore, to apply such concepts implicitly, unsystematically, and capriciously, or overtly, systematically, and carefully. This should long ago have been understood.

Broad disquisitions on method in the analysis of external conduct in general are also small in number, though on the increase since the mid 1960s.[27] They have been small for a number of reasons. "Traditionally," says one writer, "the analysis of foreign policy phenomena has consisted of a policy-oriented concern with particular situations faced by specific nations,"[28] an analysis, one might add, that ends up reported in the form of a case history. The more recent drive toward more systematic inquiry has taken the forms less of identifying variables found wherever foreign policy phenomena are found than of refining the case histories or, more commonly, enlarging the focus of concern from the individual international actor to the collectivity or system of actors.[29] As late as 1962 there were those who took the view that foreign policy variables involve a "complexity [that] makes a mockery of the few 'scientific' tools we have,"[30] thereby rejecting the premises of comparative analysis.

Representative of works on foreign policy analysis are George Modelski's *A Theory of Foreign Policy,* already referred to in Chapter 2,[31] and the more elaborate, as more recent, scheme suggested by Michael Brecher and colleagues in a 1969 article entitled "A framework for research on foreign policy behaviour." Like Modelski, Brecher and colleagues consider the making of foreign policy a process whereby a series of inputs, of demands from the operational environment as perceived through the psychological environment by the decision-making elite, is transformed into a series of decisions or outputs. Only now the array of concepts and attendant terminology has proliferated. The inputs of the operational environment divide into 10 categories: five external (the global system, subordinate systems, etc.), and five internal (military capability, political structure, etc.). These are transmuted into the images of the elite by the "attitudinal prism" of ideology. The process iself comprises "formulation" and "implementa-

27. For bibliographies see James N. Rosenau, "Comparative Foreign Policy: Fad, Fantasy, or Field?" *International Studies Quarterly* 12, no. 3 (September 1968): 296–329; and Michael Brecher, and others, "A framework for research on foreign policy behavior," *Journal of Conflict Resolution* 13, no. 1 (March 1969): 75–101.

28. Rosenau, "Comparative Foreign Policy," p. 298.

29. Brecher, "A framework for research," p. 75.

30. Rosenau, "Comparative Foreign Policy," p. 300.

31. Princeton Studies in World Politics Number 2 (New York: Praeger, 1962). For earlier reference, see pp. 34–35 above.

tion" stages, the decisions made falling into four categories called "issue areas" and differentiated by subject matter (Military-Security, Political-Diplomatic, etc.). Brecher and his colleagues, like Modelski, define their terms carefully. They then go Modelski one better, by providing a full-fledged illustration of their model's use. The illustration takes the form of taking eight decisions each of eight middle-power states, two from each of the four issue areas, and showing through content analysis of official announcements the relative influence upon them of the elite's perceptions of the various environmental factors.[32] The authors conclude, *inter alia*, that middle-power elites are marginally affected in most of their decisions by military or economic capability, by political structure, etc.

Both Modelski and the Brecher team propose sensible sets of ideas and terms for conceptualizing the flow of action that eventuates in the external conduct of a state, though the Brecher set strikes me as somewhat more elaborate than it need be. These sets, which may be said to deal with the material and efficient causes of conduct, thus constitute a welcome complement to my own scheme, which may be said to dwell particularly on formal and final causes. But they do not do more. They make little contribution, and certainly no direct contribution, to the tasks of firmly characterizing and explaining conduct which are of central concern to this essay.

Broad disquisitions on Soviet external conduct proper are few and far between. Among those few, Jan Triska's article, "A Model for the Study of Soviet Foreign Policy," is outstanding.[33] In this article Triska proposes that Soviet policy be viewed as made up of five components: ideology, strategy, operational direction, tactics, and propaganda. He proposes such an "analytical military model" because, he notes, the Soviet leaders view foreign policy as struggle, and war and peace as interchangeable periods thereof *(vide* their ideology, their constant use of warfare terminology, etc.). The first of the five components, ideology, he describes as "the essence of the matter," he reads it as standing uncompromisingly for revolutionary conquest and domination of the world, and he further describes it as unchanging.[34] Each

---

32. Brecher, "A framework for research," pp. 90–93.
33. *American Political Science Review* 52, no. 1 (March 1958): 64–83.
34. Ibid., pp. 69–71.

of the remaining four he considers an instrument for achieving the
one before. Strategy is a matter of the long-range, general direction of
movement toward the goal set by ideology, whether advance or retreat,
direct or indirect. The building of socialism in a single country and
strengthening the Soviet base instance strategic decisions. Operational
direction "receives and elaborates strategic estimates and transmits
them into practice through tactics and propaganda."[35] Examples of
decisions at this next lower level are the initiation of nonaggression
and neutrality pacts with neighbors, the generating of insecurity
abroad through the Comintern, etc. Tactics are matters of "individual-
ized actions and reactions in a given time to a given situation."[36]
Examples of tactical decisions are Soviet entry into the League of Nations, the creation of United Fronts abroad, etc. Propaganda serves as
a tool for each of the others and is the most flexible and variable of
all.

Triska's proposed method of analyzing Soviet policy is thus to plot
it in terms of a hierarchical series of targets of decreasing generality,
time horizons, and rigidity—each (after the inflexible first term) standing in the relation of means to its predecessor, end to its successor;
each calling for more short-range decisions than the one before. To
describe Soviet policy at any moment of time is to identify the long-
term direction, the short-term movement, the particular moves, and
the verbalization rationalizing the foregoing that characterize the
effort at that moment to reach the final end, which is given as world
domination. To describe the history of Soviet policy is to join together
such plottings at a number of different moments.

Triska's five-term scheme is suggestive and worth pondering. However, it suffers from a number of disabilities. The reason for choosing
his "analytical military model" is fair enough; but he is not bound so
to choose. And the difficulty with his making such a choice, tied so
closely to the specifics of the way the Soviets themselves look at the
problem, is that he complicates needlessly the important task of drawing comparisons with the conduct of other nations. Again, he jeop-
ardizes the utility of his scheme by proposing so refined a hierarchy
of objectives as is implied by his fivefold structure. The problem of

35. Ibid., p. 75.
36. Ibid., p. 77.

allocating particular phenomena between the categories Ends and Means is hard enough in a two-term hierarchy, as evidenced by the difficulty of deciding whether changes consequent upon Stalin's death are to be taken as changes of tactics or changes of goal. A doubling of terms in the structure should at least double difficulties of this sort (as indeed it appears already to have done in Triska's preliminary prospectus[37]). Finally, Triska regards as settled the final objective given by ideology, which he sees as world domination, and the direction in which influence runs among the components, which he sees as top to bottom only. These last comments are not, strictly speaking, objections to the usefulness of the scheme. But they indicate a frame of mind, along with the rationale for the choice of the military model, which has not quite broken the fetters inhibiting a rational approach to Soviet analysis. They suggest an attitude toward the subject which conceives it still as a phenomenon requiring a unique attack, a phenomenon with respect to which certain allegations, like the content and determinativeness of ideology, are not open to question, but are to be received as dogma.

A NEEDED PROGRAM

The burden of the foregoing is that neither existing disquisitions on method in analyzing the USSR and its conduct in general, nor disquisitions on method in analyzing foreign policy in general (nor yet Soviet foreign policy in particular) quite get down to issues that divide devotees of the various images scrutinized in Part II. The first speaks largely to points of conceptualization and procedure at the most abstract level, and helps to the extent of clearing away certain misapprehensions. The second speaks to points of conceptualization at a somewhat lower (but still high) level of abstraction—namely, categories for the analysis of foreign policy—and helps to the extent of suggesting additional categories. But neither the first nor the second gets down to suggesting specific categories of characterization and, most important, to devising ways of deciding the fit between concept and data. None, in short, centers on the meeting point of general concept and datum, which is the crux of the whole matter.

37. Soviet entry into the League of Nations is, among others, presented as a tactical decision (ibid., p. 68), but also as a decision of the broader, operational-direction character (ibid., p. 75).

However, systematic attacks upon particular problems, of which a few have been published in the past few years, are less barren. And the suggestions they embody, along with suggestions of my own and suggestions contained in Triska and Finley's valuable study, may fairly be presented as a preliminary program for correcting the definitions noted.

I report this program below. The report is organized on the scheme set forth in Table 4, taking up the various suggestions in the order of listing of the dimensions to which they apply. It starts with proposals concerning the basic dimensions of expansionism of ends and expansiveness, militancy, and militariness of means—deferring consideration of turpitude or immorality of means to the following chapter. It continues with proposals concerning the contextual or relational and other dimensions. It concludes with comment upon certain special problems.

The Assessment of Basic Dimensions

On the first of the basic dimensions, that of the expansionism of ends sought, the extreme positions are exemplified by Goodman and Halle. Goodman, as noted above, visualizes the aim as a Russified world state, an aim implying limitless expansion of rule, and sees the target date for achievement as about the year 2000.[38] Halle, on the other hand, denies world state or world communism to be goals, affirming that aims, if not status quo, are limited and practical (with content unspecified).[39] Others take intermediate positions.

The requirements for providing a sounder description of this variable and arbitrating the different views seem fairly clear. The question of aims, as the question of motives, is one of pictures in people's minds of the kind of order they want to bring about in the world outside.[40] As such aims can be observed only indirectly through word or deed, one must put up with uncertainty, and so one must be satisfied with the least disagreeable of a number of disagreeable alternatives. To this writer, the least disagreeable or best available procedure is to look to

38. See above, Chapter 3, p. 64.
39. *The Cold War as History* (New York, Harper & Row, 1967), p. 158.
40. Cf. William Welch, "The Puzzle of Soviet External Goals," *South Atlantic Quarterly* 64, no. 2 (Spring 1965), pp. 157–65.

and to array whatever pertinent general statements of Soviet goals are to be found in the most authoritative documents, such as Party programs, state constitutions, the 1957 and 1960 manifestos, speeches at Party congresses and other gala affairs, etc. This means systematic content analysis of the kind pursued in the Brecher article discussed above.

As I scan these authoritative documents, I find many relevant statements that point explicitly or implicitly to a world of independent and equal socialist (i.e. Communist) states at peace with one another, but none that suggest enlargement of the Soviet writ. I therefore find much that suggests the expansion of the Communist sphere and hence Soviet influence, but nothing on the expansion of Soviet rule, and so conclude that those who see world conquest, total control of the globe, to be the objectives are wide of the mark, those who see more limited objectives more nearly on it. I further see much that suggests, by indirection, the expectation of a fairly long period of coexistence, hence a target date fairly distant in the future for achievement of the desired world of Communist states.

However, these findings are provisional and subject to radical revision on the more extended and refined content analysis of the documents in question that is the method required. What is important is the method, and its ability to withstand the objections that will be raised. Among the objections to be anticipated, the most important no doubt will be the following: that the Soviets mean something different from what they say, that world communism really means world conquest, or that one has to look to the record, and the record clearly is expansionist. To the first of these, the rebuttal is that of course it is possible that what is really on the Soviets' minds is something other than what the documents suggest, but that the burden of proof is surely on those who, like Goodman, would substitute the hidden for the obvious in the meaning of words. To the second, the retort is that if we go about deriving ends from means, long-range pictures from specific acts, we in effect eliminate the distinction between the two and forgo its utility. The case for content analysis of authoritative general statements is at bottom a case for the simplest and least objectionable of the alternatives.

On the expansiveness of the means conduct employs, one may say that while there is general agreement that, on the whole, Soviet rule *has* expanded over time, there is disagreement on the magnitude, steadiness, etc., of this expansion. There are those who, like Wolfe, see continuous extension of rule, especially in the years 1945–60.[41] Again, there are those who, like Halle, see expansiveness as intermittent, marked occasionally by retreat.[42]

Of all the issues troubling the academic fraternity, this would seem most susceptible to clear-cut resolution. Provided one makes some sensible assumptions regarding the de facto control of nominally independent states commonly called the satellites, one can determine quite mathematically changes in territory (and population) under Soviet rule from year to year and graph them precisely. Assuming an area under actual Soviet control at the beginning of 1919 to have been 8,000,000 square miles, and assuming the area under her control in 1969 to be 8,650,000 square miles, then the amount she expanded during these 50 years was 650,000 square miles, or 8 percent, or an average of something less than one-sixteenth of one percent per year.[43] Adjusting for satellites largely under her control in early 1969 (putting for the sake of argument into this category Bulgaria, Czechoslovakia, East Germany, Hungary, and Mongolia), one gets a 50-year expansion figure of about 18 percent, or an annual rate something less than one-third of one percent.[44] One could, if one wanted, devise a coefficient of expansion, and draw up an index of expansion with 100 representing territory under effective Bolshevik rule in January 1919—or, alternately, November 1917, March 1918, or March 1921. Tricky points that would have to be resolved are: the status of formally independent nations as Soviet-controlled at this or that time; the reach of Soviet control in the early years within Russia, and connected with this the choice of a reasonable base period; the propriety of including temporarily occupied territory, like Austria in 1945–55, etc.; the inclusion of attempts to extend, such as the pressure exerted on Turkey in 1945–47 to retrocede the Kars district.

41. *Communist Totalitarianism: Keys to the Soviet System,* rev. ed. (Boston: Beacon Press, 1961), esp. pp. 252–58.

42. *The Cold War as History,* pp. 11, 16.

43. The 1919 figure is one (crudely rounded) given in the *New International Year Book* for 1919. The figure for 1969 is from *The 1969 World Almanac.*

44. Figures for the satellites are from *The 1969 World Almanac.*

One point that such a detailed analysis of area and population figures makes clear is the incorrectness of alleging steady expansion, the correctness of alleging intermittent expansion, broken here and there by moments of retreat. It is probably correct to speak of nine years of retreat: 1917 and 1918, with fallbacks under German, White, Allied pressures; 1941 and 1942, with retreat under Nazi pressure; 1951, with loss of control over North Korea; 1955, with relinquishment of control over Austria and retrocession of Finnish and Chinese bases; 1956, 1960, and 1963, with loss of control over Poland, Albania, and Rumania, respectively. This unsteadiness could be measured too by relating to total number of years covered the number of years respectively of expansion, retention, and contraction. On a provisional estimate, this would give results in the order given of 11 or 22 percent (1919–21, 1939–40, 1943–48), 30 or 60 per cent, and 9 or 18 per cent, years of mere retention of rule being in the majority.

On militancy, disagreement is sharp. The positions in the works of the sample range from relentless, unrelieved warfare with the rest of the world to a posture of substantial accommodation, with intermediate cases affirming a general militancy relieved now and then by a modicum of cooperativeness. Kintner, for instance, takes Soviet behavior as synonymous with political warfare, which he defines as a form of conflict that seeks to impose its will by all means except the direct use of armed force, and that therefore includes diplomatic and economic sorties, propaganda, misinformation, provocation, intimidation and sabotage, terrorism, "divide and rule" tactics, etc. Such behavior, for Kintner, has been continuous: Soviet resort to it in such apparently peaceful years as 1921–39 was simply concealed. In contrast, Fleming implies efforts at cooperation and compromise to be the norm, high militancy the exception. In between, Shulman sees strong variation in time between leftist (more militant) and rightist (less militant) mode. Tucker sees a sharp shift from the politics of aggression of Stalin's last years to the politics of persuasion of the post-Stalin era.[45]

45. William R. Kintner and Joseph Z. Kornfeder, *The New Frontier of War* (Chicago: Regnery, 1962), p. xiii; Denna F. Fleming, *The Cold War and Its Origins: 1917–1960*, 2 vols. (Garden City, N.Y.: Doubleday, 1961): the inference is based on such assertions about conciliatory behavior as those found on pp. 245, 790, 914, 1053; Marshall D. Shulman, *Stalin's Foreign*

Though the sounder description or measurement of this element and the arbitrating of the disagreement may at first sight seem difficult, here too I think there is much that can be done. Despite deficiencies of definition and application earlier noted, Shulman and Tucker have shown the way; for, as they implicitly note, Soviet conduct during any given time interval is composed of a myriad of individual acts, some of which seem on balance to breathe hostility and intransigence, some amiability and compromise, some of which are conciliatory, some refractory.[46] The requirements are to devise a sensible method of sampling the universe of such acts, sensible definitions of the two categories, perhaps a sensible weighting scheme, and to note relative frequency. And this, though difficult, is not impossible. To meet the sampling problem one can usefully rely on a respectable chronology, or a number of chronologies of divergent background to eliminate possible bias. To meet the classification problem one can usefully proceed by gauging the immediate thrust of the move, whether tending to harm or to help the bulk of other states. To meet the aggregating problem one can assign weights on a common-sense basis.

For instance, a recent thorough chronology from England, Neville Williams' *Chronology of the Modern World*,[47] culls from the universe of Soviet moves in 1948 the following as presumably the most important: (1) February, support for the Czech coup d'état; (2) March, walk out of Allied Control Commission for Germany; (3) April, beginning of interference with traffic between Berlin and West Germany; (4) April, signing of mutual assistance treaty with Finland; (5) June, expulsion of Yugoslavia from Cominform; (6) July, participation in conference on shipping in Danube; (7) July, stoppage of road and rail traffic into Berlin; (8) August, break-off of relations with United States over latter's failure to repatriate against her will a Soviet defector; (9) September, establishment of Korean People's Republic

---

Policy Reappraised (Cambridge: Harvard University Press, 1963), pp. 4–9; Robert C. Tucker, *The Soviet Political Mind: Studies in Stalinism and Post-Stalin Change* (New York: Praeger, 1963), Chapter 8.

46. For classification of postwar moves according to "conciliatory" or "refractory" see William A. Gamson and Andre Modigliani, "Some Aspects of Soviet-Western Conflict" (Paper prepared for the Annual Meeting of the Peace Research Society, Cambridge, Mass., November 1967).

47. New York: McKay, 1967, pp. 610–13.

in North Korea, claiming jurisdiction over entire country; (10) October, veto of a UN proposal to end the Berlin blockade; (11) December, support in UN General Assembly of convention on prevention and punishment of genocide and declaration of human rights.[48] Of these I would describe all but 4, 6, and 11 as militant, because in their immediate import signifying hostility rather than amiability to the world outside. The residual three I would call nonmilitant, because on the whole breathing cooperation rather than intransigence. Assigning equal weights, aggregating, and finding the ratio of militant moves to the whole gives a figure of 8/11 or 73 percent militant on the year. A similar investigation for 1958 gives 4/11 or 36 percent militant on the year, a figure one-half of the 1948 one.[49] Plotting these percentages for a number of years on graph paper would give a visual measure of change in this variable over time.

There are a number of legitimate objections that can be made to this procedure. One is the assignment of equal weights, and hence failure to distinguish magnitudes of hostility or amiability, and the treating as of equal importance, for instance, of the Berlin blockade and support for the UN genocide convention. Another is treating as separate moves what are episodes in a single, concerted drive, as in the case above, where items 2, 3, 7, and 10 are episodes in the drive against Berlin. But though legitimate and marking imperfections that need be recognized as such, these do not render the procedure worthless. The two named, it should be pointed out, tend to neutralize one another. More important, it should be remembered that a crude method is better than none, and that the proper objective is not perfection, which is out of reach, but less imperfection than we now have. The strongest treatments of the militancy topic found in the sample—Shulman's and Tucker's—essentially do what is suggested here. Conversely, what is suggested here is simply a more systematic way of doing what they do.

On militariness, disagreement is not so great, though it is still substantial. None ascribe to the Soviets the degree of addiction to the military instrument and recklessness comparable to that usually attributed to the Nazis. All emphasize a determination to avoid general

48. Ascription of moves nos. 1 and 9 to the USSR is mine.
49. Ibid., pp. 660–65.

war, especially nuclear war with the United States. On how ready they
are to employ the weapons of violence, however, and on how close to
the brink they are ready to go, there are sharp differences. As earlier
noted, Goodman speaks of a "practice . . . of subjugating nations by
means of crude military force," and Strausz-Hupé of a high, albeit
indirect and, on this account, cautious military challenge. Librach
speaks of never losing an opportunity to attack small nations in difficulties, Dallin of brinkmanship in the Stalinist era, Wolfe of willingness to risk war at the periphery, Mosely of Khrushchevian ultimatums and the manipulation of "rolling crises."[50] At the other
extreme, stressing low risk-taking propensity, low militariness, are, as
already noted: the later Kennan, who writes that the military arm was
never regarded as the *"main* agency for the spread of the world revolution"; Halle, who speaks of a general cautiousness (though his data
do not bear him out); Schuman, who emphasizes the rarity of resort to
force. Lukacs adverts both to Stalin's cautiousness and the unreality
of Khrushchev's military threats. In between, commonly stressing
moderate values of these variables on balance, marked variation in
time, and, particularly, sharp moderation on Stalin's death, are Gehlen,
Shulman, and Tucker.[51]

50. Elliot R. Goodman, *The Soviet Design for a World State* (New York:
Columbia University Press, 1960), p. xvii; Robert Strausz-Hupé, and others,
Protracted Conflict, Harper Colophon ed. (New York: Harper & Row, 1963),
Chapter 4 (for extended treatment see above, Chapter 3, pp. 77–80); Jan
Librach, *The Rise of the Soviet Empire: A Study of Soviet Foreign Policy,*
rev. ed. (New York: Praeger, 1965), p. 17; David J. Dallin, *Soviet Foreign
Policy after Stalin* (Philadelphia: Lippincott, 1961), p. 13; Wolfe, *Com-
munist Totalitarianism,* p. 23; Philip E. Mosely, *The Kremlin and World
Politics: Studies in Soviet Policy and Action* (New York: Vintage, 1960),
p. 551.

51. George F. Kennan, *Russia and the West under Lenin and Stalin*
(Boston: Little, Brown, 1961), p. 389; Halle, *The Cold War as History,* p.
11 (for discussion see Chapter 5, pp. 148–49, above); Frederick L. Schuman,
The Cold War: Retrospect and Prospect, 2nd ed. (Baton Rouge: Louisiana
State University Press, 1967), esp. pp. 19–20 (for discussion see Chapter 5,
pp. 158–63, above); John Lukacs, *A New History of the Cold War,* 3rd ed.,
expanded, of *A History of the Cold War* (Garden City, N.Y.: Doubleday,
1966), pp. 62, 208; Michael Gehlen, *The Politics of Coexistence: Soviet
Methods and Motives,* (Bloomington: Indiana University Press, 1967), for
instance, pp. 60, 208; Shulman, *Stalin's Foreign Policy Reappraised,* for instance, pp. 4–9, 259; Tucker, *The Soviet Political Mind,* Chapter 8 passim;
for discussion of the last two see Chapter 4, pp. 112–32, above.

Where it is a simple question of addiction to the military instrument proper, the method of strengthening the assessment of the variable and arbitrating between divergent views is simple. One has only to take a sample of those events or crises that might be most expected to encourage use of the armed forces and note the frequency with which the Soviets did in fact use their armed forces rather than invoke less drastic measures like verbal threats, economic help or sanctions, etc. This is what, as already noted, Gehlen has done for the post-Stalin years.[52] His conclusion, of low degree of militarism, practically resolves the matters for these years. The method is readily extensible to other periods.

A study of Khrushchevian threats of use of military force which this writer conducted in 1965 both strengthens Gehlen's finding and illustrates other investigatory possibilities.[53] This study raised the question of how ominous or malignant were a sample of five celebrated pronouncements delivered at various times of post-Stalin crisis. It defined "threat" as the declaration by one party of an intent under specified conditions to do injury to another, and it identified as the principal factors determinative of ominousness the magnitude of the injury portended, the unambiguousness of the wording, the directness of address, the tightness of language, and, finally, the probability that the conditions involved would materialize. It found that in every one of the declarations examined one or another key element is missing, thereby reducing the declaration to the status of innuendo, or one or more factors determinative of ominousness are present in low degree only, shrinking the menace latent.

Where it is the related but more complicated problem of recklessness or cautiousness, procedure is somewhat more difficult. Yet it is not insoluble, and Triska and Finley show the possibilities in their chapter on "The Soviet Union: reckless or cautious?"[54] In this chapter the authors assess Soviet risk-taking by analyzing Soviet moves in 29 crises of the period 1946–63. In the first part of the chapter they do this: (1) by defining riskiness in terms of the symmetricality (appropriateness) of the action undertaken to the harm perceived to

52. See Chapter 5, pp. 140–44, above.
53. William Welch, "The Nature of Khrushchevian Threats Against the West," *University of Colorado Studies, Series in Political Science No. 3* (Boulder: University of Colorado Press, August 1965).
54. *Soviet Foreign Policy* (New York: Macmillan, 1968), Chapter IX.

threaten, a risky act being one that is disproportionately severe vis-à-
vis the threat, a cautious act one that is disproportionately mild; (2)
by scaling in terms of symmetricality to perceived harm a number
of alternative moves the Soviets might have taken in the case of seven
groups into which the 29 crises are divided; (3) by noting where the
course actually chosen falls among the hypothetical alternatives. This
finding is that in four of the 29 cases (e.g. Hungary in 1956) the
Soviet course was symmetrical (proportional) to the perceived threat,
in 12 it was less than symmetrical (e.g. Iran in 1946, Berlin in 1948,
etc.); in nine it was "decidedly cautious" (presumably much less than
symmetrical—e.g. Poland in 1956 and Suez in 1956); and in four it
was passive-indifferent (e.g. Tibet in 1950). Their conclusion to this
first part of the chapter, in short, is one of considerable cautiousness.

In the balance of the chapter, Triska and Finley set out to measure
degrees of riskiness. They present us in turn with a schematic model
of risk-taking; a scaling and ranking of the 29 crises according to
"intensity" or "inherent riskiness"; a scaling of the maximum bids in
each crisis (highest level of violence engaged in) for the initiator,
respondent, and their respective allies; and a scaling of the level of
violence implied by the entire course of Soviet action during each
crisis. They turn next to correlations for nine different situational
contexts, between what they call dependent or behavioral variables
(bid levels of initiator, bid levels of respondent, and violence level of
Soviet course of action as a whole) and the independent or non-
behavioral—namely, stakes, geographical risk, salience of parties, etc.
They conclude this part of the chapter with a series of statements
about how Soviet risk-taking varies with Soviet status as initiator,
with crisis output, with time period, with category of crisis (whether
intersystem, intrabloc, etc.). For conclusion to the entire chapter they
reemphasize the cautiousness found in the first part.

Though very informative in data presented and suggestive in procedures employed, the Triska-Finley chapter also has a number of
weaknesses, and these I would call attention to, if only because they
are of a kind that seems often, for no good reason, to go along with
the kind of study exemplified by the chapter (i.e. behavioral or semi-
behavioral), hence to vitiate unnecessarily an otherwise highly promising mode of analysis. The second, more refined assessment of degree

of risk promised in the second part of the chapter doesn't quite materialize. Not one but several new variables, it is variously hinted, are to be considered measures of risk-taking: level of violence of actor's maximum bid, ratio of same to level of violence of maximum bid by opponent, ratio of maximum bid to stakes at issue, level of conflict implied by sum total of actor's moves during crisis, etc. But the connections are not clearly and explicitly affirmed. The application to the data of these new measures yields results not always consistent with one another, results whose implications are not always clear. Hence, just how the demonstration adds up to the more refined assessment of risk-taking, confirming in more precise fashion the conclusion of cautiousness earlier reached, is obscure.

Indeed, there is in this chapter a lack of clarity and coherence of exposition that makes one almost lose sight of the many excellent qualities. Concepts are defined at the beginning (e.g. "probability") that are not used again. Terms are used in the conclusion (e.g. "decisional time-limit") that are earlier neither discussed in connection with the data nor even defined. Sometimes data are introduced only to be subsequently ignored. Sometimes, with no explanation, the discussion shifts to broader phenomena than Soviet conduct. Above all, there is a most unusual tendency to jump to discussion of complicated relationships involving a number of variables before exhausting the discussion of simple ones, and to ignore simple conclusions that seem warranted by the data in the rush to sound complicated ones. Accordingly, one may not unfairly say of the chapter (as in fact of one or two others in this otherwise outstanding work) that it exhibits in higher degree that overcomplexity, that top-heaviness of conceptualization (and sometimes data), and that obscurantism of exposition earlier noted as mildly present in Gehlen.[55]

The Assessment of Contextual Dimensions

What I call the contextual or relational dimensions of Soviet conduct, as distinct from the essential or basic, are matters of its causes and effects, antecedents and consequences. Principal among these are:

55. Among other chapters with these faults, the writer would cite ibid., Chapters IV (on doctrine and events) and VII (on the developing areas). For earlier critique of Gehlen see Chapter 5, p. 144, above.

the addiction of conduct to initiative; the offensiveness of the driving force behind conduct, and connected therewith the role in conduct of ideology and national interest; the successfulness of conduct; the impact of conduct on the rest of the world. Although these dimensions are complex and not so directly observable as the basic ones, there are steps that can be taken here too to reduce disagreement and improve results.

On addiction to the initiative, or the location of prime causes, whether inside or out, polar positions are illustrated by the views of Wolfe and Schuman. For Wolfe virtually all Soviet behavior is initiative—intiative that emanates from the internal and specifically the totalitarian nature of the actor.[56] What other powers do to her makes no difference. Her course is set by her inner nature, and the only means by which other powers can affect her is force. For Schuman, on the other hand, Soviet behavior is predominately one of responses. Her expansion, her engagement in military action, her highly centralized and autocratic internal structure are responses to the environment and, more specifically, the fear induced by aggression upon her from that environment.[57] In between, with less extreme views, stand Tucker and Shulman.[58]

After the fashion in which the ancient problem of heredity versus environment is commonly resolved, one would have a priori to say of Soviet conduct that it is neither totally initiatory—autogenetic, as some say—nor totally responsive, but a little of both. To agree to this, one has only to think of Soviet behavior following the German attack in June 1941 and the death of Stalin in March 1953. But to pin down the degree to which it is one or the other, and to arbitrate the difference of views noted, is less easy. One possibility would be to take the major shifts in direction of conduct and see whether they connect more sensibly to changes in the international scene or to changes in the internal scene. In the traditional periodization, these shifts occurred in 1921, 1928, 1934, 1939, 1941, 1945, 1949, 1953, and possibly also 1957 and 1962. Of these 10, seven seem to connect most

56. Wolfe, *Communist Totalitarianism*, p. 295.
57. Schuman, *The Cold War*, esp. pp. 14–23.
58. Shulman accents the external, Tucker the internal factor. See discussions in Chapter 4, pp. 112–14, 123–25, above.

sensibly with shifts in the international scene: 1934, with the rising fascist threat; 1939, with the failure of collective security with the West and perceived need to buy time from Germany; 1941, with the German attack; 1945, with the war's end and the perceived opportunity to extend control over East Europe; 1949, with NATO and the buildup of Western power; 1957, with the opportunities perceived to be offered by Sputnik; 1962, with the dangers shown by the nuclear showdown over Cuba. The other three connect most sensibly with internal shifts: 1921, with economic and emotional exhaustion from the Civil War period; 1928, with the turning inward of energies in connection with the five-year plans; 1953, with the internal developments consequent upon the death of Stalin. A content analysis of speeches and other documents explaining the shifts could give a more accurate reading of the relative weights of the two factors in each case and check the aggregate reading given above.

A related issue is that of the relation between character of Soviet response and character of prior initiative from outside. Specifically, this is raised in the form of whether the two are symmetrical, a soft response answering to soft initiative, hard to hard, or asymmetrical, soft answering to hard, etc. Studies by Professors Gamson and Modigliana of Michigan show some of the possibilities for improved assessment of this relationship. These authors treat the matter in the form of a test of the relative adequacy of predictions of Soviet response flowing respectively from three different pictures of Soviet conduct in the large (pictures, incidentally, that correspond fairly closely with our Ultra-Hard, Hard, and Mixed images). What they do essentially is to take 63 major Soviet actions of the 1946–63 period (from the march on Teheran to the release of Professor Barghoorn), classify them as either refractory or conciliatory, identify and similarly classify Western actions immediately preceding, and relate the two sets. Resulting correlations are not high, but on balance (drastically simplified) they seem to favor more the symmetric view that conciliatory response follows upon a conciliatory initiative. And, while much needs to be done to take adequate account of the many other phenomena that may affect the concrete moves in question, their investigation forwards our knowledge markedly.

An important issue connected with the offensiveness of motive, the second of the "causal" dimensions, is that of the role of ideology in conduct. This issue has generated more debate than any other.[59] On one side stand those who affirm a determining role and see in the ideology a blueprint and guide to action. On the other stand those who deny it this role, and see it confined to that of rationalizer or, at most, instrument of cognition. Expounding the first position among the writers of the sample are: Bouscaren, who sees ideology as the essence of the Communist movement; Librach, who calls Marxist-Leninism a "true guide in revolutionary action, statecraft, and politics"; and Kintner, who equates ideology with faith and implies it has all the driving force faith has for the typical Communist.[60] Expounding something close to the second position are: Gehlen, who thinks Leninist theory excludes no significant range of policy choices, although it bears a relationship to policy not utterly meaningless; and Halle, for whom Soviet policy is adequately explained as mere extension of older Russian policy, and for whom, therefore, explanation requires reference to no further factor.[61] Those who affirm the first position commonly, although not always, see ideology as largely unchanging through the years; those who affirm the second commonly see significant change, usually in response to perceived inconsistencies with action.

Discussion of the role-of-ideology issue normally starts out by resolving it into the further issue of the conformity between Communist word and subsequent Soviet deed, scripture and subsequent action. And the best available procedure for more firmly assessing the dimension and arbitrating the debate, it seems to me, is to settle more carefully and systematically this further issue.[62] This requires three main steps: (1) determining, for each variable (e.g. expansionism) and for the time period chosen, whether ideology as it is at the start of the time period does not, on the whole, prescribe differentially; (2) ascertaining,

59. For partial bibliographies see William Welch, "Ideology and Soviet Conduct: A Re-examination," *The Rocky Mountain Social Science Journal* 3, no. 1 (April 1966): 96–109; and Triska and Finley, *Soviet Foreign Policy*, pp. 454–57.

60. Anthony Bouscaren, *Soviet Foreign Policy: A Pattern of Persistence* (New York: Fordham University Press, 1962), p. 7; Librach, *The Rise of the Soviet Empire*, p. 3; Kintner, *The New Frontier of War*, pp. xiv–xv.

61. Gehlen, *The Politics of Coexistence*, p. 294; Halle, *The Cold War as History*, p. 11.

62. Welch, "Ideology and Soviet Conduct," pp. 100–03.

for each variable and for the time period, what the leaders of the movement have actually elected to try to do, on the whole and on the average; (3) comparing the results. The need for the first step lies in the fact that unless ideology, as indicated by the major works of scripture, party program, etc., speaks out clearly on one or the other of these variables—unless, for instance, it prescribes clearly that treaties are (or are not) to be observed—the possibility of making any truly meaningful statement about its role disappears. In somewhat different words, if ideology is ambiguous or ambivalent, seeming to permit equally observance or nonobservance of treaties and to prohibit nothing, then it really determines nothing and to say it does is to make no sense.

A provisional application of this scheme made by this writer in the case of Soviet conduct across the boad in the period 1920–50 shows low conformity indeed between word and subsequent deed.[63] In the case of only 20 out of 50 variables was subsequent action found to conform with prior ideological prescription; in the case of the other 30 it either failed to conform (27), or ideology failed to prescribe differentially (three). Conformity was particularly low in the realm of statecraft. Ideology prescribed low reliance on coercive methods in international affairs, for instance; yet practice involved frequent resort to same. Provisional application of sound procedure, in short, calls into question the "blueprint theory."

The more important consideration of the moment, however, is not the accuracy of the results of one particular application of the method but the method itself. Despite certain obvious limitations, the method, it seems to me, can at least claim an edge over what is currently in use, especially among those persuaded of the determinativeness of ideology. For these commonly resort to certain devices (I call them the Procrustean, the Zigzag, and the Aesopic) which are at bottom forms of the sifting of words and deeds of unexamined principles of selection that is criticized in connection with Chapter 3's survey of Ultra-Hard views.[64] And the method here advocated at least avoids such caprice.

Triska and Finley tackle the problem in another way. Rather than

63. Ibid., pp. 103–07.
64. Ibid., pp. 97–99.

test the influence of doctrine by looking to conformity thereto of subsequent action, they look to the incidence of doctrinal reference in the documents in which highest Soviet authority sets and provides the rationale for future courses of action. In experimental application of this method, they take the speeches and other materials from the Twenty-second Party Congress, ascertain the ratio of doctrinally stereotyped words or phrases to total words or phrases in selected statements—a ratio to which they give the name "Doctrinal Stereotype Quotient"—and then, further, in the more limited context of passages of explicit reasoning, assess the degree in which doctrine permeates premises and conclusions. Their specific findings are, *inter alia,* that doctrine enters much into long-term analysis and decision, little into short-run and crisis analysis and decision, enters more into the thinking of foreign than domestic policy specialists, more into the thinking of older than younger members of the elite.[65] Their well-based conclusion is that doctrine, while thus having a strong though variable influence upon decision-making, has its impact mainly at the cognitive moment of apprehending the problem and alternative solutions, rather than at the moment of actually choosing among the alternatives.

The issue of the role of ideology is sometimes raised in the disjunctive form of whether ideology or national interest is conduct's prime motor, national interest being taken to mean the complex of self-centered considerations that are supposed normally to prompt the behavior of states in the nation-state system.[66] The best way of resolving this one, it seems to me, is: (1) to select key historical issues that have confronted the USSR with respect to which ideology would seem to dictate one course of action, national interest a quite different one (e.g. the Sino-Indian dispute of 1962); and (2) to note which of these alternatives the course of action actually chosen agreed with the more frequently—a procedure an experimental application of which involving 19 critical cases from the years 1939–62 produced a result approximately three to one in favor of national interest. But no doubt there are other possibilities.

65. Triska and Finley, *Soviet Foreign Policy,* Chapter IV, esp. pp. 116–27.
66. For a bibliography, some representative positions, and the study subsequently summarized, see William Welch, "The Sources of Soviet Conduct: A Note on Method," *Background* 6, no. 4 (Winter 1963): 17–20.

On the dimension of successfulness, or effectiveness in achieving aims, representative extreme views are: on the one hand, those of Bouscaren, who puts a high value on this feature, and Schwartz, whose very title, *The Red Phoenix,* suggests his similar view of the matter in the postwar period, and who stresses especially high effectiveness vis-à-vis the United States; and, on the other hand, those who like Shulman stress postwar failure (albeit within the context of a shorter period) and affirm that, as late as 1951, every effort the Soviets had made to correct a disadvantageous world position generated a reaction in the West that threatened still more serious disadvantages.[67]

Making firmer assessments of this variable and resolving this debate are matters of relating aims and expectations for a given period (as specified in authoritative documents from the beginning of the period) to actual subsequent achievements. Illustrative of the possibilities is a series of observations which Triska and Finley make as a sort of by-product of their analysis of Soviet behavior in the 29 postwar crises earlier referred to.[68] The authors estimate for each of 17 of these crises the gains that the Soviets hoped to make or the losses they hoped to avoid, calculate the results actually achieved, and compare. Their first finding is that in the nine cases in which positive gain was the objective (Iran, 1946; Greece, 1947; Czechoslovakia, 1948; Berlin, 1948; Korea, 1950; Suez, 1956; Berlin, 1958; Finland, 1961; and Cuba, 1962) the Soviets succeeded in only two—Czechoslovakia in 1948 and Finland in 1961. Their second finding is that in the eight cases in which avoidance of loss was the objective (Marshall Plan in 1947 combined with the 1955 NATO extension to West Germany; Yugoslavia, 1948; East Germany, 1953; Poland, 1956; Hungary, 1956; Albania, 1962; and China in the last several years) the Soviets avoided loss in four, failing in the cases of the Marshall Plan and NATO combination, the freezing of Western borders, and Yugoslavia, Albania, and China. Down two against four in the six cases in which clear decisions were reached, the USSR thus posted an achievement record for the postwar period that hardly adds up to an impressive success story, and Triska and Finley so conclude.

67. Bouscaren, *Soviet Foreign Policy,* pp. 2–3; Harry E. Schwartz, *The Red Phoenix: Russia since World War II* (New York: Praeger, 1961) esp. pp. 412–13; Shulman, *Stalin's Foreign Policy Reappraised* p. 175.

68. *Soviet Foreign Policy,* p. 348.

The last of the dimensions here examined is that of the impact on the world and especially on world peace. On this issue there is general agreement in respect to one point: that, all in all, the Soviets are hardly a harmonizing force. As in other cases, however, there is disagreement on the magnitude of the disturbances they created. At one extreme, there are those who speak of mortal peril to the rest of humanity, of "universal, unitary, unending war to the finish."[69] At the other stand those who speak only of a mix of disturbing and encouraging features.[70]

What can be done to assess and arbitrate is again suggested by Triska and Finley's analysis of crises.[71] Crises are by definition moments of high international tension, and of the 29 crises that rocked the world in the 18-year period 1946–1963, Triska and Finley consider the Soviets to have initiated 10 (the Iranian of 1946, the Greek of 1967, the Czechoslovakian of 1948, the Berlin crises of 1948, 1958, and 1961, the Korean of 1950, the U-2 of 1960, the Finnish of 1961, and the Cuban of 1962). This amounts to one Soviet-inspired disturbance almost every two years, and even though one can question the characterization of one or two of these as of worldwide importance (e.g. the Finnish), and though in one or two others one can doubt the attribution of the initiative to the Soviet Union (e.g. the Greek and the U-2), the list and its frequency implications are probably fair. Moreover, these 10 are of greater seriousness than the average of the 29.[72] On the other hand, it is to be remembered that Soviets acted cautiously in most of these as in other crises, keeping their actions usually below the level of resort to military force. Important too is the fact that the years covered are those of the Cold War, and that in the rest of the span of Soviet rule one would probably find comparable frequency of Soviet-inspired disturbance only in 1917–21 and 1939–40. Since 1963, for instance, of the major crises that have arisen, the continued and continuing Vietnamese and Sino-Soviet, the Indo-Pakistani of 1965, the Dominican of 1965, the Israeli-Egyptian of 1967, and the Czechoslovakian of 1968, only the last can, with

69. Wolfe, *Communist Totalitarianism*, p. 305.
70. For instance, Gehlen, *The Politics of Coexistence*, pp. 63–64.
71. Triska and Finley, *Soviet Foreign Policy*, p. 333.
72. Ibid., p. 340.

any reason, be said to have been initiated by the Soviets. If it is an understatement to dismiss Soviet behavior merely as a disturbing influence in the world, so is it an exaggeration to use Wolfe's phrase of "universal, unitary, unending war to the finish" or to speak, as Philip Mosely does, of Soviet instigation of "rolling crises." It is not inappropriate in this connection to draw attention to the fact that, whatever the terms used, the Soviets are by no means the only disturbing influence in the world. On sensible criteria—and those underlying Triska and Finley's list are that—of the crises that have rocked the world in the entire postwar period, more than two out of three are of non-Soviet origin. However, the final word in the assessment of this as of other variables must await more painstaking pursuit of the procedure suggested.

The last of the dimensions or elements of Soviet conduct require no special discussion. Analysis of the special component of conduct toward other Communist states, which together with counterpart analyses for capitalist and third-world states gives a measure of the degree to which conduct is politically differentiated, is a matter of applying separately, to the narrower universe so defined, the methods suggested for the whole. The second is the critical element of change, which is a matter of temporal differentiation. The assessment of this element is a matter of assessing the other dimensions at various moments in time and noting differences and trends.

Special Problems

Before this program of suggestions is concluded, special note should be taken of three special problems of conceptualization and definition that are involved in assessment of many dimensions mentioned above. The first is the problem of separating acts of Soviet from acts of non-Soviet authorship, the second the problem of separating acts of Soviet initiative from acts of Soviet response, the third the problem of separating Soviet acts that are of a long-range, strategic, or goal-oriented nature from acts that are of short-range significance only.

As far as the problem of authorship is concerned, the main difficulty lies with the accounting one is to give of the acts of Communist parties and states other than the Soviet. Opinions diverge. On the one side stand, *inter alia*, the authors of *Protracted Conflict*, who as

we saw treat the disturbances in Jordan, Syria, and Lebanon in 1957–
58 as Soviet-inspired; Wolfe, who treats even the acts of the Chinese
(in the early years of their coming to power) as Moscow-directed;
and Kintner, who visualizes even the Yugoslavs as under Moscow
rule—the expression is "pseudo-independence."[73] On the other side
stands, *inter alia*, Fleming, who raises a question even about the
Korean War, crediting the possibility that not Moscow but the North
Koreans acting independently of Moscow were its authors.[74] The
question is one of the existence and perdurance of Muscovite control
over other elements in the international movement. Its final determination rests on the devising of more suitable ways and means of establishing the presence or absence of such control than we now have.
Pending such devising, one does best to adopt, as conventions for the
sake of getting on with the analysis, certain assumptions about the
relationships in question. The conventions I suggest are that Soviet
control be deemed to have extended substantially (if not perfectly) to
the other Communist states as follows: Bulgaria, East Germany, and
Hungary, for the entire postwar period; China, Cuba, Yugoslavia, and
North Vietnam, never; Albania, from 1948 to 1960; Czechoslovakia,
from 1948 to the present; Poland, from 1945 to 1956; Mongolia, from
1921 to the present; North Korea, from 1945 to 1951; Rumania, from
1945 to 1963. Control of nonruling parties, I suggest, has extended
(with rare exceptions) from their origin to 1953.

With respect to the problem of separating initiatives from responses, there is similarly a lack of consensus. For the Ultra-Hards
(and many of the Hards) the Nazi Pact, the invasions of 1939–40,
the Berlin blockade, the Cold War, the shooting down of the U-2,
and, indeed, almost every militant and militarist and inimical Soviet
act are cases of initiative. For those of Mixed persuasion, on the other
hand, almost the reverse is true. To determine the matter is no easy
thing. The Berlin blockade and other acts early in the Cold War were
preceded by certain Western acts that might legitimately have been
viewed as hostile by the Soviet Union, such as currency reform and

73. Strausz-Hupé, and others, *Protracted Conflict*, pp. 50–52 (for discussion see Chapter 3, pp. 81–82, above); Wolfe, *Communist Totalitarianism*,
pp. 217–18; Kintner, *The New Frontier of War*, p. 114 n.
74. Fleming, *The Cold War and its Origins*, pp. 597–601.

consolidation in West Germany. The Nazi Pact could be seen as a reaction to the Western appeasement of Hitler in Austria, Munich, etc. The blowing up of the U-2 incident could be seen as a normal response to first success in shooting down American planes over Soviet territory. Rather than seek finally to resolve this difficult matter at the moment, it would seem best to confine the notion of response fairly narrowly, and describe as such only acts which are preceded shortly in time by the acts of the other nation against which they are directed, and which are pitched at a force level no higher than that of the predecessor's. This would place the Nazi Pact, the Berlin blockade, and the U-2 incident into the "initiative" category. It would also place in this category such Soviet accommodating moves as concessions on Austria in 1955, the disarmament proposals of that year, etc. A conventional rating of the various moves would, again, permit us to get on with the analysis pending more careful determinations.

The final problem, of separating the tactical from the nontactical, is sharpened by again noting differences between Ultra-Hards and others. For the former, all Soft moves fall in the first category, all Hard moves in the second. The major requirement here is again establishing some time period which, exceeded by the life of a given Soviet move, takes that out of the tactical category. Retreats in battle, as before the Germans in 1941, or even the signing of Brest-Litovsk, can be called tactical because they were so called by the Soviets themselves and never seen as anything but temporary. On the other hand, it hardly does to put in this category moves such as the concessions of 1955, which were described as permanent and which have remained untampered with, viewed in retrospect. It clearly does not do to do as Wolfe does and downgrade as purely tactical, of short-range significance, post-Stalin liberalization and curbing of one man dictatorship, which have remained substantially with us now for 16 years.[75] The indicated criteria, it seems to me, should be the Soviets' own assessment of the movement at the time it was made and the length of time before its reversal or other substantial alteration.

What is urgently needed to construct a firm and well-substantiated image of Soviet conduct, to bring more nearly into single focus the

75. See discussion above in Chapter 3, pp. 93–94.

images currently in force, and to improve upon the modest start in this direction made by the imagists of the sample is care in small things—this is the sum and substance of the conclusion to which the argument of this chapter points. Care in defining and differentiating concepts, to the end of being as conceptually clear as humanly possible and avoiding the error of simplism; care in matching historical data and concept and avoiding capricious sifting procedures; care in assessing the complete array of such data, or a representative portion thereof, and avoiding a biased sample; care in aggregating; and care in doing the foregoing without overdoing—these are what we who are students in the field ought to be doing to improve the quality of our product, and so the help and advice that can be offered policy-makers dealing with the Soviet Union. The Triska and Finley type of study, shorn of its excesses, exemplifies the desideratum.

Not urgently needed, on the other hand, is the kind of discussion into which most extended considerations of method in Soviet and Communist studies lapse. I refer to the debates on explanatory theories, on typologies, on Kremlinology, and on comparativism earlier recounted: issues which we should have long since stopped worrying: issues whose resolution one way or another is not essential to the effective discharge of the tasks immediately at hand. Explanatory theories, yes. But the proper time to consider them is after we have learned all we can from the data, after we have learned accurately and precisely to describe the dimensions they are to explain. Typologies, certainly. But they are not necessary. We should be past the point of arguing whether "totalitarian" should be defined this way or that, or whether it is more or less "correct" than some other concept of type. Kremlinology? By all means. Whatever we may be able to learn about relative position in the power struggle from such conventional signs as order of appearance at public festivals, so much the better. Let us not, however, suppose that the Kremlinological is the only possible approach to Soviet political data, or that there are not many pressing things to be done that can be done perfectly well without it. Comparative study? Here we have something truly of importance, the activity of comparing being one we should have long since been engaging in as a matter of course. For description of Soviet behavior in its various elements becomes meaningful and useful to the extent that it is contrasted with similar description of the conduct of other nations, similarly assessed. Yet comparing, too, is not absolutely essential: without it, too, much can be done.

I do not mean we should dispense entirely with discussion of the more fundamental issues of concept and method. On the contrary, I believe it is right that some effort be devoted to a continuing critique at this highest level of abstraction. There is cerainly need, at what might be called the next level down, of further discussion of schemata or models for analyzing conduct in general and for forwarding the comparative study of such conduct. More work like that of Modelski and Rosenau would be welcome, as would a critique of the categories that I use and block out in Table 4. Finally, there is and always will be room—at the lowest level—for historical studies, for studies verifying the basic data, temporally ordering the same and proffering explanations of particular sequences, of which Ulam's is not only one of the most recent but also one of the most illustrious examples.

Nor do I mean to imply a belief that the care in little things advocated will resolve finally the outstanding issues of substance dividing the academic fraternity in this field. It will not. It will not yield perfect knowledge. It will not answer those who claim to apprehend the essence of the Soviet animal and to have classified that animal finally and irrefutably.

No, I am urging that at least for the time being, the most efficient and productive "research strategy" for students in the field is to raise the proportion of total effort devoted to supplying, at the middle level of abstraction, a thoughtful, coherent scheme for characterizing the subject conduct. Above all, I am urging the indispensability of increasing sharply the proportion assigned to improving the operation of matching concept and datum that defines the crucial moment in inquiry—for the proper goal is the reduction of imperfections, and for accomplishing this these measures offer today the best hope.

CHAPTER 7

Illustration: An Analysis of Soviet Faithlessness

No facet of Soviet behavior has raised more hackles, provoked more unrestrained emotionalism, than its morality or rectitude. None has evoked more immediate and violent a visceral response than the two elements of this facet upon which Machiavelli expatiated so cynically, so shrewdly, so tellingly in Chapter 18 of *The Prince*—honesty and fidelity to promise. The orthodox view, buttressed by suitable quotes from Lenin, is that the Soviets are utterly immoral, that they lie and break their word as seems expedient, that the truth is not in them, that treaties to them are but scraps of paper—in short, that they are disciples of the principle that the end justifies the means. Few are those who, while conceding the existence of many instances of wrongdoing, are not sure the accusation is warranted in all its extremeness, fewer still those who believe that, in whatever the degree in which it may be warranted, the USSR is not much different from other states.

The objective of the present chapter is to explore the infidelity element of this topic, and to do so in conformity with and in exemplification of the canons of right method set forth in preceding ones. Accordingly, it proposes first to describe contending views and probe underlying procedures, then to set up and apply what appear to be the best possible definitions and analytical rules for resolving intelligently the matters at issue.

The need for such an exploration, substantial in any case, acquires added urgency from the recent Soviet invasion of Czechoslovakia. For with this clear-cut case of violation of commitments vividly before him, even the friendliest of observers must harbor some doubt as to whether Soviet observance of desirable norms of international morality can become sufficiently high to make true peace more than a vain hope. And this doubt can be dissipated one way or the other only through a thorough look at the record.

EXISTING VIEWS AND TREATMENTS

Existing academic views on the topic of Soviet infidelity range from extremely to moderately unfavorable, correlating closely with overall views of conduct. I summarize them, and the associated treatments, in the usual order, starting with those of more extreme persuasion found in the works of our sample, specifically Kintner's and Kulski's.

Kintner's view, quite briefly, is that the Soviet Union does not believe in the sanctity of international treaties, and enters into such with no intention of honoring them, but only to lull opponents to sleep while preparing their undoing.[1] The source to which he refers as authority is a staff study entitled *Soviet Political Agreements and Results* that was made in 1956 for the Subcommittee on Internal Security of the Senate Committee on the Judiciary.[2] This study not only carrying the endorsement of the Kintner book, but as well typifying a certain mode of analyzing this facet of Soviet conduct fairly common among critics of Soviet behavior along this line, academic and nonacademic alike, I give it more than passing mention.

The core of *SPAR–1956* is made up of a foreword by Senator James O. Eastland, Chairman of the Senate Subcommittee on Internal Security, which sums up the study and its conclusions, and the study itself, a 52-page chronology of Soviet political treaties and agreements entered into in the years 1917–55 and the results thereof. The essence of the foreword can be summed up in this excerpt from the first, or 1955, edition of the study:

1. William R. Kintner, and others, *The New Frontier of War: Political Warfare Present and Future* (Chicago: Regnery, 1962), p. 103.
    2. US Congress, Senate, Committee on the Judiciary, Subcommittee to Investigate the Administration of the Internal Security Act and Other Internal Security Laws, 84th Congress, 2nd Session, Document no. 125, 1956 (hereinafter cited as *SPAR-1956*). This is a revision of *Soviet Political Agreements and Violations,* 84th Congress, 1st Session, Document no. 85, 1955 (hereinafter cited as *SPAV-1955*). A more recent revision is *Soviet Political Agreements and Results, Revised to January 1, 1964,* 88th Congress, 2nd Session, 1964 (hereinafter referred to as *SPAR-1964*).

The staff studied nearly a thousand treaties and agreements . . . which the Soviets have entered into not only with the United States, but with countries all over the world. The staff found that in the 38 short years since the Soviet Union came into existence, its Government has broken its word to virtually every country to which it ever gave a signed promise. It signed treaties of non-aggression with neighbouring states and then absorbed those states. It signed promises to refrain from revolutionary activity inside the countries with which it sought "friendship," and then cynically broke those promises. . . . It keeps no international promises at all unless doing so is clearly advantageous to the Soviet Union. . . . I seriously doubt whether during the whole history of civilization any great nation has ever made as perfidious a record as this in so short a time.[3]

These words are surrounded by an almost random series of statements detailing various Communist misdeeds, reporting official America's testimony to Communist untrustworthiness, generalizing the organic evilness of communism, and exemplifying the contention that the Communists themselves frequently and openly boast of the worthlessness of their pledges. Outstanding among the last is Stalin's famous comment to the effect that "sincere diplomacy is no more possible than dry water or wooden iron."[4]

The *SPAR–1956* study itself, while a chronology, is best described as an interrupted chronology. It lists chronologically, in ordinary type, what purport to be the political agreements entered into by the USSR in the years named (1917–55). It lists violations of these agreements in boldface type. However, the violations appear not in their rightful chronological places, but follow hard upon the agreements to which they apply. A representative sequence, rephrased and somewhat abbreviated, with italics serving for boldface, reads: 1926 (April): *Germany and USSR concluded a treaty of friendship and neutrality*; 1926 (July): Latvia and USSR concluded frontier dispute agreement; 1926 (August 15): Afghanistan and the USSR settled the Urta-Tagal dispute; 1926 (August 22): Uruguay recognized the USSR; 1926 (August 31): Afghanistan and the USSR concluded a nonaggression

3. *SPAR*-1956, p. viii.
4. Quoted in ibid., p. ix.

pact; *1946 (June 14): Afghanistan was forced to cede the border terri-tory of Kushka to the USSR;* 1926 (September): Lithuania and the USSR concluded a nonaggression pact, protocols of 1931 and 1934 extending the life of the treaty until 1945; *See p. 2, Under Lithuanian-Soviet treaty of April 12, 1920* (reference to Soviet imposition of mutual assistance pact on Lithuania in 1939 and invasion of same in 1940).[5] Of the total number of entries in the study (in round numbers, 580), 350 refer to agreements entered into, 230 to the results thereof, which, it is apparent from the context, the authors consider violations.[6]

SPAR–1956 lists many Soviet actions whose categorization as treaty violations few would contest. At the same time, close inspection reveals a number of weaknesses in the data and the treatment given them, and, these corrected, the conclusion then pointed to would be one somewhat milder than the one drawn by Chairman Eastland.

In the first place, some of the acts of commitment called "pledges" or moves called "violations" are based on constructions of dubious value or no value at all. It is hardly useful to consider on a par with a specific promise to a specific country such acts of commitment as accession to broad principles of general applicability, such as those constituting the Atlantic Charter or the Kellogg-Briand Pact.[7] For the question of whether subsequent deed has or has not conformed almost vanishes in a fog of obscurity. Similarly, some more specific pledges, as that made by Soviet leaders at the 1955 summit meeting to consider "reunification of Germany by means of free elections . . . carried out in conformity with the national interests of the German people and the interests of European security," are too vaguely worded to support the charge of violation later brought against the Soviets by Secretary Dulles for their refusal to discuss German reunification before settlement of the problem of European security.[8] Downright error is it to classify the Soviet vetoes in the UN as violations of the UN Charter.[9] Reprehensible though these may be, they

5. Ibid., p. 5.
6. They were so labeled in *SPAV*-1955 (above, n. 2).
7. *SPAR*-1956, pp. 6, 14.
8. On this point cf. John M. MacIntosh, *The Strategy and Tactics of Soviet Foreign Policy* (New York: Oxford University Press, 1963), p. 114.
9. *SPAR*-1956, p. 32.

clearly conform to that instrument. Also erroneous is it to describe
aggression by a flesh-and-blood army as a violation of a convention
defining aggression.[10] Action in the realm of the concrete and historical can violate only agreements referring to the concrete and historical. Agreements referring to the realm of the conceptual, like
agreements on definition, can be violated only by actions referring to
the conceptual realm, such as announcement of acceptance of a different and inconsistent definition.

In the second place, the record of Soviet malefactions is inflated by
a rather considerable amount of double counting. A single action is
at times seen as a violation of a number of different versions of one
and the same pledge. Invasion of Polish soil in September 1939, for
instance, is conceived to be in violation of the 1932 Nonaggression
Treaty beween the two countries, the 1934 renewal of the treaty, and
a 1938 reaffirmation of adherence to that treaty.[11] Nothing is said to
explain why a treaty and a protocol of extension should be considered
separate instruments, and an act inconsistent with the provisions of
the treaty-as-extended should be counted as two violations—especially
when the treaty as originally drawn up would, absent the extension,
have lapsed by the time the act in question was committed. Sometimes, too, what might seem to be a single act, constituting a single
infraction, is broken into several components, constituting several
infractions. So counted as infringements of the USSR-Polish Nonaggression Treaty (in its various forms mentioned above) are the
Soviet-German secret protocol concerning spheres of influence in East
Europe of August 23, 1939, the Soviet invasion of Poland of September 17, the incorporation of southeastern Poland into the Ukrainian
Republic on November 1, 1939, and the incorporation of northeastern
Poland into the White Russian Republic on November 2, 1939.[12] In
consequence of these proliferations in combination, the Soviet action
against Poland in August and September 1939 is marked down as 15
violations of one and the same instrument. This is somewhat exag-
gerating matters.

In the third place, even if the foregoing are overlooked, the aggre-

10. Ibid., p. 7.
11. Ibid., pp. 7, 10, 12.
12. Ibid., p. 3.

gating of the data into a judgment of a total turpitude overlooks the evidence of observance also contained in the study. Although many of the instruments listed (about 100) are counted as having been violated one or more times during their existence, many more (about 250) are not so listed, and those that are, are also implicitly presented as having no violation charged against them for periods of varying length. The presumption in these cases is of observance rather than nonobservance.

Kulski deals with the matter in a section, "Soviet Respect for Treaties," that heads a long chapter measuring Soviet behavior against the "Pancha Shila" or five basic principles governing the relations of states first announced in the Sino-Indian agreement of 1954.[13] This section he introduces with the observation that the Soviet record in this area is long and "far from encouraging." He then proceeds to back up this observation with a survey of the "most glaring examples" of disrespect. The acts constituting the violations in question turn out to be the following familiar 14: in Asia, the conquest of Georgia in 1921 and of Bukhara and Khiva in 1925, and the denunciation of the Treaty of Neutrality with Japan in 1945; in Europe, the attacks upon Finland and Poland in 1939 and the incorporation of parts of Rumania and all the Baltic states in 1940, the unilateral denunciation of the pact with Yugoslavia in 1949, the retention of troops in Hungary and Rumania following the removal of troops from Austria in 1955, and the intervention in Hungary in 1956. Kulski's survey, while on the whole more careful than that on which Kintner bases his position, nevertheless exhibits some of the same defects. Like *SPAR–1956*, he makes much of the fact that the Soviets "systematically violated" the precise definitions of aggression incorporated in the Convention on the Definition of Aggression of 1933 (which he reproduces almost in full)—unmindful of the absurdity of the notion of definition-violation. Moreover, like the authors of *SPAR–1956*, he feels that mere enumeration of violations is all that is required of him to substantiate a generally negative conclusion.

Other than Kintner and Kulski, adherents of the extreme view stop short of full consideration of the matter, normally confining themselves to unsupported generalization or the more or less random nota-

13. Wladyslaw W. Kulski, *Peaceful Coexistence: An Analysis of Soviet Foreign Policy* (Chicago: Regnery, 1959), pp. 303–12.

tion of particular instances of violation. The Overstreets affirm flatly that the Soviet Union has "never been known to respect a treaty which it has signed"; that Stalin broke every agreement he made with respect to the East European countries; that the USSR holds the world's record for treaty violation.[14] They also detail violation of the Yalta and Potsdam agreements on Germany, though somewhat mysteriously and inconsistently claiming that (apparently, as hard as he might try) Stalin never succeeded in breaking the four-power agreement on Berlin.[15] Wolfe generalizes that the Soviets carry out only such agreements as are self-enforcing, elsewhere pointing to the postwar seizures in East Europe as contrary to the pledges made in the Atlantic Charter and other pacts.[16]

Those who hold less extreme though still dim views of Soviet behavior in this dimension are rarer and commonly have less to say. Commonly they mention in passing certain violations without giving undue emphasis thereto or generalizing therefrom. Kennan, for instance, mentions violations of Brest-Litovsk, of early promises to China, and of the Roosevelt-Litvinov agreements with the United States; and Mosely mentions violations of Yalta and the postwar agreements.[17] But neither proceeds to generalization, though Mosely does advert vaguely late in his work to Soviet lack of moral restraints.[18] One should add at this point the views of Professors Triska and Slusser, for though their excellent works on Soviet treaties are of too specialized a nature to form part of the sample scrutinized by this essay, their judgments obviously merit high respect. On balance, this view finds the Soviet record poor.[19] Yet the authors note that in certain

14. Harry and Bonaro Overstreet, *The War Called Peace: Khrushchev's Communism* (New York: Norton, 1961), pp. 84, 175, 327.

15. Ibid., p. 175.

16. Bertram D. Wolfe, *Communist Totalitarianism: Keys to the Soviet System,* rev. ed. (Boston: Beacon Press, 1961), pp. 300, 253.

17. George F. Kennan, *Russia and the West under Lenin and Stalin* (Boston: Little, Brown, 1961), pp. 42, 262, 299; Philip E. Mosely, *The Kremlin and World Politics: Studies in Soviet Policy and Action* (New York: Vintage, 1960), p. 313.

18. *The Kremlin and World Politics,* p. 542.

19. Jan F. Triska and Robert M. Slusser, *The Theory, Law, and Practice of Soviet Treaties* (Stanford, Cal.: Stanford University Press, 1962), Chapters 26 and 27. Hereinafter cited as *Soviet Treaties.*

parts of the record—that is, in respect to certain categories of treaties and certain stretches of time—the reverse is true and the record fair.[20]

Those who suggest mixed or mildly favorable views of Soviet fidelity to promise—who find it neither outstandingly good nor outstandingly bad—are also rarer, also have less to say. Halle claims that the Soviets did not necessarily renege on the Yalta pledge to hold free elections in East Europe, advancing the curious argument that in Soviet terminology "the people" excludes all but workers, that the Communist Party is considered to articulate the will of this group, hence that what was done in the "elections" of 1945–48 that established Communist rule in these lands was not inconsistent with the instrument to which the Soviets subscribed. Schuman hints at something of the same argument. Fleming, when he does touch on the subject, as likely as not refers to instances of Soviet observance rather than violation of pledge. Triska and Finley, whose four pages on the subject deal less with violations themselves than with Soviet justifications thereof, conclude with the backhanded observation that clearly the USSR has not broken *all* its treaties. Lukacs takes the most reflective view; while noting that many agreements have been violated (such as the Yalta Declaration on Liberated Europe), he notes also that some agreements have been kept (e.g. the Yalta provisions on the Far East), pointing out that a fair investigation of the matter should attend to the latter as well as the former.[21]

The official Soviet view of the treaty relation and their behavior in connection with it lies at the other extreme from that of Kintner and Kulski. Treaties and the observance principle, *pacta sunt servanda,* are sacrosanct on this view, while the performance record is immaculate. To the charges of violation brought against them by other nations,

20. Ibid., pp. 394–95.
21. Louis J. Halle, *The Cold War as History* (New York: Harper & Row, 1967), pp. 69–70; Frederick L. Schuman, *The Cold War: Retrospect and Prospect,* 2nd ed. (Baton Rouge: Louisiana State University Press, 1967), p. 83; Denna F. Fleming, *The Cold War and Its Origins: 1917–1960,* 2 vols. (Garden City, N.Y.: Doubleday, 1961), pp. 116, 172–73, 267; Jan F. Triska and David D. Finley, *Soviet Foreign Policy* (New York: Macmillan, 1968), pp. 418–21; John Lukacs, *A New History of the Cold War,* 3rd ed., expanded, of *A History of the Cold War* (Garden City, N.Y.: Doubleday, 1966), pp. 55, 89 n., 144, 331 n.

the Soviets make one or another of four standard rejoinders.[22] In the case of alleged violations of treaties originally entered into by the tsarist government (as repudiation of debts), the standard rejoinder is that they are not bound by such treaties, that profound revolution such as that of 1917 absolves a new government of the duty of observance, conferring upon it the right of annulment. In the case of alleged violations of an obligation to refrain from hostile propaganda, the standard rejoinder is that the promise binds only the state, and that not state but Party is responsible for the acts in question. In other cases—depending upon the particular circumstances—the rejoinders have been the extinction of or prior violation by the other party. The former was used as excuse for entering eastern Poland on September 17, 1939, in prima facie contravention of the treaties of 1921 and 1932, the line of thought being that German invasion from the west earlier in the same month had effectively eliminated the Polish state. The latter was used, for instance, in justification of the attack on Finland in November 1939, the particular line of argument being that Finland had "systematically violated" its obligations under the Non-aggression Treaty of 1932 through actions showing no intention of complying with the provisions of the treaty. In short and in sum, the Soviets rebut allegations of violation and maintain their claim to a 100 percent fulfillment record by contending that what appear to be violations are really not such, either because the Soviet State is not properly speaking party to the commitment infringed upon, or because though a party it has been released by the extinction or prior violations of the partner. This position makes unnecessary, of course, any detailed examination of the topic.

The foregoing testifies to the fact that views of the fidelity element in Soviet conduct, like views of Soviet conduct in general, (1) diverge sharply and (2) are poorly substantiated if indeed substantiated at all. The topic is not always considered in general terms. Where it is, it is either dispatched unceremoniously with a quick, unsupported generalization or, if supported, given support shot through with defects of one kind or another. Even Professors Triska and Slusser's major work, admirable as it is, barely brushes the topic, disclaiming

22. Triska and Slusser, *Soviet Treaties,* pp. 390–94.

extensive treatment.[23] A new investigation is therefore very much in order, starting with a reexamination of concept and method.

CONCEPTUALIZATION AND METHOD

A careful study of the fidelity-to-promise facet of the behavior of a state or regime might usefully begin by considering the objective of analysis and clarifying, in its light, the terms and method to be used. The student's interest in the faithlessness or faithfulness of a given regime to its obligation is not, to begin with, the statesman's interest in scoring points for immediate advantage, nor yet the moralist's or lawyer's interest in assessing ethical standing or measuring against some abstract standard of perfection. A student's ultimate concern, I would suggest, is to learn how well or poorly the regime has contributed or now contributes to a stable international order, how well it is likely to contribute in the future, and what conditions may improve, what tarnish, that contribution. Accordingly, the student is interested in pledge-making and implementation not for its own sake, but for the light they throw on this larger concern. Terms are well defined, method well devised, to the extent that they enable him to determine whether, or to what degree, on the whole and on the average, the regime he is examining is in this respect a stabilizing influence within the larger global society, playing the game according to the rules.

The foregoing considerations suggest that the terms for analyzing a regime's record of pledge-fulfillment be given a somewhat more practical definition than is customary. Specifically, they suggest that "pledges" be confined to promises that are (1) strictly ascribable to the regime in question or its agents, (2) unambiguously obligational and (3) specific in character, (4) encased in formal instruments like treaties and, moreover, such instruments as (5) may reasonably be considered to have remained in force and not, practically speaking, annulled by an act of the other side that the regime in question might plausibly consider a prior violation. On the other hand, and further, they suggest that the label "violation" *not* be withheld from an act on the grounds either (6) of its being ascribable to an agent who is not so in law or (7) of its being consistent with the pledge on the actor's constructions thereof.

23. Ibid., p. 389.

The reasoning behind these constructions can be quickly explained. Confining the analysis to promises that are (1) strictly ascribable to the regime itself, as against those authored by a previous government, is to take note of the fact that the regime's standing as contributor to a stable international order is far more affected by how well it fulfills its own promises than how well it fulfills the promises of a predecessor. Granted that there is in general a stabilizing value in a rule of international law which requires a new regime, even a radically new one, to assume the obligations of an old. Still and all, it makes little sense to convict a government of infidelity when, as in the Soviet case, what is involved is repudiation of the debts, treaties, etc., not only that it never contracted but that were contracted by a predecessor whose philosophy and existence were anathema to it and, in fact, were held in general disrepute. This is a little like holding the son responsible for the sins of the father. If immorality is involved, it is immorality in a narrow, legalist sense only, not in a broad one.

Confining the analysis to promises that are (2) unambiguously promissory in character, that is, to statements clearly implying acceptance of an obligation, is to take note of the fact that to consider statements ambiguously promissory in character, like statements of intent or belief, is to resolve, or rather dissolve, the fidelity question into the broader question of conformity of practice and preachment. And this in turn is to do two things: to replace a fairly definite and clear-cut question with one stickier and harder to determine, and to apply a standard only distantly related to standing as contributor or noncontributor to a stable international order, all nations falling short in some measurable degree of practicing what they preach. To treat statements comprising the Atlantic Charter, for instance—statements of fact, desire, endeavor, hope, and commitment to principle—as unequivocal pledges, unequivocal assumptions of obligation, is to introduce considerable confusion into the discussion and to obscure the real issues.

By promises that are (3) specific in character are meant pledges tendered other states specifically named, rather than the generality thereof. Confining the analysis to such pledges registers the fact that, from the point of view of contributing to a stable order, it is more important that a nation abide, say, by a commitment to neighbor X to respect neighbor X's boundaries than by some vague promise to the

world at large to behave itself for ever and ever. A Soviet commitment
to respect the territorial integrity of Poland is a weightier matter than
a Soviet commitment under Article 10 of the Charter of the League
of Nations to "respect and preserve . . . the territorial integrity . . . of
all Members of the League."

Confining the analysis to promises that are (4) encased in formal
instruments is to take note of a qualitative difference, insofar as contribution to stability is concerned, between adherence to promises
given in exchange and under the most solemn of conditions and adherence to promises not so given. A unilateral pledge not to resume
nuclear tests, for instance, such as the three nuclear powers individually made in the summer of 1959, is one thing;[24] a signature on the
test-ban treaty, such as was later concluded, is quite another. Sub-
scription to an oral understanding not to use capriciously the veto
power granted by the UN Charter is a less binding matter than sub-
scription to a written agreement not to do so. These comments, and
those of the preceding paragraph, are not to be understood as arguing
that observance of general pledges, or of pledges unilaterally given,
or of pledges given in oral form only is a matter of no consequence.
They argue rather that disregard of pledges of these types, to which
all nations even as all men are prone, do not—unlike disregard of
pledges specific, reciprocated, and written—seriously and directly
threaten achievement of a viable international order.

Confining the analysis to promises that (5) may reasonably be considered to have remained in force and not, practically speaking, annulled by what might plausibly be construed a violation of the *quid
pro quo* on the other side is, again, simply to note the reasonableness
of the position that violation of a contract by one side releases the
other and terminates the arrangement, and that commission then of
the act proscribed is commission under conditions that differ radically,
from the point of view of contribution to stability, from commission
under the earlier conditions. Release because of prior violation by the
other side is a reasonable defense. This we recognize, for instance,
when we defend Western rearmament of West Germany against the
charge of violating the Potsdam agreements. For the defense runs in

24. Or were supposed to have made. The statements in question were
declarations of resolve or intent only. See Richard P. Stebbins, *The United
States in World Affairs 1959* (New York: Random House, 1960), p. 162.

terms of prior violation of the same instruments, through earlier Soviet rearmament of East Germany.

The rules implying looser construction also find their defense in the common sense of the matter. Refusing to withhold the label "violation" from an act (6) on grounds of its being ascribable to an agent who is not so in law hardly requires justification. It is simply to insist upon what should be insisted upon in all investigations political—namely, that one look to the actualities rather than to the legalities of the matter, that one not, for instance, refuse to treat the Bay of Pigs invasion as an American move simply because it was carried out by an organization not legally an agent of the American government. Inadmissible, too, is the refusal to withhold the label "violation" from an act (7) on grounds of the act's being consistent with the pledge on the actor's construction. Questions of construction, and of conformity of the generality of the pledge and the particularity of the act, are questions for the analyst to settle. And although in making this determination he should take account of the construction put on the pledge by party X, this is not the only factor he need take account of (there is party Y's construction of the pledge too), and he need give it no greater weight (indeed, *should* give it no greater weight) than seems reasonable to him, all things considered. One doesn't decide a case involving violation of a contract between individuals on grounds of one party's interpretation of the terms, especially when such interpretation involves definitions that border on the meaningless.

As to method, considerations respecting the end for the sake of which the analysis of a regime's pledge-keeping is undertaken reinforce what simply equity requires—namely, that the student look at and weigh the record as a whole. Whatever will do as sensible measure of pledge-fulfillment, even the most superficial reflection shows one thing that clearly will *not* do—namely, simply citing and enumerating instances of violation. It will not do to convict country A as a chronic violator, whose word is not to be trusted, on the grounds that it violated one treaty in year X, another two years later, etc., for a grand total of 17 violations. That a business firm in the course of its career has reneged 17 times on its contracts tells us little about its trustworthiness save that it is not perfect, a quality which hardly distinguishes it from others of its kind. Nor, *mutatis mutandis,* does it tell us much about performance along this line to learn that a given nation or corporation adhered faithfully to this or that contract, this or that many contracts. Clearly, more information is needed to reach a reasoned judgment on the matter. That more is the *total* number of instances in which pledge-keeping is at issue, including both the number of instances in which pledges have been kept and the number in which they have not been kept. One wants to know of the business firm whether it is a large one, part to hundreds of contracts, each of many years' duration, or a small one, party to few, of short duration. Of a state or regime one wants to know the same. What has been the full range of its obligations? How many have there been in the various categories? How long were they or have they been in force? Frequency is of the essence. The proper method is unavoidably statistical.

To these rules of procedures should be added an injunction against such obvious distortions as double-counting. If counting is of the essence, as the necessary means of appraising frequency, things counted should be carefully discriminated, duplication avoided. To convict a country of a treaty violation because it seized an area on the treaty partner's border in defiance of a nonaggression clause is one thing. To convict it of 10 or 20 violations because it seized one-half of the town one day, the other half the next, and because the nonaggression treaty had been recently renewed and still more recently reaffirmed in an exchange of notes, is to impart to its offenses spurious magnitude. To applaud it for a record of treaty observance similarly compiled is to do the same to its virtues.

The first five of these rules tend to give the accused the benefit of the doubt. And it may be that, on balance, the entire set has this tendency. Fairness to the accused is not, however, the reason for invoking them. That reason, to repeat, is that the more limited set of criteria involved promise best to contribute to a proper understanding of the behavior under scrutiny. The less limited set, besides making more difficult the assessment of observance or nonobservance in specific cases, in effect ties fidelity to a perfectionism neither met by nor to be anticipated of any nation. What is even more important, it ties fidelity to a standard of performance above what is required to secure a viable international order. The world is a world of competing sovereignties, each with a somewhat biased view of its own behavior, each with the imperfections of the normally self-assertive. Before deciding whether this or that regime contributes on balance to stability, intelligent procedure demands that one take account of these norms of self-assertiveness, these imperfections.

APPLICATION: PLEDGES IN GENERAL

If the foregoing is correct, sound procedure for analyzing infidelity requires assembling all unambiguous, specific, formalized pledges entered into by the Soviet regime or its agents, or a suitably devised sample thereof; estimating their duration and, in the case of termination due to Soviet abrogation, giving due regard to the possibility of prior violation by the partner; enumerating violations on the rules of construction given; and, finally, relating the pledges and violations in some meaningful way.

At first glance, this appears a herculean task indeed. The Soviet Union has been party to a very large number of treaties and other instruments comparable or near-comparable in legal status. According to supplements to Professors Triska and Slusser's excellent work already cited, the Soviet government put its signature to 2,586 such instruments in the 41-year period 1971 through 1957 and to an added 1,058 in the succeeding 1958-through-1962 quinquennium.[25] This gives a grand total of 3,644 for the years 1917 through 1962, and provided the annual rate for 1958-through-1962 (210) has been maintained, the grand total as of the end of 1968 exceeded 4,900 and as of this moment of writing (early 1970) has gone over the 5,100 mark. Totals, it might be added, exclude secret treaties. For although, as Professors Triska and Slusser neatly put it, "That they [the Soviets] have engaged in secret diplomacy is a matter of public record," the record is apparently not quite public enough to permit an exact calculation of the number of agreements thus entered into.[26]

Soviet treaties fall into a number of diverse groups. Of the total of 2,475 instruments entered into during the 40-year period 1918 through 1957, those of an economic type (treaties of trade and com-

25. Triska and Finley, *Soviet Foreign Policy*, p. 422.
26. *Soviet Treaties*, p. 375.

merce, payments agreements and treaties of economic aid, etc.) numbered 850, or about 34 percent.[27] At the same time, instruments of a political character (treaties of alliance, neutrality, or nonaggression, of the establishment of diplomatic relations and demarcation of spheres of influence, etc.) numbered 588, or 24 percent, while instruments of the residual category, called "functional-technical" and made up of treaties on communication and transportation, on legal and cultural matters, on repatriations, etc., numbered 1,037 or 42 percent. For the ensuing five-year period, 1958 through 1962, on the other hand, when a stepped-up rate produced 1,058 more instruments, respective numbers and percentages were as follows: economic—528, or about 50 percent; political—163, or about 16 percent; and functional-technical —360, or about 34 percent.[28] The comparison is important, for it documents two important conclusions respecting trends elsewhere explicitly set forth by Professor Triska—namely, that the share of economic instruments in the total has been increasing significantly, that of political instruments declining.[29]

Yet if the task at first seems herculean, on second look it appears more manageable. For more extended scrutiny reveals two considerations that narrow appreciably the scope of legitimate disagreement.

The first of these considerations is that those who have studied the subject with care and whose opinions are entitled to respect seem to agree that Soviet observance of nonpolitical treaties is fair to good. Writing in 1946, Michael Florinsky quotes a number of flattering statements from Western traders on performance in the commercial category and concludes that, "The observance by the Soviet Union of her economic commitments is on the whole satisfactory and offers little ground for legitimate suspicion and complaint."[30] Writing in 1962, Triska and Slusser, in their chapter on violations, assert that in these nonpolitical categories violations have been "much less fre-

27. Jan F. Triska, "Soviet Treaty Law: A Quantitative Analysis," *Law and Contemporary Problems* 29, no. 4 (Autumn 1964): 904.
28. Calculated from data in ibid., pp. 902–04, and in Triska and Finley, *Soviet Foreign Policy*, p. 422.
29. "Soviet Treaty Law," p. 903.
30. "The Soviet Union and International Agreements," *Political Science Quarterly* 61, no. 1 (March 1946): 88.

quent" than in the political, and that trade agreements carefully limited and defined have "enjoyed a relatively high standard of performance on the part of the Soviet Union."[31] They assert the same, or something close to it, of cultural exchange agreements.[32] Harry Schwartz reports in 1963 that in the commercial field the Soviet Union has a reputation as a good commercial risk.[33] A listing of important postwar treaties which as of 1963 the Soviet Union had kept, according to the State Department, bears this out. Of this list of 27 instruments, 25 fall in the economic and functional-technical categories (the cultural exchange agreements for 1960–61 and 1962–63, the International Sugar Agreement, etc.).[34] It is also noteworthy that the more or less standard citations of demerit put out by State, Defense, and other interested US agencies include virtually none from these categories.

Final judgment on performance in the economic and functional-technical fields must await more intensive assembling and arraying of the data. But there is a presumption that throughout this range of pledges the Soviet fulfillment record is at least reasonably good. And this in turn means—to draw out the really important implication of the first consideration—that throughout a range of pledges that amounted to over 75 percent of the total for the 1918 through 1957 period, that rose to nearly 85 percent of the total for the quinquennium 1958 through 1962, and that for the six years in the immediate past would at the same relative rate of growth have exceeded 90 percent, the fulfillment record is at least reasonably good. And this further suggests that even if the Soviet Union is shown in default in respect to every single political treaty she has entered into, her overall performance record would still remain fair and improving.

The second consideration that helps narrow the scope of legitimate

31. *Soviet Treaties,* pp. 395, 400. See also Triska and Finley, *Soviet Foreign Policy,* p. 421.

32. *Soviet Treaties,* p. 401.

33. *New York Times,* July 26, 1963, p. 9.

34. Memorandum from the Department of State on Soviet Treaty Violations, August 22, 1963, cited as Appendix to US Congress, Senate, Committee on Foreign Relations, *Nuclear Test Ban Treaty: Hearings,* 88th Congress, 1st Session, 1963, pp. 967–68.

disagreement is that insofar as the political category is concerned, a rough-and-ready method is at hand for gauging fulfillment, and applying it leads to the provisional conclusion that the record, if not perfect, is no worse than mediocre or at least falls short of that perfidy ascribed to it by those of Ultra-Hard persuasion.

The rough-and-ready method comprises two major steps: taking an estimate of the overall magnitude of Soviet obligations in the category, and relating to it a second figure representing a generous estimate of the totality of violations, the result being what I might provisionally call an infidelity ratio. For making the first of these estimates the logical unit is the bound year, an obligational unit defined as 365 days of commitment to a single discrete pledge like a promise not to attack. Estimating the grand total of bound years is a matter, for a given period of time, of multiplying the number of political treaties entered into by an estimate of the average number of pledges per treaty, and the product in turn by an estimate of an average number of years of life per pledge. For making these calculations adequate materials are at hand in the form of Triska and Slusser's invaluable work already cited and the texts of Soviet treaties as found in such collections as the *British Foreign and State Papers*. A generous estimate of the totality of Soviet violations is already at hand in the form of *SPAR–56*, the *Soviet Political Agreements and Results* of the Senate subcommittee already referred to. For reasons noted above, *SPAR–1956* almost certainly overstates the case for Soviet infidelity, hence serving the valuable function of constituting a maximum indictment and establishing the upper limit of Soviet malfeasance.

Applying the method to the 38-year period 1917–55 (the period covered by *SPAR–1956*) yields the calculations and results that follow. Conservative estimates for the number of political treaties, the number of pledges per treaty, and the temporal life of an average pledge during this period are respectively 400, 5, and 10 years. The number of political treaties I derive by taking Triska and Slusser's figure of 588 for 1918 through 1957 (above), reducing it by 88 to give an estimated counterpart (500) for the period 1917–55, and further reducing it by 20 percent to allow for possible inflation due to inclusion of ambiguous, too general, and nonformalized pledges, the separate counting of protocols of extension, etc.[35] The number of pledges per treaty (5) and average life per pledge (10 years) are calculated on the approximately 40 separate political treaties for the period noted in Tables 7, 8, and 9 below. The total Soviet commitment of political character for the 38 years is therefore conservatively estimated at 20,000 pledge years. On the other side, the liberal estimate of total number of violations for the period that is provided by SPAR–1956 —liberal because the sum of all allegations, no allowance at all being made for the rules of construction and procedure outlined above—is 230. The infidelity ratio for the period therefore works out to 11.5 per thousand, or somewhat less than 1.2 percent. This is to say that the USSR fails to honor a political promise, on the average, in only about one month out of every 120 (or 10-year period) over which it is bound, observing the promise the other 119 months.

Because of the manner in which most uncertainties have been resolved, these quantifications of faithlessness are almost surely maximum figures. Yet if one were to argue otherwise, urging that SPAR–1956 overlooks some derelictions and compresses others into a single allegation when it should more properly treat them as several, the overall conclusion would change but slightly. For increasing the above ratio by a factor of 2 (or, for that matter, even 5) gives a product (2.5 percent or 6 percent as the case may be) that on the surface still hardly supports a judgment of utter perfidy.

The two considerations, while narrowing legitimate disagreement and raising a substantial presumption against an extreme and for a moderate view of the matter, nevertheless rest on data highly aggregative in nature, data which fail to discriminate the more critical types of pledge from the less critical types, that is, those more important to international stability from those less important. An adequate probe requires more than this. Needed also is a more selective effort, an effort directed at asesssing the record in respect to the more critical types referred to. Since the latter are to be found largely in the political field, one turns next to the subdivisions of this category.

35. Triska, in "Soviet Treaty Law" (p. 897), gives 175 as the average annual number of treaties of all types entered into in the 1953 through 1957 quinquennium. By applying to this figure the 25 percent estimated from the distribution data cited on p. 225 above, I get the figure 44 for political treaties for each of these years, or 88 for two of them.

APPLICATION: CRITICAL PLEDGE TYPES

Soviet treaty law distinguishes the following categories of political treaties: on the substantive side, treaties of alliance, mutual assistance, regional problems, nonaggression, neutrality, peace, guaranties of fulfillment; and, on the formal side, treaties establishing diplomatic relations.[36] Triska and Slusser supply a 10-class breakdown of treaties or agreements: (A) of alliance, mutual assistance, and friendship; (B) of neutrality and nonaggression; (C) of peace and armistice; (D) of recognition and diplomatic relations; (E) on general principles, future relations, etc.; (F) on questions of territory and spheres of influence; (G) on matters military and naval; (H) based on Great Power negotiations; (I) on international organization; and (J) on the political and military organization of the USSR and the Soviet bloc.[37] The range and character of individual pledges is fairly well, though not completely, suggested by these labels.

From the various pledge types incorporated in these treaty subcategories I choose as the most critical these five: (1) pledges of nonintervention in the partner's internal affairs, which are found in treaties of a number of the subcategories listed, but mainly in A and B; (2) pledges to other great powers incurred in the interests of establishing the general peace, which are found mainly in treaties of subcategories C and H; (3) pledges of mutual aid to a partner in case of aggression, found almost exclusively in treaties of subcategory A; (4) pledges of neutrality in the face of an attack upon a partner, and nonalignment, that is, nonparticipation in an alliance or coalition directed against a partner—pledges found largely in treaties of subcategory B; and (5) pledges of nonaggression against a partner, found also largely in treaties of subcategory B. Other kinds of pledges involved in the treaties of the various subcategories are commonly too general, as those found in treaties of subcategories E and I, or are too trivial in content (e.g. those of subcategories D and G), or have an objective hard to reconcile with a stable international order (those of subcategory F), or because of Soviet dominance of the partner(s) are more justly to be considered unilateral declarations than true promises (subcategory J).

36. Triska and Slusser, *Soviet Treaties,* p. 228.
37. Ibid., p. 568.

I take up the types in the order listed. Although incompletely carried out in the case of the first two for reasons to be made clear, the procedure is to apply the rules of conceptualization and method set forth on pp. 219–24 of the chapter and implicitly extended in the demonstrations on pp. 224–28. That is to say, the procedure (except in the case of the first two types) is to construct an exhaustive or near-exhaustive enumeration of unambiguous, specific, formal commitments of the Soviet regime, estimate their lives (in the case of termination due to Soviet abrogation giving due regard to the possibility of prior violation), juxtapose a maximum indictment, that is, a list of violations on constructions least favorable to the USSR, and relate violations to years-in-force in the form of infidelity ratios.

Nonintervention Pledges

In a typical nonintervention pledge, the Soviet government commits itself "not to interfere in any way in . . . [the] internal affairs" of the partner state and "to abstain more particularly from action of any kind calculated to promote or encourage agitation, propaganda, or attempted intervention designed to prejudice . . . territorial integrity or to transform by force the political or social regime of all or part of its territories."[38] Pledges of this character date back to the early days of the Soviet regime, and at least as far back as the 1921 Treaty of Riga with Poland.[39] They are found not only in the peace treaties ending the 1917–21 period of international turmoil, but in practically all of the mutual aid, neutrality, and nonaggression treaties (see Tables 7, 8, and 9 below for list), and as well in instruments of recognition and the establishment of diplomatic relations like the Litvinov-Roosevelt agreement of 1933 with the United States.

Insofar as nonintervention pledges are concerned, it can hardly be argued but that the Soviet record is close to perfect—perfectly faithless.[40] Relating years in which violation occurred to bound years in the period 1917–63, after the fashion suggested on pp. 224–28

---

38. Taken from Article V of the 1932 Treaty of Nonaggression with France, text of which is found in Leonard Shapiro, ed., *Soviet Treaty Series* (Washington, D.C.: Georgetown University Press, 1955), Vol. II (1929–39), p. 61.

39. Triska and Slusser, *Soviet Treaties*, p. 198.

40. Ibid., p. 395.

above, would almost certainly yield high ratios, maybe even ratios as high as 80 percent or more.

Of cases that might be cited in exemplification of this poor record, subsequent Soviet actions in the face of the Litvinov-Roosevelt agreement of 1933 are among the best known. In the interchanges constituting this agreement the Soviets promised to refrain from propaganda or other acts disturbing American tranquillity, prosperity, order, or security, to abstain from propaganda whose object was the bringing about by force of any change in the political or social order of the United States, and to refrain from permitting the formation of any group whose aim was the overthrow of the American political or social order. They nevertheless harbored the Third International on Soviet territory, controlled it, and through it directed the Communist Party of the United States in its intermittent campaigns to foster discontent and encourage violent overthrow of the American political and social order.[41] But this was standard operating procedure. They have done the same through the Comintern or more directly to most of the many other states, Communist and non-Communist alike, to whom they similarly have bound themselves over the course of their history. For instance, in contravention of their 1945 pledge to the Yugoslavs, they strove mightily to subvert the government of that country in the late '40s, using every conceivable means toward this end; in contravention of their pledge to Nationalist China in 1945, from 1948 on they contributed heavily to the overturn of that regime by the Chinese Communists in 1949; in contravention of their pledge to Czechoslovakia in 1943, they contributed materially to the overthrow of the democratic regime in 1948, and more recently, in the spring of 1969, to the overthrow of the humanely Communist regime of Alexander Dubcek.

The standard Soviet defense against allegations of this type is not that interventions of the kind elaborated did not occur—that they did has been admitted—but that they were the acts not of the Soviet government, but of the Comintern or, at best, the Soviet Party leadership.[42] In other words, such acts, though authored by Stalin, Zino-

41. Florinsky, "The Soviet Union and International Agreements," pp. 74–75.

42. Triska and Slusser, *Soviet Treaties*, p. 393.

viev, Molotov, etc., were authorized by these gentlemen in their capacity as Secretaries of the Comintern or, at best, the Communist Party of the Soviet Union, rather than as officials of the Soviet state. But this is a legalistic quibble of a kind inconsistent with our Rule 6. If one and the same group (the CPSU) is in control both of the Soviet government and (whether through the Comintern or not) of the Party apparatus of the partner to the treaty containing the nonintervention clause, then the pledge not to intervene and the intervening are essentially acts of one and the same party, however one slices it, and a violation has occurred. And that the CPSU was thus in control of parties in the partner state for much of the period at issue is a matter hardly open to question.[43]

At the same time, let us be clear that the validity of the indictment depends on showing the existence of the control relation in question. And although this can be demonstrated for most of the time under scrutiny (1917–63), it cannot be said to have existed all the time in all of the states to whom the USSR in this fashion has been bound. To find out for how long, in what particular cases, it may have lapsed requires a more extended study, partner by partner, year by year, than has yet been made. And for this reason the assessment of the high degree of faithlessness here reached must be considered provisional. On the other hand, we do know it has been lapsing in recent years. For the growth of polycentrism within the international Communist movement now obvious to all is another name for the dwindling control extending from the CPSU to national parties in the other states of the world: a development one clear implication of which is that, however high one places the overall infidelity ratio for this type of pledge for the 1917–63 period as a whole, that ratio has in recent years been a declining one.

Establishment-of-Peace Pledges

This second category of political pledge is really a catchall for specific engagements concerning the restoration of peace in Europe and the Far East entered into by the Soviet Union with the Western Allies in the war against Germany and Japan. These engagements are

43. See, for example, Bernard Morris, *International Communism and American Policy* (New York: Atherton, 1966), esp. pp. 35–43.

so numerous that an exhaustive listing is neither possible nor desirable. Suffice it to list as representative: under the armistice agreements of late 1944 and early 1945 with Rumania, Bulgaria, and Hungary, a commitment to act in concert with the other Allies on the Allied Control Commissions to be formed; under the Yalta agreements of February 1945, a commitment to assist liberated peoples to form interim governments broadly representative of all democratic elements and pledged to the earliest possible establishment through free elections of responsible government; under the Potsdam decisions of July 1945, commitments to the destruction of German militarism, the wiping out of nazism, the punishment of war criminals, the decentralization of the German political structure, the dissolution of concentrations of Germany's economic power, the treatment of Germany as a single economic unit, the limiting of reparations, etc.; under an agreement reached at the Moscow meetings of the Council of Foreign Ministers of April 1947, a commitment to the repatriation of all German prisoners of war by December 1, 1948; under the peace treaties of 1947 with Hungary, Bulgaria, and Rumania, a commitment to the establishment of the human rights of freedom of expression, of the press, of religion, of political association, etc., in these nations.

Insofar as this category too is concerned, it can hardly be argued but that the Soviet record has been bad, and that relating violation years to bound years would probably yield high infidelity ratios. Sound are the cases for alleging that the Soviets were in violation of the Yalta, Potsdam, and other late-war and early-postwar agreements in doing the following in the immediate postwar years: refusing to allow free elections to be held in Poland and the other East European countries occupied by her troops; refusing to consult other Allied members on the Allied Control Commission for these countries; interfering in the internal affairs of these countries; forcing discriminatory economic agreements on these countries; creating an East German "police force" trained and armed in quasi-military fashion; refusing to participate in the Four-Power meetings of the Berlin *Kommandatura* and the Control Council for all of Germany; blockading the ground access routes to Berlin; restricting to controlled parties the rights of political participation in East Germany; taking an undue amount of repara-

tions out of East Germany and refusing to report thereon; tendering
final recognition to the Oder-Neisse boundary, etc. The defense put
up by Schuman and others in the case of interference with democratic processes is not convincing. To acquit the Soviets of the charge
of violating the Yalta declaration on the grounds that they understand something different by the terms "democratic" and "free elections" than do we is inadmissible under our Rule 7. To do this is
utterly absurd when one takes account of the particular constructions
they favor. For to treat as a free and democratic election one in which
participation is confined to one or two Communist or Communist-
dominated parties is to make the terms in question meaningless and
so completely useless for analytic purposes.

There are certain considerations related to the matter of prior
violation that taken into account would probably modify these results
somewhat. As we know, some Western moves that appear to be violations of the agreements in question are excusable within our fifth
rule by virtue of being responses to prior violations from the Soviet
side—such, for example, as rearmament of West Germany. It is altogether likely that the same prove to be the case of certain Soviet
moves. Which ones, and how many, must await a rational ordering of
events, final ascription of terms "action" and "reaction," "challenge"
and "response," and final assignment of initial responsibility. But
some are likely to be found, even if the general conclusion of high
Soviet malefaction is not materially disturbed. It is also in point to
observe that, whatever the finding from such an inquiry, there is a
point in the ceaseless alternation of moves and countermoves, violations and counterviolations, where, the original agreements having
been so thoroughly honored rather in the breach than in the observance, it becomes senseless any longer to consider them in effect.
In the writer's judgment, that point should be placed at about the
year 1948, when the Berlin blockade brought the two sides close to hot
war, when Soviet control of East Europe had become consolidated,
and when the moves had been consummated or were on the way to
being consummated to accord the two parts of Germany separate
juridical status. In this view it is pointless to speak of subsequent
moves—as West German rearmament, the erection of the Berlin Wall
in 1961, etc.—as violations by either side. But how much these con-

siderations would soften the generally unfavorable results remains to be seen.

Mutual Assistance Pledges

Mutual assistance pledges (alternately, mutual aid or alliance pledges) to which the Soviet is party are of fairly uniform character. In a typical pledge of this type, the Soviets commit themselves to come to the aid of the partner should "notwithstanding" its "peaceful intention" said partner be "the object . . . of an unprovoked aggression" from some stated source.[44] The stated source may be generalized (any third country), semiparticularized (for instance, any European state), or particularized (e.g. Germany).

The Soviet regime has been party to about 30 unambiguous, specific, formalized mutual aid pledges in the 52 years of her existence, 23 major ones in the period 1917–63.[45] These latter Table 7 lists by period and year (Column 1), noting in each case the partner or promisee (Column 2), the threat the USSR is obligated to help repel (Column 3), the encasing instrument and clause (Column 4), and other data further commented on below. The earliest of these 23 were not entered into until the period of interest in collective security (1934–39), when the USSR bound itself in the manner indicated to France (1935), Czechoslovakia (1935), and Mongolia (1936). The 1939–41 period saw pledges extended to the Baltic countries, the war years to major-power allies Britain, France, and China, to the smaller East European countries which were invaded and took up arms against Germany (Poland, Czechoslovakia, Yugoslavia), and with Iran in a special three-way deal involving Britain. These pledges extended generally beyond fighting the war to helping repel renewed aggression from German or Japanese quarters in the postwar period. In 1948, in the post-war period of 1945–53, the USSR extended the com-

---

44. Taken from Article II of the 1935 Treaty of Mutual Assistance with France, the text of which is found in Shapiro, *Soviet Treaty Series,* Vol. II, p. 128.

45. Taken from Triska and Slusser, *Soviet Treaties,* pp. 569–70, the gentleman's agreement with Mongolia in 1934 being excluded because originally cast in verbal form only. The listing is not quite exhaustive: there should be added to it 1941 agreements with Czechoslovakia and France similar to the British and Polish ones cited.

TABLE 7

USSR: Mutual Assistance Pledges to Which a Party and Their Violation, 1917–63[a]

Period & Year[b] (1)	Promisee[c] (2)	Threat USSR Is Pledged to Help Repel[d] (3)	Encasing Instrument & Clause[e] (4)	Termination: Year & Manner[f] (5)	(6)	YIF Given[g] (7)	YIF Adjusted[h] (8)	Violation Years[i] (9)	Infidelity Ratio[j] (10)
1917–21	None								
1921–28	None								
1928–34	None								
1934–39									
1935	France	Aggr. by Eur. state	T/MA 2	1938	CET USSR	3	3	None	0
1935	Czech.	Aggr. by Eur. state[k]	T/MA 2	1938	CET USSR	3	3	None	0
1936	Mongolia	Any military attack	Pr./MA 2	1946	Repl.	10	0	None	—
1939–41									
1939	Estonia	Aggr. by Eur. power	P/MA 1	1940	Abro. USSR	1	1	1940	100
1939	Latvia	Aggr. by Eur. power	P/MA 1	1940	Abro. USSR	1	1	1940	100
1939	Lithuania	Aggr. by Eur. power	T/MA 2	1940	Abro. USSR	1	1	1940	100
1941–45									
1941	Britain	Germany during war	Agr./JA 1	1942	Repl.	1	1	None	0
1941	Poland	Germany during war	D/Coop. 2	1943	Abro. USSR	2	2	1943	50
1942	GB, Iran	Germany during war	T/A 3	1946	Expiry	4	4	None	0
1942	Britain	Germany during war; Renewed Ger. aggr.	T/A,C,MA 1,4	1955	Abro. USSR	13	13	1955	8
1943	Czech.	Germany during war; Renewed Ger. aggr.	T/F,MA,PWC 1,3	—	IF–1963	20	5	None	0
1944	France	Germany during war; Renewed Ger. aggr.	T/A,MA 1,4	1955	Abro. USSR	11	11	1955	9
1945	Yugo.	Germany during war; Renewed Ger. aggr.	T/F,MA,PWC 1,2	1949	Abro. USSR	4	4	1949	25
1945	Poland	Germany during war; Renewed Ger. aggr.	T/F,MA,PWC 1,4	—	IF–1963	18	7	None	0
1945	China	Japan during war; Renewed Jap. aggr.	T/F,A 1,3	1950	Abro. USSR	5	5	1950	20
1945–53									
1946	Mongolia	Any military attack	T/F, MA 2	—	IF–1963	17	0	None	—
1948	Rumania	Renewed Ger. aggr.	T/F,C,MA ... 2	—	IF–1963	15	0	None	—

TABLE 7 (Continued)

Period & Year[a] (1)	Promisee[c] (2)	Threat USSR Is Pledged to Help Repel[a] (3)	Encasing Instrument & Clause[e] (4)	Termination: Year & Manner[f] (5)	(6)	YIF Given[g] (7)	YIF Adjusted[h] (8)	Violation Years[i] (9)	Violation Infidelity Ratio[j] (10)
1948	Hungary	Renewed Ger. aggr.	T/F,C,MA 2	—	IF-1963	15	0	None	—
1948	Bulgaria	Renewed Ger. aggr.	T/F,C,MA 2	—	IF-1963	15	0	None	—
1948	Finland	Aggr. by Germany	T/F,C,MA 1	—	IF-1963	15	15	None	0
1950	China	Renewed Jap. aggr.	T/F,A,MA 1	—	IF-1963	13	13	None	0
1953–63									
1955	7 in East Europe[l]	Armed attack in Eur., any source	T/F,C,MA[m] 4	—	IF-1963	8	0	None	—
1961	N. Korea	Any armed attack	T/F,C,MA 1	—	IF-1963	2	2	None	0

a. Compiled, with addition of Warsaw Pact pledge of 1955 and North Korean treaty of 1961, from Triska and Slusser, Soviet Treaties, pp. 569–70. For sources of treaty texts, data on termination and alleged violations, see respectively nn. d, f, i below.

b. Periodization follows more or less standard Western and Soviet lines: the year 1939 breaks at August 1, the year 1941 at June 1, the year 1945 at September 1. Year of pledge is year of signature of instrument containing it.

c. The other state which the USSR has pledged herself to help.

d. Source for texts of treaties is British Treaty Series (London: H.M.S.O.).

e. Abbreviations: A = Alliance; Agr. = Agreement; C = Collaboration; Coop. = Cooperation; D = Declaration; F = Friendship; JA = Joint Action; MA = Mutual Aid; P = Pact; PWC = Postwar Collaboration; Pr. = Protocol; T = Treaty.

f. Termination of treaty or treaty-as-extended. Abro. = Abrogated; CET = Considered Effectively Terminated; Repl. = Replacement by another instrument (below in table); IF-1963 = In Force as of end of 1963. For data on termination see Triska and Slusser, Soviet Treaties, pp. 228–40.

g. Years in Force calculated on Columns 1, 5, and 6.

h. Years in Force calculated by reducing the figure of the preceding column (7) by the number of years the partner was

under effective Soviet control, hence the pledge not a true one (see text, p. 239, for further explanation).

i. Years in which violations are alleged to have occurred, on a maximum indictment, for which main sources are:

1. US Congress, Senate, Committee on the Judiciary, Subcommittee to Investigate the Administration of the Internal Security Act and Other Internal Security Laws, Soviet Political Agreements and Results Revised to January 1, 1964, 88th Congress, 2nd Session, 1964.

2. US Congress, House, Committee on Foreign Affairs, Background Information on the Soviet Union in International Relations, 87th Congress, 1st Session, 1961.

3. US Department of Defense, Armed Forces Information and Education, Alert No. 5—Soviet Treaty Violations, November 5, 1962, cited as insert in US Congress, Senate, Committee on Foreign Relations, Nuclear Test Ban Treaty: Hearings, 88th Congress, 1st Session, 1963.

j. The ratio (as a percentage) of number of years in which a violation occurred to the total number of years a pledge was in force—computed on Columns 9 and 8.

k. USSR aid conditioned on prior fulfillment by French of similar provision in Franco-Czechoslovak Alliance.

l. Albania, Bulgaria, Czechoslovakia, East Germany, Hungary, Poland, Rumania.

m. The so-called Warsaw Pact.

mitment to help repel renewed German aggression to Rumania, Hungary and Bulgaria; also in 1948 it extended a general commitment of this nature to Finland (renewed in 1955), while in 1950, in Stalin's final years, it transferred to the new Communist regime the commitment to China originally made to the Nationalists in 1945. The Warsaw Pact of 1955, in the immediate post-Stalin era, generalized the pledges given the individual East European countries, enlarged them to cover aggression from any source, and brought East Germany and Albania within their protection. A commitment to North Korea in 1961 completes the list: a list which, it might be added, has since 1963 been extended by a pledge to East Germany in 1964 and by renewals in 1963–67 of the Czech, Polish, Mongolian, Bulgarian, and Hungarian pledges.[46]

The pledges in question had lives of varying length. Ten of the 26, those to Finland and other Communist states, remained in force as of the end of 1963 (Column 6). The rest lapsed as a result of replacement by similar commitments, expiry, or termination by the USSR of the encasing instrument (Columns 5 and 6). Those that lapsed because of Soviet termination include all those contracted before the end of the Second World War save only the Mongolian. Terminating action can in some cases be considered reasonably justified, in others hardly justified, in still others wholly unjustified.[47] I take as reasonably justified Soviet abrogation in 1938 of the 1935 agreements with France and Czechoslovakia, inasmuch as it is reasonable to consider that, practically speaking, these had been made inoperative by Western conduct at Munich in 1938. I take as hardly justified, on the other hand, Soviet annulment in 1950 of the 1945 treaty with Nationalist China, and of the British and French alliances in the spring of 1955. Quite unjustified I take to be: abrogation in 1943 of the 1941 agreement with the Polish government in exile, an action taken in reply to Polish accusations concerning the Katyn Forest executions; abrogation in 1949 of the Yugoslav treaty of 1945—a judgment to which subsequent Soviet governments themselves agreed; and the abrogation in 1940, on the plea of voluntary incorporation within the Soviet

46. Cf. *International Affairs* (Moscow), no. 10 (October 1967): 102–03.

47. For data on termination see Triska and Slusser, *Soviet Treaties,* pp. 228–40, 248–70.

Union, of the Baltic pacts of 1939. Years-in-force calculated on the various terminal years as cited appear in Column 7.

These years-in-force figures, however, refer only to the realm of the formal. Some adjustment downward is needed to account for the fact that in some cases, for certain periods of their existence, the partners to whom the Soviet Union committed itself were so much under its control as not to be independent second parties, and that in these cases the pledges therefore did not have the standing of promise-to-independent-second-party usually understood by the term. Such I take to be the case, consonant with the discussion on control of the preceding chapter, with the pledge to Czechoslovakia for the years 1948–63, the pledge to Poland for the years 1945–56, and the pledges to Mongolia, Rumania, Hungary, and Bulgaria for the entire period of formal duration up to 1963. In these cases, the commitment in question is to be seen as a unilateral guarantee or declaration rather than a genuine pledge. Column 8 records the adjustments required by these considerations.

"Violation" may be construed strictly or loosely, insofar as concerns application to Soviet acts bearing on these pledges. The term may be limited to "real" violations, that is, to full-fledged failures to render the stipulated help against aggression. Or it may be expanded to include also what might be called "technical" violations, that is, failure to observe ancillary provisions, of which practically speaking those having to do with the term of the promise are most important. On the broad construction, which is the one I adopt here as the more reasonable and is the one reflected in Column 9, the Soviets broke their word (once) in the case of each of eight of the 17 genuine pledges for all or part of their formal duration (or eight out of the grand total of 23). These violations consisted of the partly or wholly unjustified abrogations in the years 1940 through 1955 of the pledges to the three Baltic countries, of the first Polish and Chinese pledges, of those made to Britain and France under the wartime alliance, and of the Yugoslav wartime pledge. Of these eight, that which concerned Poland was substantive, for in this case abrogation meant withdrawal of recognition and deprivation of aid. In the other seven, abrogation had no substantive consequences.

On the positive side, as the table shows, the Soviets apparently kept their word in the remaining nine of the genuine cases (15 of the total). The Polish case apart, they observed their wartime pledges of mutual aid in the face of the Nazi and Japanese aggressions of 1941–45. To this many Western leaders testify.[48] In fact, not the least illustrious of these leaders, the redoubtable Churchill, in a testimonial the Soviets never tire of repeating, said on this point that "I know of no government which stands to its own obligations, even in its own despite, more solidly than the Russian Soviet Government."[49] By all outward signs, too, the Soviets stood ready to honor the Czech pledge in the teeth of Hitler's threatened aggression of 1938. In this case, to be sure, where Soviet fulfillment was conditioned on fulfillment by the French of a similar pledge, the issue was not finally joined, the French having chosen the course of appeasement. But public pronouncements, etc., leave the Soviets technically "in the clear," as Triska and Slusser somewhat grudgingly put it.[50] It is not entirely inappropriate in the general connection to mention too the backing given Mongolia in 1939 against Japanese aggressions through Manchuria. For although the Mongolian promise is more rightly construed as a unilateral guarantee than as a true pledge, its observance may be said to have the same general import.

The overall violation or infidelity ratios that are obtained by relating total number of years in which violations occurred (violation years) to total number of years during which the pledges were in force (pledge or bound years) are accordingly not impressively high. As shown in Column 10 these amount to 100 percent in the case of the three Baltic countries, a technical violation having occurred in each case during the single year the pledge was in force. And in the case of the Polish pledge of 1941, the ratio is 50 percent. But in the other cases ratios are below 50 percent, and in many are 0 percent. All in all, for the entire period 1917–63, on the constructions here adopted, out of a total of 91 years during which the Soviets were bound by genuine pledges, those marked by violations numbered only eight, or 9 percent. A construction of "violation" that excluded the technical,

48. See, for example, Herbert Feis, *Churchill, Roosevelt, Stalin* (Princeton: Princeton University Press, 1957), pp. 310–11.

49. Statement to House of Commons on February 27, 1945, *Parliamentary Debates,* Commons, 5th Series (1909–) Vol. 408, p. 1284.

50. *Soviet Treaties,* p. 233.

and/or a construction of "pledge" that included the unilateral guarantee, would make this figure even lower.

It may be said, in legitimate objection to the above, that it is misleading to calculate the life of a pledge on the years during which a state is conditionally bound to help, that is, bound on the condition an aggression has been committed against the partner; rather, it should be calculated on the years in which the state is actually bound, that is, years in which the condition is fulfilled, and an aggression has actually occurred. There is force to the objection, and it might have been better to proceed along the alternative lines suggested. Fortunately, thus proceeding makes little difference. Calculating on this basis yields a figure for years actually bound of about 16—roughly that component of total years bound represented by the years in which Germany and Japan were actually making war on the treaty partners. But the number of violations assignable to these years dwindles to the single one of abrogation of the Polish agreement, and the infidelity ratio remains low—in fact, sinks still lower, to 6 percent.

Neutrality and Nonalignment Pledges

Neutrality and nonalignment pledges to which the Soviets are party are also of fairly uniform character. In a typical pledge of neutrality, the USSR agrees to "observe neutrality" should the partner "become the victim of aggression on the part of one or more third powers."[51] Sometimes, as in the treaty of 1939 with Germany and that of 1941 with Japan, the condition stipulated is broadened to include involvement in war or hostilities with a third party, regardless of which side initiated the conflict. In a typical nonalignment pledge, the USSR undertakes "not to be a party to any alliances or agreements of a military or political character with one or more powers which might be directed against [the partner]."[52] The arrangement in question is sometimes alternately called a coalition or a grouping.

Sustained Soviet neutrality policy dates from 1925. Although Soviet

---

51. From Article II of the 1927 Treaty of Nonaggression and Neutrality with Persia (Iran), the text of which is found in Shapiro, *Soviet Treaty Series*, Vol. I (1917–29), p. 341.

52. From Articles I and II of the 1931 Treaty of Neutrality and Nonaggression with Afghanistan, text in Shapiro, *Soviet Treaty Series*, Vol. II, p. 33.

diplomacy had known earlier pledges of this kind, in 1925 the Soviets adopted the device in a big way, in order to form an effective barrier against possible hostile action from the West and South, and thus to stabilize relationships with the capitalist world.[53] According to Professors Triska and Slusser, neutrality came now to be more than a temporary expedient and represented a sort of preventive insurance against the forming of hostile coalitions by the capitalist enemy.[54] It appeared the best way of giving form to the doctrine of peaceful coexistence to which following the period of consolidation the USSR had reconciled itself as the most practicable relationship with the capitalist world available for the time being.

In the years 1917–63 the Soviet Union subscribed in all to some 35 unambiguous, specific, and formalized neutrality type pledges of genuine nature, 14 of the wartime category, and 21 of the more general nonalignment category. (Comparable figures for pledges both genuine and unilateral are 14 and 25.) As Table 8 shows, between 1921 and 1934 she signed pledges of one or both of the two types with all limitrophe nations in Europe and the Middle East save only Rumania and, besides, the great European powers of Germany, France, and Italy: pledges of both types with Turkey, Afghanistan, Lithuania, Persia, Finland, Poland, and Italy; pledges of the strictly wartime type alone with Germany and France, and of the nonalignment type alone with Latvia and Estonia, neutrality provisions with these two having been written into the peace treaties of 1920. Between 1934 and her engulfment in the Second World War she entered into pledges of the strict type with her Far East neighbors China and Japan, and in Europe with Yugoslavia and, again, Germany (in the infamous Ribbentrop-Molotov Pact). Since June 1941, she has contracted no more of the strict neutrality type, considering it no longer possible and/or desirable that she stay out of wars involving parties whose security is most closely tied to her own. Pledges of the nonalignment types, on the other hand, she has incorporated into all her mutual aid treaties, which means that she has been bound for some period or other since the war by such pledges to all her European neighbors save Norway; also in Europe to Britain, France, Yugoslavia, Bulgaria, East Germany,

53. Triska and Slusser, *Soviet Treaties,* p. 265.
54. Ibid., p. 264.

TABLE 8

USSR: Neutrality and Nonalignment Pledges to Which a Party and Their Violation, 1917–63[a]

Period & Year[b] (1)	Promisee[c] (2)	Action USSR Is Pledged to Stay out of[d] (3)	Encasing Instrument & Clause[e] (4)	Termination: Year and Manner[f] (5)	(6)	YIF Given[g] (7)	Adjusted[h] (8)	Violation Years[i] (9)	Infidelity Ratio[j] (10)
1917–21									
1921	Afghan.	TP agreement against	T/F 2	1926	Repl.	5	5	None	0
1921–28									
1925	Turkey	TP military action vs	T/N,NA 1	1945	Expiry	20	20	None	0
1925	Turkey	TP alliance against	T/N,NA 2	1945	Expiry	20	20	None	0
1926	Germany	TP attack against	T/F 2	1939	Repl.	13	13	None	0
1926	Afghan.	TP war with	T/N,NA 1	1931	Repl.	5	5	None	0
1926	Afghan.	TP union against	T/N,NA 2	1931	Repl.	5	5	None	0
1926	Lithuania	TP attack on	T/NA,F 3	1940	Abro. USSR	14	14	None	0
1926	Lithuania	TP agreement against	T/NA,F 4	1940	Abro. USSR	14	14	1939	7
1927	Persia	TP aggression against	T/G,N 2	—	IF–1963	36	36	None	0
1927	Persia	TP alliance against	T/G,N 3	—	IF–1963	36	36	None	0
1928–34									
1931	Afghan.	TP war with	T/N,NA 1	—	IF–1963	32	32	None	0
1931	Afghan.	TP alliance against	T/N,NA 2	—	IF–1963	32	32	None	0
1932	Finland	TP aggression against	T/NA 2	1939	Abro. USSR	7	7	None	0
1932	Finland	TP Treaty hostile to	T/NA 3	1939	Abro. USSR	7	7	1939	14
1932	Latvia	TP alliance against	T/NA 2	1940	Abro. USSR	8	8	1939	13
1932	Estonia	TP accord against	T/NA 2	1940	Abro. USSR	8	8	1939	13
1932	Poland	TP aggression against	T/NA 2	1940	Abro. USSR	8	8	1939	13
1932	Poland	TP agreement hostile to	T/NA 3	1939	CET USSR	7	7	1939	14
1932	France	TP aggression against	T/NA 2	1938	CET USSR	5	5	None	0
1933	Italy	TP aggression against	T/F,NA,N 2	1941	CET USSR	8	8	None	0
1933	Italy	TP combination against	T/F,NA,N 4	1941	CET USSR	8	8	None	0

(*Continued*)

TABLE 8 (Continued)

Period & Year^b (1)	Promisee^c (2)	Action USSR Is Pledged to Stay out of^d (3)	Encasing Instrument & Clause^e (4)	Termination: Year and Manner^f (5)	(6)	YIF Given^g (7)	YIF Adjusted^h (8)	Violation Years^i (9)	Infidelity Ratio^j (10)
1934–39									
1937	China	TP aggression against	T/NA 2	1950	Abro. USSR	13	13	1941	8
1939–41									
1939	Germany	TP warlike action vs	P/NA 2	1941	Abro. USSR	2	2	None	0
		TP grouping against	P/NA 4	1941	Abro. USSR	2	2	None	0
1941	Yugo.	TP attack on	P/NA 2	1945	Repl.	4	4	None	0
1941	Japan	TP military action with	T/N 2	1945	Abro. USSR	4	4	1945	25
1941–45									
1942	Britain	TP alliance against	T/A,C,MA 7	1955	Abro. USSR	13	13	None	0
1943	Czech.	TP alliance against	T/F,MA,PWC 5	—	IF–1963	20	5	None	0
1944	France	TP alliance against	T/A,MA 5	1955	Abro. USSR	11	11	None	0
1945	Yugo.	TP alliance against	T/F,MA,PWC 4	1949	Abro. USSR	4	4	None	0
1945	Poland	TP alliance against	T/F,MA,PWC 6	—	IF–1963	18	7	None	0
1945	China	TP alliance against	T/F,A 4	1950	Abro. USSR	5	5	None	0
1945–53									
1948	Rumania	TP alliance against	T/F,C,MA 3	—	IF–1963	15	0	None	—
1948	Hungary	TP alliance against	T/F,C,MA 3	—	IF–1963	15	0	None	—
1948	Bulgaria	TP alliance against	T/F,C,MA 3	—	IF–1963	15	0	None	—
1948	Finland	TP alliance against	T/F,C,MA 4	—	IF–1963	15	15	None	0
1950	China	TP alliance against	T/F,A,MA 3	—	IF–1963	13	13	None	0

TABLE 8 (Continued)

Period & Year[b] (1)	Promisee[c] (2)	Action USSR Is Pledged to Stay out of[d] (3)	Encasing Instrument & Clause[e] (4)	Termination: Year and Manner[f] (5)	YIF Given[g] (6)	YIF Adjusted[h] (7)	YIF (8)	Violation Years[i] (9)	Infidelity Ratio[j] (10)
1953–63									
1955	7 in East Europe[k]	Incompatible alliances and agreements	T/F,C,MA[1] 7	— IF-1963	8	0		None	—
1961	N. Korea	TP alliance against	T/F,C,MA 2	— IF-1963	2	2		None	0

a. Compiled, with addition of Warsaw Pact pledge of 1955 and North Korean treaty of 1961, from Triska and Slusser, *Soviet Treaties*, pp. 569–72. For sources of treaty texts, data on termination, and alleged violations, see respectively nn. d, f, i below.

b. Periodization follows more or less standard Western and Soviet lines: the year 1921 breaks at March 18, the year 1939 at August 1, the year 1941 at June 1, the year 1945 at September 1. Year given for pledge is year of signature on instrument containing it.

c. The other State whose involvement with third parties (TP) the USSR has pledged herself to stay out of.

d. Source for texts of treaties is *British Treaty Series* (London: H.M.S.O.).

e. Abbreviations: A = Alliance, C = Collaboration, F = Friendship, G = Guarantee, MA = Mutual Aid, N = Neutrality, NA = Nonaggression, P = Pact, PWC = Postwar Collaboration, T = Treaty.

f. Termination of treaty or treaty-as-extended. Abro. = Abrogated; CET = Considered Effectively Terminated; Repl. = Replacement by another instrument (below in table); IF-1963 = In Force as of end of 1963. For data on termination see Triska and Slusser, *Soviet Treaties*, pp. 228–40, 248–70.

g. Years in Force calculated on Columns 1, 5, and 6.

h. Years in Force calculated by reducing the figure of the preceding column (7) by estimated number of years the partner was under close Soviet control, hence the pledge not a true one (for further explanation see text, p. 239).

i. Years in which violations are alleged to have occurred, on a maximum indictment, for which main sources are:
1. US Congress, Senate, Committee on the Judiciary, Subcommittee to Investigate the Administration of the Internal Security Act and Other Internal Security Laws, *Soviet Political Agreements and Results, Revised to January 1, 1964*, 88th Congress, 2nd Session, 1964.
2. US Congress, House, Committee on Foreign Affairs, *Background Information on the Soviet Union in International Relations*, 87th Congress, 1st Session, 1961.
3. US Department of Defense, Armed Forces Information and Education, *Alert No. 5—Soviet Treaty Violations*, November 5, 1962, as inserted in US Congress, Senate, Committee on Foreign Relations, *Nuclear Test Ban Treaty: Hearings*, 88th Congress, 1st Session, 1963.

j. The ratio (as a percentage) of the number of years in which a violation occurred to the total number of years a pledge was in force—computed on Columns 9 and 8.

k. Albania, Bulgaria, Czechoslovakia, East Germany, Hungary, Poland, Rumania.

l. The so-called Warsaw Pact.

246 PART III: MELIORATION

and Albania; to Iran and Afghanistan in the southeast (the prewar pledges having carried over), and to China and North Korea in the Far East. She has in this period bound herself in this way therefore to all neighbors save only Norway, Turkey, and Mongolia, and to all other Communist states save Mongolia, North Vietnam, and Cuba.

The pledges in question continued in force for periods ranging from one to 36 years. Thirteen of the 39—the strict neutrality pledges to Iran (Persia) and Afghanistan, and the nonalignment pledges to these two states, Finland, and the other Communist states—were active as of 1963. The rest lapsed as a result of either replacement, expiry, or termination by the USSR (Columns 5 and 6). As in the case of the mutual aid pledges, Soviet termination can in some cases be considered justified, in others not.[55] Reasonably justified I take to be these abrogations: in 1938 of the Czech and French treaties, on grounds of their having been effectively nullified already by Western action at Munich; in 1941 of the Italian treaty, on grounds of Italy's alliance with the invader Nazis; and in 1941 of the Ribbentrop-Molotov Pact, on grounds hardly requiring specification. Hard to justify (though there are some extenuating circumstances) are her abrogation in 1950 of the treaty with Nationalist China and her abrogation in 1955 of the treaties with Britain and France. Clearly unjustifiable are her abrogations of the following: the Polish treaty, in 1939, on grounds of Poland's extinction; the Finnish treaty, also in 1939, on spurious accusations of prior violation; the Baltic Pacts, in 1940, on grounds of incorporation voluntarily acceded to; the pact with Japan, in 1945, on grounds of Japanese hostility to Russian allies in the war against Germany; and the pact with Yugoslavia, in 1949, again on spurious accusations of prior violation. Years-in-force calculated on the various terminal dates as cited appear in Column 7. Adjustments downward to allow for periods when the partner was under Soviet control, on the assumptions explained in the discussion of mutual aid pledges, are reflected in Column 8.

As for violations, the Soviets broke their word (once) in the case of eight of the 35 pledges that were genuine for all or part of their formal duration, or eight out of a grand total of 39. As noted in Column 9 of the table, three of these were violations of the strict,

55. See n. 47 above.

wartime type of pledge. Contrary to the promise she made in the treaty of 1932 not to give aid or assistance, either directly or indirectly, to an aggressor attacking Poland, the USSR signed the agreement of August 23, 1939, that cleared the way for Nazi Germany's invasion of September 1, and later (on September 17) she too attacked. Again, contrary to the promise she made in the pact of 1937 to "refrain from taking any action or entering into any agreement which may be used ... to the disadvantage of China by one committing aggression against her," the USSR in the declaration appended to the similar 1941 pact with Japan promised that aggressor against the Chinese to respect the territorial integrity and inviolability of the Empire of Manchukuo, Chinese territory the Japanese had seized back in 1931. Finally, contrary to her promise in the Japanese treaty of 1941 to observe neutrality, should Japan become involved in military action with third parties—a pact the entire purpose of which, from the Soviet side, was to buy Japanese abstention from the conflict between Russia and Germany—on August 5, 1945, she entered the lists against Japan by attacking the Japanese armies in Manchuria. As for the residual cases involving the neutralist or nonalignment type of pledge: in initialing the secret protocol attached to the Nazi pact of 1939 that divided East Europe into German and Russian spheres of influence (plus the protocol of October reallocating Lithuania), the USSR was in effect entering a coalition directed against or treaty hostile to Poland, the Baltic states, and Finland within the common-sense meaning of the agreements of 1932 with those powers (1926 with Lithuania).

On the positive side, the Soviets have apparently, as the table shows, kept their word in the remaining 27 of the genuine cases (31 of the total). True, they did enter into negotiations with Nazi Germany in the fall of 1940 with a view toward getting German approval for pressure on Turkey for a base within range of the Straits and for bringing the area southeast of Batum within the Soviet sphere.[56] Such a "deal" would have constituted something close to an anti-Turkish coalition which the Soviets had pledged themselves not to join in the treaty of 1925 and subsequent protocols of extension. But the "deal" was not consummated, the Germans coveting Turkey for their own sphere of influence. In short, the USSR fulfilled its neutrality pledge

56. Kulski, *Peaceful Coexistence*, pp. 356–58.

to China during all but one year of the course of the latter's war with Japan, its pledge to Japan for four and one-half of the five years it was to remain in force, and its pledge to the Nazis for the two years in which it was in force—a point the Nazis themselves conceded. As for pledges of the nonalignment sort, as nearly as can be determined there have been no other violations than those of 1939 already noted, nor any alleged. In other words, the Soviets kept all the pledges of this sort made in 1921–33 up to 1939, kept the pledge made to Germany in 1939 for the two years of its duration, have kept from 1926 and 1927 respectively pledges made to Afghanistan and Iran (still in force), and have kept without exception the pledges made in the war and postwar eras (also still in force).

Overall violation or infidelity ratios are accordingly quite low—in fact, lower than those prevailing in the case of the mutual aid pledges. As shown in Column 10, these are all 0 percent where pledges of the strict or wartime type are concerned save only in the Polish, Chinese, and Japanese cases, where they are 14 percent, 8 percent, and 25 percent respectively. Where the neutralist type is involved, they measure between 7 and 14 percent in five cases, in the rest 0 percent. All in all, for the entire period 1917–63, out of a total of 170 years during which the Soviets were bound by genuine pledges to observe neutrality in case of war involving a partner, those years marked by violations number only 3 or 2 percent. Out of a total of 227 years during which the Soviets were bound by genuine pledges to stay out of coalitions directed against a partner, those years marked by violations number only five, or 2 percent. Proceeding on a construction of "pledge" that includes the unilateral declaration would make these figures even lower.

To the manner of calculating the life of a pledge of the strict or wartime neutrality type, the same objection might be made that was considered in the discussion of the preceding section. That is, the objection might be made that the more meaningful calculation is one based on the years in which not only was the pledge in force, but the condition activating the pledge fulfilled, and the partner actually involved in war. On this basis, the figure for years bound comes to only 16, and the violation ratio to 3–16 or 19 percent.

Nonaggression Pledges

The last of the critical categories of political pledges is the nonaggression. Nonaggression pledges are found in two forms, one rather vague, the other fairly definite. On a typical formulation of the first, the USSR pledges itself "to respect, in all circumstances, the sovereignty and territorial integrity" of the partner.[57] On a typical formulation of the second, the USSR undertakes "to refrain from any act of aggression directed against . . . " the partner.[58] Variants of the first are to maintain friendly contact or friendly relations, of the second to refrain from an attack upon or hostile acts or violence against the partners. "Aggression" came to acquire a still more specific meaning when a Soviet initiative a convention on the definition of aggression was written in 1933 and subsequently subscribed to by many of her treaty partners.[59] In the definition of this convention, one State is said to commit aggression against another when it does any of the following: declares war upon the other; invades by armed forces the other's territory, with or without a declaration of war; attacks with its land, naval, or air forces the other's territory, vessels, or aircraft; erects a naval blockade around the other's coasts or ports; supports on her territory armed forces which have invaded the territory of the other, or refuses on the other's demand to take on her own territory all measures needed to deprive those bands of assistance or protection.

Some exceptions from the early period of consolidation aside, Soviet pledges of nonaggression date from the second period of the development of her foreign policy (Table 9), when she sought to stabilize her relations with the capitalist world and to minimize the chances of her being drawn into wars therewith, which practically speaking meant wars involving states on her borders. The nonaggression treaties embodying the pledges were considered pacts of peace, and their acceptance by other parties to whom they were offered was looked upon as the acid test of peacefulness.[60] In the period 1921–28 the USSR extended such pledges to the three states on her southern border, to Lithuania, and to Germany. In the period 1928–34 she renewed these (save in the Persian case) and added to the list of promises Finland,

57. From Articles II and III of the 1926 Treaty of Nonaggression with Lithuania, text in Shapiro, *Soviet Treaty Series,* Vol. I, p. 323.

58. From Article I of the 1932 Treaty of Nonaggression with Finland, text in Shapiro, *Soviet Treaty Series,* Vol. II, p. 46.

59. Ibid., pp. 69–70.

60. Triska and Slusser, *Soviet Treaties,* pp. 248–49.

TABLE 9

USSR: Nonaggression Pledges to Which a Party and Their Violation, 1917–63[a]

Period & Year[b] (1)	Promisee[c] (2)	Character of Action USSR Pledged to[d] (3)	Encasing Instrument & Clause[e] (4)	Termination: Year and Manner[f]		Given[g] (7)	YIF Adjusted[h] (8)	Violation Years[i] (9)	Infidelity Ratio[j] (10)
				(5)	(6)				
1917–21	None								
1921–28									
1925	Turkey	No aggression	T/N,NA 2	1945	Expiry	20	20	1945	5
1926	Germany	Friendly touch	T/F 1	1939	Repl.	13	13	None	0
1926	Afghan.	No attack	T/N,NA 2	1931	Repl.	5	5	None	0
1926	Lithuania	Respect for sov., ti., inv.; no aggression	T/NA,F 2,3	1940	Abro. USSR	14	14	39,40	14
1927	Persia	No aggression	T/G,N 2	—	IF-1963	36	36	45,46	6
1928–34									
1931	Afghan.	No aggression	T/N,NA 2	—	IF-1963	32	32	1946	3
1932	Finland	No aggression	T/NA 1	1939	Abro. USSR	7	7	1939	14
1932	Latvia	No act of aggression	T/NA 1	1940	Abro. USSR	8	8	39,40	25
1932	Estonia	No act of aggression	T/NA 1	1940	Abro. USSR	8	8	39,40	25
1932	Poland	No act of aggression	T/NA 1	1939	CET USSR	7	7	1939	14
1932	France	No war, aggression	T/NA 1	1939	CET USSR	6	6	None	0
1933	Italy	No war, aggression	T/F, NA,N 1	1941	CET USSR	8	8	None	0
1934–39									
1937	China	No war, aggression	T/NA 1	1950	Abro. USSR	13	13	None	0
1939–41									
1939	Germany	No aggressive action	P/NA 1	1941	Abro. USSR	2	2	None	0
1941	Yugo.	No attack	P/NA 1	1945	Repl.	4	4	None	0
1941	Japan	Respect for inv., ti.	T/N 1	1945	Abro. USSR	4	4	1945	25
1941–45									
1943	Czech.	Respect for ind., sov.	T/F,MA,PWC 4	—	IF-1963	20	5	45,48	40
1945	Yugo.	Friendship, coop.	T/F,MA,PWC 5	1949	Abro. USSR	4	4	48,49	50
1945	Poland	Respect for ind., sov.	T/F,MA,PWC 2	—	IF-1963	18	7	1956	13
1945	China	Respect for sov., ti.	T/F,A 5	1950	Abro. USSR	5	5	48,49	40
1945–53									
1948	Rumania	Respect for ind., sov.	T/F,C,MA 5	—	IF-1963	15	15	None	—
1948	Hungary	Respect for ind., sov.	T/F,C,MA 5	—	IF-1963	15	15	1956	—

TABLE 9 (Continued)

Period & Year[a] [b] (1)	Promisee[c] (2)	Character of Action USSR Pledged to[d] (3)	Encasing Instrument & Clause[e] (4)	Termination: Year and Manner[i] (5)	(6)	YIF Given[g] (7)	YIF Adjusted[h] (8)	Violation Years[i] (9)	Infidelity Ratio[f] (10)
1948	Bulgaria	Respect for ind., sov.	T/F,C,MA 5	—	IF-1963	15	0	None	—
1948	Finland	Respect for ind., sov.	T/F,C,MA 6	—	IF-1963	15	15	None	0
1950	China	Respect for sov., ti.	T/F,A,MA 5	—	IF-1963	13	13	None	0
1953–63									
1955	Austria	Respect for ind., ti.	T/State 2	—	IF-1963	8	8	None	0
1955	7 in East Europe[k]	Respect for ind., sov.	T/F,C,MA[l] 8	—	IF-1963	8	0	1956	—
1961	N. Korea	Respect for sov., ti.	T/F,C,MA 4	—	IF-1963	2	2	None	0

a. Compiled, with addition of Warsaw Pact pledge of 1955 and North Korean treaty of 1961, from Triska and Slusser, Soviet Treaties, pp. 569–72. For sources of treaty texts, data on termination and alleged violations, see respectively nn. d, f, i.

b. Periodization follows more or less standard Western and Soviet lines: the year 1939 breaks at August 1, the year 1941 at June 1, the year 1945 at September 1. Year given for pledge is year of signature on instrument containing it.

c. The other state to whom the USSR has made the pledge.

d. Source for texts of treaties is British Treaty Series (London: H.M.S.O.). Abbreviations: coop. = cooperation; ind. = independence; inv. = inviolability; sov. = sovereignty; ti. = territorial integrity.

e. Abbreviations: A = Alliance, C = Collaboration, F = Friendship, G = Guarantee, MA = Mutual Aid, N = Neutrality, NA = Nonaggression, P = Pact, PWC = Postwar Collaboration, T = Treaty.

f. Termination of treaty or treaty-as-extended. Abro. = Abrogated; CET = Considered Effectively Terminated; Repl. = Replacement by another instrument (below in table); IF-1963 = In Force as of end of 1963. For data on termination see Triska and Slusser, Soviet Treaties, pp. 228–40, 248–70.

g. Years in Force calculated on Columns 1, 5, and 6.

h. The figure of the preceding column (7) adjusted downward by estimated number of years partner was under close Soviet control, hence the pledge not a true one (for further explanation see text, p. 239).

i. Years in which violations are alleged to have occurred, on a maximum indictment, for which main sources are:
1. US Congress, Senate, Committee on the Judiciary, Subcommittee to Investigate the Administration of the Internal Security Act and Other Internal Security Laws, Soviet Political Agreements and Results, Revised to January 1, 1964, 88th Congress, 2nd Session, 1964.
2. US Congress, House, Committee on Foreign Affairs, Background Information on the Soviet Union in International Relations, 87th Congress, 1st Session, 1961.
3. US Department of Defense, Armed Forces Information and Education, Alert No. 5—Soviet Treaty Violations, November 5, 1962, as inserted in US Congress, Senate, Committee on Foreign Relations, Nuclear Test Ban Treaty: Hearings, 88th Congress, 1st Session, 1963.

j. The ratio (as a percentage) of the number of years in which a violation occurred to the total number of years a pledge was in force—computed on Columns 9 and 8.

k. Albania, Bulgaria, Czechoslovakia, East Germany, Hungary, Poland, Rumania.

l. The so-called Warsaw Pact.

Latvia, Estonia, Poland, France, and Italy. In the period 1934–39 she renewed the pledges to states on the Baltic littoral, renewed again those to the states on her southern flank (Persia again excepted), and extended the pledge to China (in 1937). In 1939–41 she added Germany, Yugoslavia, and Japan to the list of promisees. In the war years she revived the pledge to Czechoslovakia and extended it to the new Communist governments of Poland and Yugoslavia; while in the immediate postwar years she incorporated the pledge into the mutual aid treaties with Finland, Rumania, Hungary, and Bulgaria. Nineteen fifty saw the 1945 Chinese pledge reenacted for the benefit of the new Communist government. Nineteen fifty-five saw the Finnish and Afghani pledges renewed, and the pledge written into the Austrian State Treaty and Warsaw Pact. North Korea (1961) and East Germany (1964) are the most recent additions to the list of promisees. Table 9 gives details for the period 1917–63.

The lives of Soviet nonaggression pledges vary from two to 36 years. Twelve of the 28—with Persia (Iran) and Afghanistan, Finland and Austria, and with the other Communist states—remained in force as of 1963. The others lapsed for one or another of the usual reasons (Columns 5 and 6). As in the case of the other types, the Soviets terminated a number of them unilaterally, or rather the instruments encasing them.[61] And as in the case of the other types termination seems sometimes reasonably justifiable (the French, Italian, and 1939 German), sometimes hardly justifiable (the 1945 Chinese), sometimes quite unjustifiable (the 1932 Finnish, the 1932 Polish, the Baltic, the Japanese, the 1945 Yugoslav). Years-in-force calculated on the various terminal dates as cited appear in Column 7. Adjustments downward to allow for periods when the partner was under close Soviet control, on the assumptions explained in the discussion of mutual aid pledges, are reflected in Column 8.

On a loose construction, such as includes moot as well as clear cases, the Soviets broke their word once each in the case of six of the 24 genuine nonaggression pledges for all or part of their formal duration, twice each in the case of seven others, violations therefore totaling 20. Column 9 of the table gives the details. Enlargement of the calculation to include all 28 pledges, both genuine and unilateral, gives a corresponding total of 22.

61. See n. 47 above.

Unambiguous violations number 11 in all, or half the total. The invasion of Poland in September 1939, and of Finland in November of that year are as clear cases of infidelity as one could find, for in the treaties of 1932 with these two countries (extended in 1934) the USSR herself was committed to refrain from taking any aggressive action against them, and the convention on the definition of aggression to which all three subscribed, as well as the treaties themselves, had named invasion as one of the primary forms of aggression. Action against the Baltic countries in 1940 is only slightly less clear, for although the Soviets only threatened attack and invasion, the threat itself was so clear and present, armies being drawn up on the borders of the victim states, and the design was so clearly reduction to vassalage at a minimum, that in any common-sense view the action directly countered the pledge made to Lithuania in 1926 (renewed in 1934 and 1939) to "respect, in all circumstances, [her] sovereignty and territorial integrity and inviolability," and only slightly less directly countered the pledges made to Latvia and Estonia in 1932 (renewed in 1934 and 1939) to "refrain from . . . any acts of violence directed against [their] territorial integrity and inviolability or . . . political independence."[62] Action against Japan in 1945 supplies another clear case. Entry into the war against that power in the beginning of August, a number of months before expiry of the 1941 treaty, unambiguously contravened the pledge made in that treaty "to maintain peaceful and friendly relations . . . " and to respect Japan's "territorial integrity and inviolability."[63] Finally to be noted in this connection are: the retention of troops in Iran in 1945 and 1946 in contravention of the 1927 pledge against aggression; the pressure brought on Poland in 1956, through troop movements, etc., in contravention of the 1945 pledge to respect her sovereignty; and the invasion of Hungary in 1956 in defiance of pledges to respect her sovereignty incorporated in both the 1948 treaty with her alone and the multilateral Warsaw Pact of 1955. (These last two deserve mention, even though in the terms used here they represent violations of declarations unilaterally made rather than true pledges.)

The remaining 11 cases, counted nevertheless, consist of violations

62. Shapiro, *Soviet Treaty Series,* Vol. I, p. 323, and Vol. II, pp. 47, 52.
63. *British Treaty Series,* Vol. 144, p. 839.

that are not unambiguous, the Soviet action in question bearing as much the character of internal intervention as external attack, or external pressure of a kind that falls short of the extremes of attack or the prelude thereto. These 11 include, first, Soviet contributions in February 1948 to the overturn of the Czech democracy, and Soviet actions against Yugoslavia in 1948 and the Nationalist Chinese in 1949—moves which, though justly considered in contempt of the wartime treaties with the three states in question, seem to be so more because of inconsistency with the nonintervention than with the non-aggression clauses of the latter. These cases include, second, the pressures brought on the Baltic states in September 1939 to cede bases (successful), on Czechoslovakia in 1945 to cede Ruthenia (successful), on Turkey in 1945 to cede Kars and Ardahan and a base on the Straits (unsuccessful), and on Afghanistan in 1946 to cede the border area of Kushka (successful)—moves which, while no doubt meriting condemnation, hardly are to be construed as aggression within the meaning of the definition of the convention (or the prelude thereto); moves which differ little in kind from behavior only too regrettably normal to a great power in its dealings with small. The nature of the Soviet action in the Turkish affair makes the allegation of violation in this instance particularly weak. The USSR had "denounced" the controlling treaty on March 19, 1945, which meant she gave the notice, according to procedures detailed in the treaty itself, that she did not agree to its automatic extension beyond the date of expiry (November 7, 1945) set 10 years earlier. The high point of the campaign for the retrocession of territory on the Georgian border and cession of a base on the Straits did not come until the following years, when the treaty had expired. The only action that could reasonably be viewed as raising a question of violation was the transmission of the notes of March–June 1945 informing Turkey of a desire and readiness to negotiate a new treaty incorporating the changes referred to.

On the positive side, the Soviets have apparently (as the table shows) kept their word in the remaining 11 of the 24 genuine cases (13 out of the total of 28). They kept without exception their pledges to Germany, France, Italy, their first pledges to Afghanistan, China, and Yugoslavia, and all their postwar pledges save those to Hungary. They kept all their prewar pledges up to 1939, all their postwar pledges (the Hungarian again excepted) since 1949. To their keeping of the pledge on Austria our own State Department has testified.[64]

Overall infidelity ratios, while higher than those of the previous two categories, are not greatly so. As shown in Column 10, they range from highs of 50 percent (the second Yugoslav case) and 40 percent (the second Czech and Chinese cases) down to 0 percent (12 cases), the remaining nine cases varying between 3 percent and 25 percent. All in all, for the entire period 1917–63, out of a total of 246 years during which the Soviets were bound by genuine pledges of this type, those marked by violations numbered 20, or about 8 percent. Proceeding on a construction of "pledge" that includes the unilateral declaration would raise the totals to 325 and 22 respectively, but lower the ratio to between 6 and 7 percent.

For the political agreements as a whole, the conclusion to be drawn from the survey of the five critical subcategories is therefore a mixed one—not overly good, but yet not overly bad. High infidelity ratios for the nonintervention and establishment-of-peace categories, percentage ratios possibly in the eighties, are balanced by a composite ratio of 5 percent for the other three. An overall ratio for all five would, therefore, on a fair assessment occur about one-third of the way up the scale. The separate findings rest on lists of violations that may fairly be called maximum indictments within the rules set forth at the beginning of this chapter, and the overall figure therefore also is probably a maximum. Hence the conclusion to be drawn for the entire category of political pledges is one of performance not completely intolerable.

The net effect of the foregoing is to modify the orthodox view and show this facet of Soviet behavior to be appreciably less black than commonly made out to be. Violations there have been: no amount of verbal legerdemain can absolve the USSR from the accusation of breaking its word on a number of notable occasions, of which the most notable are those of 1939 and 1940. But on the whole and on

64. Memorandum from the Department of State on Soviet Treaty Violations, August 22, 1963, cited as Appendix to US Congress, Senate, Committee on Foreign Relations, *Nuclear Test Ban Treaty: Hearings,* 88th Congress, 1st Session, 1963, p. 967.

the average performance has squared reasonably well with promise. Considerations set forth above suggest that bound years in which promise has been substantially kept far outnumbered those in which promise has not been kept. In respect to economic and functional-technical matters—and treaties of these types comprise more than three-quarters of all treaties—that record is acknowledged to be good even by American critics of Hard persuasion like Harry Schwartz. In respect to three critical pledge subcategories (pledges of mutual aid, neutralization, and nonaggression arrangements), which constitute a substantial portion of the third or political category and are found incorporated in the residual 20 to 25 percent of all treaties, it is at least fair: infidelity ratios remain below 10 percent even when doubtful cases are resolved in a manner unfavorable to the USSR. Only in respect to the remaining critical subcategories, nonintervention pledges and special war-liquidation pledges, is the record poor, and some reservation should be attached to the judgment on the latter of these two.

Moreover, what evidence there is bearing on trends suggests improvement in this record, and decreases in infidelity ratios. As earlier noted, the percentage of nonpolitical treaties in the total is rising, that of political treaties decreasing. As suggested by the tables for mutual aid, neutrality and nonalignment, and nonaggression pledges, and as independently reported by Triska and Slusser, violations cluster around war years: the aftermath of World Wars I and II, and the eve of World War II.[65] With the post-Stalin thaw in East-West relations, they have become fewer in number. The action in Czechoslovakia in 1968 and the doctrine attempting to legitimize interference in the internal affairs of the bloc must, of course, make one wary of projecting this trend into the future. But it seems real enough for the period 1953–68.

And so those who take the more moderate view of Soviet behavior along this line (they are usually students of the Mixed view on conduct as a whole, such as John Lukacs) appear to have the right of it. Assuredly it is wide of the mark to claim with the more extreme Western analysts that Soviet pledges are made only to be broken, or that the Soviets have never been known to respect a treaty they have

65. *Soviet Treaties*, p. 395.

committed themselves to, or that the fulfillment record is "far from encouraging." On careful scrutiny that record turns out to be considerably better. It turns out, in fact, to be better even than moderates like Triska and Slusser make it out to be. For their generally critical view is scarcely borne out by a close look at their data. On the other hand, and equally assuredly, it is wide of the mark to claim with the Soviets themselves that the fulfillment record is perfect. That claim remains what it seemed to be at the start—pure nonsense.

These conclusions so rather surprisingly favorable to the Soviets have their limitations, it should be clearly understood. And removal of these limitations may make them (and the broader position on Soviet morality of which they are part) less favorable, bringing them closer to those of the USSR's harsher critics and the public at large.

In the first place, the conclusions are provisional. The procedures on which they rest, though sounder than those underlying earlier surveys, are still rough in places, and needed refinements may modify results. Two refinements particularly are needed. The first and less important is to extend the treatment above accorded pledges of mutual aid, neutrality and nonalignment, and nonaggression for the time period 1917–63 to the years before and since, and to extend it as well to other types of pledges, both political and economic, for the entire span of Soviet history. Either this, that is, or extend it to some sample of the pledge universe suitably devised and selected. That the first of these extensions may well lead to a weakening of the conclusion of recent improvement is only too apparent: on any reasonable basis the 1968 invasion of Czechoslovakia contravened the nonintervention and nonaggression pledges of both the Soviet-Czechoslovak treaty of 1943 (extended in 1963) and the Warsaw Pact.

The other and more important of the two needed refinements of method is to work out some means of taking into account the qualitative factor or relative importance of individual instances of fulfillment or nonfulfillment. Manifestly, some pledges are more important than others, their observance in one set of circumstances more important than their observance in some other. Manifestly Soviet abrogation of her mutual aid agreement with Britain in 1955, in which no substantive matter of a refusal to give aid was involved, is not a violation of the same import as the abrogation of her mutual aid agreement with Poland in 1943, when a substantive matter was involved. Nor is her pressure on Afghanistan for cession of the Kushka district in 1946 a breach of a nonaggression pledge of the same importance as the attack upon Finland. Some system of weighting individual moves in question is needed, such as one running in terms of estimated impact on international stability, or populations or areas involved, or degree of coerciveness used. Introduction of such a scheme into the analysis might make dimmer the overall record, since some Soviet violations (e.g. the invasion of Poland in 1939) are of the first magnitude however they are calculated.

In the second place, the conclusions say nothing about causes or motives, and enlargement of the scope of inquiry to include these phenomena (another needed step) may leave untouched some of the other tenets of the harsher critics of Soviet conduct along this line. Perhaps in unconscious realization of some of the more favorable data presented above, these critics sometimes qualify their indictment to read, "The Soviets keep their word only so long as it is in their interest to do so." This remark has at least the merit of acknowledging obliquely that the Soviets make promises for reasons more substantial than throwing other nations off their guard or for the sake of having an agreement which they can then break with malicious glee. And, even after deflating that flexible, accordionlike term "interest," it still has truth in it. For the Soviets do make and keep agreements because of advantages they see accruing to themselves—what state has done so for other reasons? There can be no quarrel over the proposition, for instance, that they have kept their commercial agreements, by and large, because shipment of goods wanted by the trading partner has been the necessary condition of receiving goods they themselves need; or that they have stood by their pledge of nonaggression toward Austria because they have seen this as a necessary means of keeping Western military power out of that country; or that they have honored cultural exchange agreements, by and large, because of useful information gained from greater contact with the USA. Nor should one cavil at the notion that perception of immediate advantage is the most important reason for keeping their pledges (when they have kept them), taking precedence over some abstract devotion to the principle of fidelity to promise.

More challengeable is the notion usually intended by the remark—
namely, that the Soviets keep their promises *only* for reason of private
advantage and not for reason of respect for the principle of pledge
fulfillment, and that they cease to observe them the moment their
calculation of net immediate advantage shifts against observance.
While motives are extraordinarily hard to get at, the opposite hypothesis is at least tenable. That is, it is not unreasonable to suppose the
USSR opts for treaty violation only with reluctance, and not only out
of a lust for quick benefits. For a totalitarian even as for a democratic
state, future credibility is a factor to be reckoned with. Yet the critics
may be right on the point in general, and the further investigation in
this direction that is needed may show them so to be.

Finally, in the third place, these conclusions say nothing about
comparative performance. They leave untouched another contention
of the harsher critics of Soviet behavior along this line—namely, that
the USSR holds the world's record for treaty-breaking. Extension of
the scope of inquiry to include comparisons, another step desirable
from the point of view of enhancing our understanding, might provide corroboration for the harsher position on this point too.

Needed in this case is the application of identical procedures to the
conduct of other states. Should the United States be taken as the other
state, this procedure would involve: (1) arraying American pledges
meeting the desiderata of unambiguous, specific, and formal promises
clearly authored by our government or its agents; (2) estimating the
life span of these promises with due regard for the possibility of lapse
on account of prior violation by the other side; and (3) relating to the
years-in-force alleged violations on some maximum indictment, of
which official or quasi-official Soviet publications provide a rich
supply.[66] Preferably this would involve further subdivision by pledge
types on a breakdown close to that used in the Soviet analysis. How
such an investigation would come out and how resultant American
infidelity ratios compare with their Soviet counterparts, one can only

---

66. For instance, V. Durdenevsky and S. Krylov, "Violation by the Imperialist States of the Principle of Observing International Treaties," *International Affairs* (Moscow), no. 2 (February 1955): 63–70. Also see article
by Professor Krylov reproduced in Triska and Slusser, *Soviet Treaties*, pp.
409–11.

conjecture. That we too have erred at times is clear. Our leaders testify as much.[67] Applying the same criteria to American as well as to Soviet conduct, one can hardly escape the conclusion, for instance, that the interventions in Guatemala in 1954, the Bay of Pigs in 1961, and the Dominican Republic in 1965 are cases of pledge violation, conflicting with the provisions of the OAS charter against intervention in the internal affairs of another country. (And, indeed, not many in this country tried to escape the conclusion.)[68] Such malefactions of so unambiguous a character one would think, as one would hope, are fewer than Soviet equivalents. And in qualitative terms, it is probably correct to contend that we have not as yet been guilty of violations leading to the awful end of Soviet violations of 1940 of their pacts with the Baltic nations. On the other hand, American commitments of this sort have been less extensive than Soviet equivalents. Non-fulfillment ratios may turn out not to be much lower than Soviet counterparts. But whatever turns out to be the case, comparative assessment is needed; the conduct of the non-Soviet party must be evaluated on precisely the same terms, by precisely the same method, as that of the Soviets.

On the other hand, removal of the limitations referred to may have the opposite effect. Deepening and broadening the inquiry may reinforce the generally favorable tendency of the conclusions. "The path of history is littered with broken treaties . . . , " said Dean Rusk in testimony on the Test Ban Treaty before the Senate Foreign Relations Committee.[69] And the Soviet record may turn out to be little or no worse than others. Or Soviet violations, though more numerous than those of other countries, may turn out to be more excusable. Triska and Slusser may be quite correct in urging that " . . . in the short history of its existence . . . Soviet Russia experienced more political tensions and conflicts than any other state in the same period of years," and that " . . . more Soviet political treaties were subject to more conflicts and tensions than any other political treaties."[70]

67. See, for example, remarks of General LeMay in *Nuclear Test Ban Treaty: Hearings*, p. 414.

68. For example of acceptance of the conclusion, see Arthur Krock, *New York Times*, May 11, 1961, p. 34.

69. *Nuclear Test Ban Treaty: Hearings*, p. 70.

70. *Soviet Treaties*, p. 282.

Or a complete examination of the Soviet record, in respect to all political categories, on the procedures indicated refined to take account of the qualitative factor, may show even lower infidelity ratios. Adjusting for magnitude means weighting by some measure of importance instances of fulfillment as well as instances of nonfulfillment, and the Soviet record of fulfilling its wartime commitments would loom large in any accounting. In any event, although possible, it is by no means certain that improved and expanded treatment would harden the judgment.

The conventional American wisdom—to use a patronizing term—rates Soviet faithfulness high. The reasons for this are easily conjectured. One of them is the distorting effect of the Cold War intellectual milieu, an effect which only the strongest-willed and most self-critical are able to recognize and conscientiously offset. But besides this stands another reason of less subjective character. Many of the Soviet violations in question have, like the recent moves against Czechoslovakia, been spectacular and unambiguous, involving invasion, death, and sometimes even deportation to millions and national extinction. They have been carried out brutally, with callous disrespect for individuals. They have been rationalized in terms absurd on their face. In other words, many of the malefactions constituting the negative side of the Soviet record—and these are the events that make news—have been crimes in the grand manner, brutally executed, ludicrously rationalized. Not blunders worse than crimes, but blunders superimposed upon crimes. The stigma attached to the size, implementation, and attendant explanation of the wrongdoing has in short, I believe, been unwittingly allowed to color the record as a whole.

But once appearance is probed and analyzed, the reality turns out to be something milder. Fidelity, not infidelity is the norm. While a final evaluation must await the more intensive and extensive investigation outlined, the record does not warrant the extreme charges brought against it. And while unclouded optimism is foolish, as Czechoslovakia should constantly remind us, still, insofar as concerns the possibility of the USSR's contributing steadily along this dimension to international stability, the future is not without hope.

EPILOGUE: RECONCILIATION

CHAPTER 8

The Mediation of Differing Views

Care in small things—in the definition and differentiation of concepts, in the specification of rules for their application to the historical record, in the aggregating of results—will go far toward producing the clearer generalizations of Soviet external conduct, the firmer substantiation of those generalizations, and so the better disciplined learning to which all who profess the ideals of scholarship aspire. Such care, exemplified in the treatment accorded the facet of infidelity to promise by the preceding chapter, will do much to reduce the considerable differences now prevailing among students in the field and to bring closer together the divergent images—the images of Great Beast, Mellowing Tiger, and Neurotic Bear—which they have severally developed.

But it will not do all one would like. Particularly will it not where the reduction of differences and the development of what we are pleased these days to call "consensus" are concerned. For differences of conclusion depend on more than failure to abide by the canons of right method. They depend also on differences in the choice of starting points and in the resolution of a myriad of procedural issues too numerous to be covered by even the most exhaustive book of rules. And these may, in fact these are, likely to trace ultimately to deep-seated differences in emotional commitment and mind sets.

More needs to be done if gaps between images are truly to be narrowed and the images themselves brought close to a single focus. And that more required, it seems to me, is effort quite differently directed. That more is meliorative effort directed no longer at the point of the investigatory process individually pursued, but at the point of communication and exchange of results. That more is the kind of positive attempt to iron out, to reconcile, or at least to understand differences between individuals that is implied by the term "mediation."

The general problem of mediating between divergent views and viewers and mitigating the attendant discord is more familiar in other contexts. George Kennan gives us a trenchant example in the opening chapter of the work constituting part of our sample. With his customary insight and felicity of phrase Kennan there points out that the discord that grew between Soviet Russia and the West in the immediate postrevolution period over such events as Soviet adherence to the Treaty of Brest-Litovsk, Western interventions in Murmansk and Archangel, etc., derived in considerable measure from the fact that the Soviets saw these events mainly as helps or hindrances to the survival of their fledgling regime, while the Western nations saw them primarily as helps or hindrances to the prosecution of the war against Germany.[1] In other words, whereas the conceptual framework for drawing meaning from the events in the first case assigned primary importance to Soviet domestic security, in the second it assigned primary importance to Soviet (and Western) external security. Kennan does not get into the specifics of how this particular conflict of views might have been mediated, beyond suggesting that a little imaginative insight on both sides might have softened the discord and its repercussions through succeeding years. He nevertheless points up the issue neatly.

Types of image of Soviet external conduct correlate fairly closely with types of perception of the international order as a whole and with types of prescription for American conduct, as suggested at the end of Chapter 2. Consideration of the topic in broader context appearing to me the more useful mode of treatment, the present and final chapter begins with a description of these correlates and with a symbolic portrayal of and commentary upon the properties of the continuum which they form.

CORRELATIVE TYPES OF WORLD VIEW

Types of perception of the international order associated with the image types abstracted from the works of our sample include three or four primary elements. There is, first, some concept of desirable world order. There is, second, some concept of a structural factor or

1. *Russia and the West under Lenin and Stalin* (Boston: Little, Brown, 1961), pp. 10–11.

factors having to do with individual states or groups of states that contribute to or detract from the end. There is, third, some concept of other favoring or nonfavoring factors such as size. There is, fourth and last, a concept of the modifiableness or nonmodifiableness of the foregoing three.

Perceptions differ from one another to the extent that they incorporate differing values of one or more of these elements. The desirable order may be perceived as one predominantly of justice, one of peace, or one combining the two. Structural attributes believed conducive or not conducive to the end may be attributes of internal structure— whether "open" or "closed," "totalitarian" or "democratic," "capitalist" or "socialist"—or attributes of external interstate relationship— whether aligned or unaligned. Other factors favoring or not favoring the goal may include the power of states, whether great or small, the intensity of nationalism, whether high or low, and the level of technology, whether prenuclear or nuclear. The last three factors may be considered easily modifiable, modifiable through slow or radical change, or not modifiable at all.

The Ultra-Hard image of Soviet external conduct, it will be remembered, sees that conduct as expansion-minded without limit, extremely expansive, militant, and immoral in implementation, and highly tyrannical toward its own.[2] It sees it as relentlessly initiatory, motivated by the lust for power, posing mortal danger to the rest of mankind. It sees it, *in toto*, as utterly aggressive, and it sees it, moreover, as unchangeably, irrevocably so.

The type of world view embracing the Ultra-Hard image considers Soviet conduct typical of a broader category of states called Communist or, sometimes, one yet broader called totalitarian and bound up with a "closed" society.[3] Contrasted sharply with that conduct is the conduct of states of a diametrically opposed category variously called democratic, nontotalitarian, or non-Communist, and integrally bound up with an "open" or "free" society. Democratic states characteristically behave quite differently: they are preservation- rather than expansion-minded, pacific rather than militant, cooperative rather than tyrannical

2. Cf. Table 6, p. 56.

3. Robert Strausz-Hupé, and others, *Protracted Conflict,* Harper Colophon ed. (New York: Harper & Row, 1963), p. 133.

toward their own. They respond rather than initiate and are driven by a zeal for human welfare rather than a lust for power. They are amenable to entreaty and persuasion rather than force alone. They are capable of a genuine evolution rather than being unmodifiable.[4] Communist states do not vary significantly one from another in their external behavior.[5] So with states in the democratic or even broader non-Communist category. "Communist" and "democratic" exhaust the possibilities insofar as behavior on the international scene is concerned; there is no genuine third category.[6]

External alignments and interstate groupings follow naturally, in composition, structure, and functioning, upon internal structure, by which they are generated. The biggest and strongest of Communist states welds the lesser ones into a single organism, the better to pursue its aggressive aims, and it imposes on this bloc a tyrannical control. The biggest and strongest of the democracies thereupon seeks, in reaction, to rally around it the lesser democracies and non-Communist states, and to unite them in collective-defense alliances, which it leads through persuasion and exhortation as the first among equals.[7] The two groupings exhaust the possibilities. There is no significant third category of state, as defined by internal structure, and so there is no true third alignment category. Those who claim to be neutral are not truly such: if not clearly favoring the democratic camp, they are for all intents and purposes in the enemy's.[8]

The overall picture of the world that thus takes shape is one in which those forces friendly or contributory to the desired future order of peace and justice, and those forces not friendly or contributory to such order, are quickly, clearly, and finally identifiable and distinguishable from one another. The grounds of distinction are internal structure and the interstate groupings derivative therefrom. Contributing to that order, and alone so contributing, are the democratic states and the alliances they form.[9] Threatening that order, and alone

4. Ibid., pp. 143–44.
5. Ibid., p. 139.
6. Ibid., passim. This is an inference from the work as a whole.
7. Ibid., p. 145.
8. In ibid., p. 131, neutrals are referred to as "so-called," on p. 57 the term being put in quotes.
9. Ibid., p. 146.

so threatening, are the Communist states and the alliances they form. States of the second group, under the shrewdly calculating command of its strongest element, strive ceaselessly and ubiquitously, through force and through guile, to communize and reduce to vassalage the states of the first group.[10] Such is their nature, moreover, that barring cataclysms within or without, they will continue so to do into the indefinite future. States of the first group, depending upon their perceptiveness of the reality as here outlined, upon their ability to contain the subversion sponsored by their opponents, upon their ability to submerge their differences, etc., respond strongly or weakly, as the case may be. In the conflict that thus develops the existence of a third force—of a third role in the drama—is an illusion. Those who profess to the status of neutral are essentially aiders and abettors of the Communist camp, the preferred term being "pawn," or "proxy," or "neutral" qualified by a "so-called."[11] The controlling maxim is, "He who is not for us is against us." The global condition is therefore one of a straight, two-sided war, and of a war, furthermore, that is "a unitary, unending war to the finish."[12]

The course of action advocated by this world view flows logically from these systems. As the challenge is total, varying only in mode, undifferentiated as to space or time, integrated, so must the response be. If we are to stand any chance whatsoever of achieving the desired future order, the democracies, and especially the strongest, must remain stronger than the Communists.[13] Facing the options open to them, the free world, and especially its leaders, must choose firm and resolute policies over weak and irresolute ones. They must counter promptly, steadily, the initiative of the other side, without squeamishness as to means, casting aside neurotic fears of nuclear holocaust.[14] Wherever or whenever the Communists or their proxies seek to advance—no matter how inconvenient the moment or disadvantageous

10. Ibid., passim.
11. Ibid., p. 57 for use of "so-called" and pp. 57–66 for treatment of "proxy" concept.
12. Bertram D. Wolfe, *Communist Totalitarianism: Keys to the Soviet System*, rev. ed. (Boston: Beacon Press, 1961), p. 305. See also Strausz-Hupé, and others, *Protracted Conflict*, pp. 109–10, 149.
13. Strausz-Hupé, and others, *Protracted Conflict*, p. 127.
14. Ibid., pp. 123, 126.

the battlefield—there and then they must stand firm. For present superior force and resolve, and the Communists will back down and peace be preserved until such time as internal revolt returns them to the ranks of non-Communists, if not democracies. But absent such force, such resolve, and with each success their appetites will increase, they will become ever more emboldend, and they will end forcing their opponents to choose between nuclear war and total surrender.[15] The further implications, for American policy in particular, are too clear to require elaboration.

This kind of world view is sometimes labeled dichotomous or, yet more esoterically, Manichaean. I prefer chiaroscuro, however, with the esthetic connotation. Its elements I have abstracted largely from *Protracted Conflict,* discussed earlier and at some protractedness in Chapter 3. But other works developing the Ultra-Hard image of Soviet conduct, where they reveal themselves at all in this matter, express themselves in very similar terms. Bouscaren, Goodman, Kintner, Overstreet, and Wolfe say almost exactly the same thing. Dallin's, Kulski's, and Librach's views are both less extreme and less explicitly developed.

The Mixed image of Soviet external conduct—the third of the three—I take out of order in order to enhance the contrast with the Ultra-Hard. The Mixed image sees conduct as moderately expansion-minded only. It sees it as generally militant in implementation, intermittently expansive and militarist, not particularly immoral, moderately hegemonic toward its own.[16] It sees it as largely responsive rather than initiatory—particularly so where expansion and resort to military force are concerned. It sees it as driven by fear, posing moderate threat to mankind, and moderately changing.

The world view of which the Mixed image is part does not associate the conduct described with a certain internal structure.[17] Nor does it distinguish such conduct radically from another sort of conduct associated with another structure. It sees Soviet conduct as fairly typical of all states, however organized they may be internally. It sees

15. Ibid., p. 130.
16. Cf. Table 6, p. 56.
17. Louis J. Halle, *The Cold War as History* (New York: Harper & Row, 1967), pp. 157–60.

all states and their variants, democracies, Communist, or other, as expansion-minded, intermittently expansive and militarist, but responsively so, and driven more by fear than by ambition—on the whole, self-assertive, but defensively and restrictedly so. The same it finds true of the various and shifting interstate groupings which they form.

The overall picture of the world that thus takes shape is one in which action contributory toward the desired future order and action detracting therefrom are not surely prefigured. Action in one direction or the other is not the product of a structure that can be readily marked, but the product of the contingencies of time, circumstance, and, indeed, accident. All states are potentially disruptive. The fact of statehood, of sovereignty, generates a heightened concern for security, and this concern may embroil two nations in damaging conflict whether through misreading of intentions, the accident of alliances, or sheer inadvertence.[18] This conflict may then intensify and spread—in fact, it is quite likely to.[19] At the root of the problem are misunderstandings of purpose so well symbolized by the simile of the bottled scorpion and tarantula seeing murderous intent in each other's moves—misunderstandings so tartly summarized by the observation that "the process of driving the (encircling) danger back becomes, to the eye of the outsider, the process of imperial expansion."[20] At the same time, states are capable of learning and exercising a measure of self-restraint in the interests of maintaining a viable equilibrium.[21] The global condition is thus a variegated one, alignment patterns shifting with the tides, periods of stress alternating with periods of calm, local wars sometimes waxing into general ones but sometimes not.

It follows from this that the optimum strategy for achieving the desired future order cannot be plotted easily once and for all. Such strategy is not a simple matter of wholesale support for the free world and wholesale opposition to the Communist. It is generally, on the part of all states, a matter of exercising restraint and forbearance in dealings with one another. In somewhat greater detail this is taken to

18. Frederick L. Schuman, *The Cold War: Retrospect and Prospect*, 2nd ed. (Baton Rouge: Louisiana State University Press, 1967), p. 72.
19. Halle, *The Cold War as History*, pp. 413–14.
20. Ibid., p. 17.
21. Schuman, *The Cold War*, p. 129.

mean acceptance of a moderate view of security requirements, the preference of diplomacy over violence and the confinement of the latter to immediately threatening situations, respect for neutrals, the seeking of accommodation with enemies on global problems like arms control, the building up of international organizations, etc.[22] It is further taken to imply prompt and firm, yet measured, action to safeguard the peace on occasions when the power equilibrium may be menaced by megalomaniacs of the Hitler stripe.[23] But the contents cannot be spelled out completely. Application to the concrete situation depends on the contingencies of time and place, on a pragmatic assessment of particular circumstances. Such policy and action, while incumbent upon all states, whatever their internal structure or ideology may be, are particularly so upon the great powers, upon whom especially the future rides.[24]

This world view associated with the Mixed image of Soviet conduct pictures a global scene of many tones and shades grouped largely around the center of the white-black scale. Let us call it therefore the multigrayed or multitoned view. I have abstracted it largely from Halle and Schuman. But the others of Mixed persuasion seem to reflect similar positions, though they speak rarely in general terms.

The Hard image of Soviet conduct, lying between Ultra-Hard and Mixed, assigns to conduct values intermediate between those of the other two, with the notable exception of capacity for change. As described in Table 6, the Hard image sees conduct as expansion-minded, militant, ambition-driven, etc., but in lesser degree than does the Ultra-Hard. It concedes that responsiveness to the environment has some place in behavior and the element of fear in motivation, though in lesser degree than does the Mixed. It sees a greater capacity for change than either of the others.

The cognate world view is correspondingly intermediate. Internal structure remains as with the chiaroscuro a factor of primary importance insofar as contribution to the desired future is concerned; democratic and Communist or totalitarian are the leading types, the former being evaluated positively, the latter negatively.[25] External

22. Ibid., pp. 72–81, 93.
23. Halle, *The Cold War as History*, Chapter III.
24. Ibid., p. 24.
25. Marshall D. Shulman, *Beyond the Cold War* (New Haven: Yale University Press, 1966), p. 100.

arrangements reinforce characteristic internal tendencies: alliances, interstate organizations, etc., enhance both the democracies' benign impact upon the environment and the Communists' malignant impact. Only now other factors make their appearance, the picture growing less simple. As implied by the image of the Soviets, the behavior of the leading types is less extreme, and variation, evolution, and proliferation come in varying degrees to be taken into account. Significant variation within types is noticed, absolute statements having to be converted accordingly into generalizations. Democracies do not always behave peaceably *(vide* Britain and France at Suez), nor Communist states aggressively *(vide* Yugoslavia). Some evolution of species, even totalitarian species, takes place, and more is possible.[26] Third categories of state (the underdeveloped) and third categories of alignment (the neutrals) begin to play independent roles.[27] Virulent nationalism becomes a force independently to be reckoned with, since any state—democratic, Communist, or underdeveloped (although especially the last mentioned)—is vulnerable to the virus.[28] The level of technology, especially military technology, also becomes a force.[29] In short, the nonstructural factors and the contingencies of place, time, and accident featured by the multitoned world view begin to enter into calculations.

In consequence, threats to the desired future of peace and justice, while they are seen still to come primarily from Communist sources, no longer come exclusively from there. They come also from excessive ethnocentrism, from nuclear advance. The global condition is no longer a two-sided, total war to the finish between democracies and Communist states, open and closed societies.[30] The relationship between these two groups is now a "limited adversary relationship."[31] This relation changes—has changed and may change again; indeed, the entire scene is in flux.[32] And there are other conflicts in progress.[33]

In further consequence, the indicated imperative for the democra-

26. Ibid., Chapter 3.
27. Ibid., p. 20.
28. Ibid., pp. 29–30.
29. Ibid., pp. 29–31.
30. Ibid., p. 20.
31. Ibid., p. 100.
32. Ibid., Chapter 2.
33. Ibid., p. 31.

cies, and particularly the United States, is not just to keep their defenses up, to strengthen their alliances, and to stand firm in the face of
any or all Communist initiatives—although these things come first.[34]
Required is a more flexible, discriminating course.[35] On some matters
(e.g. arms control) a conciliatory approach is the order of the day, with
agreements to be sought with all but the most unregenerate of Communist opponents. Not all non-Communist states are to be hugged to
the democratic bosom, nor all Communist states repulsed.[36] Neutrals
are no longer to be viewed as per se immoral but tolerated, if not wel-
comed, in the new spirit of "Who is not against us is for us." Individual cases, in brief, are to be viewed more on individual merit.

The lineaments of this semichiaroscuro or pluritoned world view
are abstracted from Shulman's *Beyond the Cold War*. But Kennan,
Mosely, Schwartz, Tucker, and Ulam, where they speak to the subject,
suggest positions close to Shulman's.

While not represented in the works of the sample, the fourth and
fifth views that fill out the spectrum of logical possibilities should be
noted, for they are to be found in the writings of some American
students, they may some day be reflected in more, and, however this
may be, consideration of all the possibilities enhances the analysis.

The Ultra-Soft view of Soviet conduct, at the other end of the scale,
sees that conduct as preservation-minded only, as utterly nonexpansive,
conciliatory, and moral, resorting to force only *in extremis,* through
and through cooperative with its own. It sees conduct as largely responsive to the moves of others, motivated solely by concern for
mankind, exerting a stabilizing influence upon the world. It sees it,
in toto, as peace-loving, and it sees it as permanently, unchangeably so.

The world view embracing this image postulates two types of state
only and two camps of alliance systems built thereon, the socialist
(Communist), to which the Soviet belongs, and the capitalist, of completely opposite (i.e. aggressive) nature. Third types, significant variation within the existing two, significant transformation short of the
preordained cataclysm of proletarian revolution—these things are denied. In consequence, threats to the desired future order are clearly

34. Ibid., pp. 101–02.
35. Ibid., pp. 88, 110.
36. Ibid., pp. 104–05.

and finally identifiable: they come from the capitalist camp only (and the pseudo-neutrals siding with it). The courses of action prescribed for both sides are to do what in any case their inner natures compel them to do—the capitalists to attack, the Communists to defend the peace. This world view, which may be styled reverse chiaroscuro, is of course the official Soviet-Stalinist view of the world, exemplified in the US by the writings of Party members and sympathizers.[37]

Finally, between the reverse chiaroscuro and multitoned world views lies the last of the five possibilities. This view, while retaining an essentially two-valued scheme, with states of the socialist (Communist) side identified as the Children of Light, those of the capitalist (democratic) side as the Children of Darkness, tones down the contrast measurably. It does so in the usual manner: by characterizing less crudely and extremely, by conceding some variation of consequence between and within types, by admitting some evolution.[38]

Interrelationships and Acceptance

The five kinds of perception of the international order and attendant prescriptions for the attainment of the desired future that have been distinguished above are related to one another in an orderly way, and the academic community's adherence to them exhibits an orderly pattern. The better to bring out these relationships and this pattern, I take the continuum they form and give it pictorial representation.

The continuum which the five views form is, like the continuum of the five views of Soviet conduct which they respectively embrace, a continuum defined in terms of the hardness attributed to the Communist structure. If for convenience one represents this continuum as a 10-point scale, then the chiaroscuro view may be located at point 9, the pluritoned at point 7, and so forth.

Figure A is my pictorialization of this continuum. Columns 1 and 2 list the viewpoints and their numerical values in the appropriate order. Columns 3–7 spell out, in pictographic form, each view's ideas

---

37. For instance, a summary of this position in late Stalin years is found in David A. Shannon, *The Decline of American Communism* (New York: Harcourt Brace, 1959), pp. 23–33.

38. Cf. almost any article on the international situation in the Communist periodical *Political Affairs*, as, for instance, Herbert Aptheker, "Theory of Peaceful Coexistence," 46, no. 7 (July 1967): 47–58.

Name	Rating	Content				
		Kinds of State and Their Bearing on Desired Future				
		DEMOCRATIC			COMMUNIST	
		Pure and Aligned	Modified and Semialigned	Intergrade and Neutral	Modified and Semialigned	Pure and Aligned
(1)	(2)	(3)	(4)	(5)	(6)	(7)

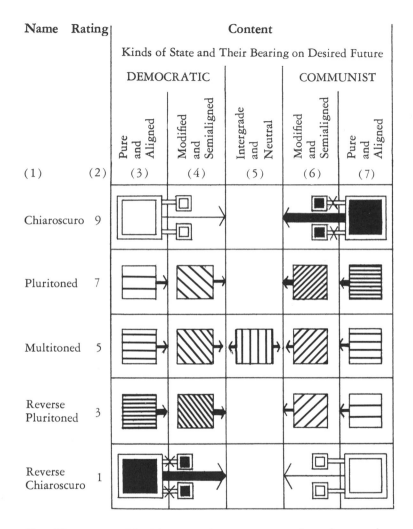

Chiaroscuro	9
Pluritoned	7
Multitoned	5
Reverse Pluritoned	3
Reverse Chiaroscuro	1

Note: Names are explained in text; ratings are on a 10-point scale measuring Communist hardness. Shading indicates degree of hostility toward desired future of peace and justice; width of arrow, degree of resort to coercion and guile in day-by-day conduct; number of enclosing lines, degree of invariancy; ties between great and small squares, ✳ and =, relations respectively of domination and equality.

of the roles of different categories of state in the quest for global peace and justice (the classification running in terms of internal structures). Occupied squares indicate categories which the viewer regards as playing independent roles in the drama, unoccupied squares those he does not. Shading indicates degree of hostility to the desired future order, black meaning extreme enmity, white complete amity. Size of arrow stands for degree of addiction to coercion and guile in day-by-day behavior, broad meaning high militancy and deception, narrow low. Size of squares in the extreme cases (they are left out of the others for clarity's sake) distinguishes the great powers from the small, the character of the rule relation between the two being marked by the symbols (for unequal) and = (for equal). Number and indefiniteness of boundaries indicate invariance or incapacity for change, two or more meaning high, one low. The figures opposite the chiaroscuro view, at point 9 on the scale, thus portray a view which sees the world as composed of only two categories of nations, the democratic or free which are peace-loving, addicted to persuasion and honesty, and grouped cooperatively about the leading power, and the Communist, which are aggressive, addicted to force and guile, and dominated by the leading power. Members of both categories are on this view rigid and unalterable. The figures opposite the multitoned view, at point 5 on the scale, by contrast portray a view which sees the world as composed of several categories of nations, authoritarian as well as democratic on the non-Communist side, Communist-revisionist and Communist-dogmatist on the other. On this view none are inherently inimical to the desirable world order; all are potential threats thanks to nationalist forces, to the accidents of miscalculation and unwise decisions, etc.; and all are potentially modifiable, transformable into other structures. The figures opposite the reverse chiaroscuro view, at point 1 of the scale, finally, portray a view which, again, sees the world as composed of only two categories of nations, but this time finds the capitalist (democratic) to be the ones that are inherently aggressive, addicted to force and guile, and grouped submissively around the leader, the Communist to be the peace-loving, etc.

Of the various interrelationships among world views which Figure A brings out—properties of the continuum, as I shall call them—three are particularly instructive, it seems to me.

The first of these properties is the bilateral symmetry that is exhibited by each of the world views and which revolves about the intergrade column as axis. Each view differentiates about equally on each side, and assigns to counterparts on the two sides equal and opposite values. Thus the chiaroscuro, embracing the Ultra-Hard view of Soviet conduct, sees Communist states as in the extreme inimical to the desiderated order of the future, and motivated by a lust for power and conquest, but sees democratic states as in high degree friendly to that order, being motivated by a beneficent desire to achieve it; sees Communist states as forming a sun-and-satellite system dominated by the largest power, but democratic states as forming a loose alliance of equals in which the largest power leads by persuasion and example; sees Communist states expansion-minded and in high degree militant, immoral, and intractable, but non-Communist states preservation-minded, in high degree pacific, moral, and tractable. So too the pluri-toned. The differentiation of subtypes now noted in the Communist world is matched by a similar one in the democratic. The lesser degrees of inimicality to the desired order, of selfish motivation, of hegemony, of militancy now noted of some Communist states and the system they form, are matched by the lesser degrees of friendliness, selfless motivation, and cooperativeness now noted of some democratic states and their system. Lesser degrees of expansionism, militancy, immorality, and intractability assigned to some states of the first category are offset by lesser degrees of the corresponding opposites assigned to some states of the second. And as with the chiaroscuro and pluritoned, so, *mutatis mutandis,* with the other three. Throughout the array, what is true of the second type is the opposite of what is true of the first. Second differs from first as left hand differs from right, mirror reproduction from original. One implication of this is that views of Soviet and American conduct are functionally related to one another, and the continuum may alternately be considered as defined in terms of softness of view of American conduct, point 9, for instance, representing also the most charitable concept of American behavior.

A second and associated property is the bilateral symmetry about the pattern as a whole, revolving about the central position as axis. The most conspicuous mark of this symmetry is the fact that as the names imply, the reverse chiaroscuro world view is the mirror image of the chiaroscuro. Both are two-valued, denying independent roles to third types or variants of the two main ones, considering claims to a neutral status to be covers for partiality to the other side and hence essentially spurious. Both ascribe essential goodness and benignity to one side, essential badness and malignity to the other. But the bad qualities which view 9 assigns to Communist societies, view 1 assigns to capitalist (democratic) ones; the good qualities which view 9 assigns to democratic societies, view 1 assigns to socialist (Communist) ones. Again, where an adherent of view 9 considers a claim to neutrality spurious because he believes it simply a cover for essential pro-Communism, an adherent of view 1 reaches the same conclusion because he believes the claim a cover for essential pro-capitalism (pro-democracy). Both, finally, see the structures as essentially unmodifiable or, to be more precise, modifiable only by some catastrophic event such as revolution or crushing military defeat.

The symmetry noted between views 9 and 1 prevails also between views 7 and 3. For partisans of both these views, the world, while in a broad sense recognized still as bipolar, nevertheless in detail is considered plurivalued and more malleable. Both recognize significant variation of type and intergrades in respect both to internal structure and alignment status. Both see some variety of internal structure on both sides and believe some structures better placed in a third category than in either of the two dominant ones. Both see the relation of large to small, on both sides, as neither uniformly one of utter subordination nor yet one of complete equality. Upright neutrality may still be nonexistent, neutrals being conceived as leaning one way or the other. But the status is no longer conceived as spurious, a mask for essential alliance with or subservience to one side or the other. As with structure and alignment status, so with shade. True, one side remains essentially peaceful, using force and deception only in defense, the other essentially warlike, using force and deception in the cause of self-aggrandizement. But there are exceptions: the essentially peaceful sometimes "aggress," the essentially warlike sometimes agree to and abide by measures serving objectively the desired goal. The mirror imagery relation is, of course, marked by the fact that while adherents of view 7 continue to ascribe essential goodness or peaceableness to the democratic camp, essential aggressiveness to the Communist, and while they see the first as only on infrequent occasion aggressive, and the second only on infrequent occasion peaceable, these affirmations are reversed by adherents of view 3.

The third property to be noted of the array of world views is that moderate findings in respect to hardness of conduct and contribution to world order go along with a sense of the diversity and modifiableness of structures and alignment possibilities. The world of partisans of the multitoned view is a more complicated world than that of chiaroscuro or its opposite. Whereas the latter group structures into two extreme categories, considering deviation apparent and not real, for the partisans of the multitoned deviation is real and makes a difference. For instance, whereas for both extremes Yugoslav departures from presumed Communist norms are either of no consequence or an outright Communist deception or capitalist trick; and whereas for both her neutrality is an illusion, making her a Trojan horse or imperialist lackey, as the case may be; for the partisan of the multitoned, internal variation and nonalignment are real and, indeed, are evaluated as positive contributions to the sought-for end. Again, the gray world of the multitoned view is a more fluid one than that of the extremes. For the partisan of the extreme views, change can only be catastrophic. Structures do not alter through slow evolution: they are transformed suddenly by the agency of revolution from within or military defeat from without. For the partisan of the multitoned view, on the other hand, gradualness is the norm. Structures do alter significantly by degrees: post-Stalinist liberalization in the Soviet Union is just such a case for them. So also do alignments, which tighten or weaken significantly—*vide* the erosion of both Eastern and Western blocs since 1956. And so, finally, do policies, which harden, loosen, then perhaps harden again, in near endless sequence.

The pattern of adherence to and acceptance of the various views follows that for the images of Soviet conduct. If our sample is a good one, a preponderance of serious students adhere in fairly equal proportions to the first three, and the corporate view for the community —academic orthodoxy, if you will—therefore falls in the range of pluritoned or semichiaroscuro, or say, at a point roughly between 7 and 8 on the continuum. Judging, moreover, from the phasing within the 1959–68 decade of the works of the sample and the content of works published since 1968, the median or corporate view has moderated perceptibly, shifting down the spectrum. The official position of the United States government, it is worth noting, has behaved similarly. Under Foster Dulles this was straight chiaroscuro, correlating impact on peace almost perfectly with internal structure, denying independent role to the "immoral" neutral. Under Kennedy and Johnson, on the other hand—and Dean Rusk to the contrary nothwithstanding—the outlines have softened. These considerations suggest the not surprising theorem that academic orthodoxy is not much more moderate than the official position and moves with it, both movements being rather obviously tied to the tension level of the global system and, more especially, of the actual, working Soviet-American relationship.

The five world views and the continuum they form have a wider applicability—they describe attitudes and opinions within broader, supra-American contexts. A brief consideration of them within two of these contexts (the Soviet-American and the global) may, I hope, strike the reader less as a digression than as an illuminating extension of remarks of, say, the character of a coda to a musical structure.

There have been two major Soviet postwar viewpoints, the Stalinist and the Khrushchevian. The Stalinist, which prevailed until the death of the old tyrant, received its classic formulation in the so-called two-camp speech given by Andrei Zhdanov at the founding meeting of the Cominform in 1947.[39] In this view, the impact of the various states of the world upon the desired future is perfectly correlated with type of internal structure and the "camps" to which particulars of the type belong; there exist only two of these types and camps, socialist (Communist) and capitalist or imperialist (democratic), the first being inherently peace-loving, the second inherently aggressive; and the unavoidable destiny of man is a war to the finish between the two, a war ending in socialist victory. Here is reverse chiaroscuro, crude and simple, belonging at point 1 on the continuum. The Khrushchevian world view, formulated originally at the Twentieth Party Congress in 1956, is more moderate.[40] In this view, generalization on the two types replaces universalization; proliferation, variation, modifiable-

39. Excerpted in Alvin Rubinstein, ed., *The Foreign Policy of the Soviet Union* (New York: Random House, 1960), pp. 236–39.

40. Leo Gruliow, ed., *Current Soviet Policies* (New York: Praeger, 1957), Vol. II, pp. 29–38.

ness enter. Capitalist states are not invariably aggressive nor socialist states invariably peace-loving (the Chinese, for instance, ultimately turn out to be aggressive). A third category of state, called national-bourgeois, and a third camp, called neutral, take their stands between socialist and capitalist. The final transition to socialism within each nation is no longer necessarily a matter of violence, nor is the showdown between major camps inevitably a matter of war. Here is a pluritoned view, answering to a point close to 3 on the continuum. The Soviet Union being a highly authoritarian society, the academic community has formally accepted these officially promulgated views, and only then, unanimously shifting with officialdom from the first to the second in the immediate post-Stalin years.

Within the larger context of the Soviet-American relationship, acceptance of the various viewpoints thus has tended to polarize around mirror images first near the extremes of points 9 and 1, and later near the more moderate points 7 and 3 (Soviet acceptances are of course more highly concentrated). On the whole, the two nations tend to view the world, themselves, and one another in very much the same way—with only the signs reversed. And their views have shifted in much the same degree, and at much the same time, with only the direction reversed. As the median view of American academia and officialdom has moderated with the onset of the '60s, moving down from a point beween 9 and 8 to one near 7 or so on the continuum, the median Soviet view has moved up, from point 1 to 3.[41] As the median American view has become more discriminating and tolerant, more affirmative of complexity, so has the Soviet. On this point, of the relation of world views, the tendency is pronounced, if modest, toward convergence.

This characteristic of mirror imagery between median American and Soviet views, which has been commented upon before not infrequently, should not be misinterpreted.[42] The symmetry prevails only

41. For changes from Stalinist position that mark the variants of Khrushchev and his successors, see William Zimmerman, "Soviet Perceptions of the United States," in *Soviet Politics since Khrushchev,* ed. Alexander Dallin and Thomas B. Larson (Englewood Cliffs, N.J.: Prentice-Hall, 1968), pp. 163–80.

42. For such other commentary, see, for example, Herbert Spiro, *World Politics: The Global System* (Homewood, Ill.: Dorsey Press, 1966), pp. 301–10.

approximately, and only in respect to the factors incorporated in the definition of the types rather than wholesale. The Communists, for instance, are necessitarian in their outlook, as their opposite numbers in the US are not. The Communists affirm as inevitable the triumph throughout the world of their kind of society. Partisans of democracy do not. To the question of whether democracy will triumph, the latter answer, "This depends."[43] Specifically, it depends for them on whether or not the democracies resolve correctly the choice open to them, opting for military strength and firm resistance to the other side's initiatives over weakness and "appeasement." No less important is it to point out that the mirror-image relationship between these two says nothing about relative truth: the chiaroscuro view of Foster Dulles and *Protracted Conflict* may turn out to be, as Americans hope, a truer picture of affairs than its opposite.

Beyond American and Soviet views lie those of the other Western powers, and of China, Yugoslavia, and the Third World. The views of the other Western powers, one can presume, occupy ranges more moderate than that of American views, the median nevertheless falling in the upper half of the continuum. Maoism is, of course, ultra-Stalinism, hence reverse chiaroscuro standing at the opposite end of the scale from the views of the work of Ultra-Hard persuasion that takes its name from Mao—*Protracted Conflict*. While the caveats noted above apply here too, the mirror imagery can be striking down to very detail. The statements in which Mao and company exalt socialism and excoriate capitalism could, with simple transposition of terms, as well have been written by our authors of Ultra-Hard persuasion. Consider, for instance, the Chinese complaint that the imperialists "have been pursuing their policy of nuclear blackmail in order to realize their ambition of enslaving the people of all countries and dominating the world."[44] With the appropriate substitution of "Communists" for "imperialists," such a statement would fit smoothly into the text of *Protracted Conflict*.

If the Chinese stand may aptly be called ultra-Stalinist, the Yugo-

43. For instance, Strausz-Hupé, and others, *Protracted Conflict*, pp. 150–51.
44. The quote is from a letter of June 14, 1963, from the Central Committee of the Chinese Communist Party to the Central Committee of the Soviet Communist Party, quoted in the *New York Times*, July 5, 1963, p. 7.

slav may be called infra-Khrushchevian. The various Khrushchevian modifications of Stalinism—the differentiation of types and variants within types, the conversion of statements about types from absolutes to generalities, the affirmation of gradualism—all these the Yugoslavs carry a step or two further.[45] Besides national-bourgeois structures, they find the welfare capitalism of the Belgian or Scandinavian kind also to be third categories, way stations between full-blooded capitalism and full-blooded socialism. Among socialist states they find a number of gradations from the pure Marxist variant (exemplified by Yugoslavia, *mirabile dictu*) through to the dogmatic or Trotskyite variant exemplified by the Chinese. Not all capitalist states are aggressive, nor all socialist states peace-loving. A socialist state can conceivably be aggressive, say the Yugoslavs with the Chinese in mind. Change by degree or evolution is now no longer the exception but the norm: the Yugoslavs see no inevitability to, as they abhor, violent change. Most important, by way of amendment to the Khrushchevian view, is the shift in the relative assessment of internal and external structural variables. For the Khrushchevian, internal structure remains the main determinant of impact on the desired order of the future: one looks first to the question of whether a state is socialist or capitalist, second only to the question of whether it does or does not belong to a bloc or military alliance. With the Yugoslavs this relationship is reversed: bloc participation is the more important factor ("bloc" being a term which for the Yugoslavs, in contradistinction to the Soviets, includes any alliance, capitalist or socialist, however "defensive" the nominal purpose). Correlatively, neutrality or nonalignment is a more important condition than socialist structure from the point of view of world peace. The difference is of capital importance, as it puts the Yugoslavs on balance nearer point 5 than point 3 on the scale and makes their position not far from that, say, of Halle or Schuman.[46]

45. See Edvard Kardelj, *Socialism and War* (London: Methuen, 1961), for a full statement of the Yugoslav view.

46. The difference, and the importance which both sides attributed to the difference, lies behind the acerbity of the dispute between the USSR and Yugoslavia over the League of Yugoslav Communists' Ljubljana Program of 1958, for which see Robert Bass and Elizabeth Marbury, eds., *The Soviet-Yugoslav Controversy, 1948–1958: A Documentary Record* (New York: Prospect Books, 1959), Chapter IV.

Leading views from the third world develop this last point to its logical conclusion. Taking as a fair exposition of the general position a 1961 statement of the then Ghanian ambassador to Ethiopia, one finds that the factor upon which achievement of the desired future preponderantly depends is alignment status.[47] Alignment, participation in military alliances and similar exclusive organizations, is a grave threat to that future; nonalignment, participation in organizations that are not exclusive but transcendent (e.g. the UN), contribute positively to that future's advent. Internal structure, per contra, means nothing. Whether a state is capitalist or Communist apparently makes no difference at all insofar as achievement of the global goal is concerned. Beyond alignment status, what a state does at specific junctures is the important thing. "Positive neutralism," the name given the general approach, means "the conscientious exercise of judgment strictly in accordance with the merits of each issue, rather than with any regard to who the contesting parties are."[48] Finally, and consequent upon the above, the world of states is a malleable one. Since alignment is an act of will, states can choose to forgo joining others or, having joined, choose to withdraw. A future order marked by the disappearance or near disappearance of blocs is accordingly a possibility. Says the Ghanian ambassador, "The world needs more uncommitted countries; and the larger the number, the safer the world will be."[49] The world needs more; it has been getting more, and though the future is not pre-determined, the possibility of getting still more is there to be seized. This view corresponds precisely to point 5, the midpoint on the continuum.

Within the broadest context of all, the global context, one therefore finds a rich variety of world views, answering to every point on our continuum. While adequate materials are not ready at hand to establish the point beyond doubt, it seems clear that whereas the distribution within either the strictly American or the strictly Soviet context is heavily skewed (the latter especially so), and the distribution

47. E. M. Debrah, "Will Most Uncommitted Nations Remain Uncommitted?" *Annals of the American Academy of Political and Social Science* 336 (July 1961): 83–97.
48. Ibid., p. 85.
49. Ibid., p. 87.

within the Soviet-American context therefore largely bimodal, within this new and broadest context it is quite even throughout the range. It seems equally clear that, with the recent development of Titoist and neutralist views as well as shifts earlier noted in American and Soviet medians, the global trend of the last 15 years also has been toward the moderate center, hence closer approximation to the normal frequency pattern. This reinforces the case for the not surprising theorem already advanced, namely, that the polarization and dispersion of views are linked to an increase in international tensions, concentration to a decrease, moderation to peace.

These various interrelationships, properly understood, not only provide a deepened understanding of the differences between images. They also serve the further salutary purpose of reminding persons of one view that elsewhere others look at things in exactly the same way, only with the signs reversed. They may thus encourage the process of selfexamination advocated below.

Toward a Modicum of Consensus

To mediate is to interpose between parties to a conflict with a view to bringing about a reconciliation. Mediating between different schools of thought or, more accurately, the adherents of different schools of thought, is a matter of trying to see whether the differences can be reconciled, whether and to what extent the adversaries can reach some common ground or at least come to disagree amicably. Mediating between differing views of Soviet external conduct I take to mean seeing what can be done to maximize points of agreement, minimize points of disagreement, to the end of achieving not consensus in any total sense—for that would be no more desirable than it is possible—but a modicum of consensus or at least a tolerable and respectful sort of coexistence.

There are, it seems to me, three main things that partisans of the different images of Soviet conduct and correlative world views can and should do to move in the direction named. These may in sum be described as developing habits of recognizing at progressively deeper levels of thought and consciousness the bases of their differences, and then making allowance for what they find, each in his own thought and the communication thereof.

The first of these steps is to recognize the differences in the argument (its assumptions and reasonings) upon which differences of image are founded, and address oneself directly to them. Only some of the works of the sample do this (Kennan, as already noted, is outstanding). Works of Ultra-Hard persuasion particularly are apt to dismiss contrary argument out of hand as "wishful thinking," if indeed they recognize its existence at all.[50] In respect to basic assumptions, this is particularly true. Too few seem to be aware that there are problems of deciding which of contrasting categories to assign certain individual decisions to, whether initiative or response, strategic or tactical, and whom to assign ultimate authorship to, the formal agent or some presumed boss thereof. Is establishment of the Cominform in the fall of 1947 to be considered an initiative, or is it to be considered a response to the promulgation of the Truman Doctrine earlier that year? Is post-Stalin liberalization to be construed as a development of long-range, strategic significance, or one of tactics alone? Is the entry of Chinese volunteers into Korea in the fall of 1950 a move of Chinese or of Soviet authorship? Too few see that there are questions to be pondered before an answer is attempted. It is not claiming too much to say, in consequence, that to a considerable degree adherents of the different images and world views just are not talking to one another. There is an absence of true communication, a lack of dialogue, in the new vernacular.

This lack of true debate is particularly unfortunate where it relates to what emerges (thanks in good part to the elaboration and discussion of world views) as the most radical issue of all underlying the divergence of views—namely, whether Soviet Russia's activities are to be explained mainly as behavior generic to the category "state" or as behavior specific to a certain type of state, totalitarian, Communist, or however labeled. This writer must confess to strong opinions on this issue. The activities of Soviet Russia in the foreign field do not appear to him, in their principal features, to be different enough from those of other states, and especially other great states, to require special explanation. He looks upon the issue much as did the *Manchester Guardian* in the following satirical comment upon British

50. For example, Wladyslaw W. Kulski, *Peaceful Coexistence: An Analysis of Soviet Foreign Policy* (Chicago: Regnery, 1959), esp. pp. xvi, 88, 564.

reaction to the arrival of its first official Soviet visitors, a trade delega-
tion of 1920:

> The blow has fallen. A Bolshevist, a real live representative of
> Lenin, has spoken with the British Prime Minister face to face.
> A being . . . erect upon two legs and bearing the outward form
> and semblance of a man was seen to approach 10, Downing
> Street, yesterday, to ring at the door and gained admission. . . .
> The Bolshevist pretends to go downstairs like any ordinary
> mortal, but without doubt in doing so he conceals some deep
> design. Probably if scrutinized his method of locomotion would
> be found to depend on some inhuman device. Meanwhile, Mr.
> Lloyd George has seen him and lives.[51]

The writer accordingly, and with due obeisance to the principle of
Occam's Razor, opts for the generic explanation, or first of the two
alternatives. But this resolution of the issue is not above challenge.
What is above challenge, to get back to the main point, is the need for
all hands, whatever their beliefs, to engage the argument, and to engage it directly, clear-sightedly, and firmly. The debates over whether
conduct is primarily Communist or Russian, whether motivation is
based on ideology or national interest—while partially meeting the
need—do not quite get to the heart of the matter.

Direct address to points of difference entails accurate summation of
the rationale behind the opposing image, reasoned evaluation of the
rationale. It also entails doing such things in a spirit of civility, free of
ill-tempered remarks, *argumenta ad hominem,* and the like. Kennan's
treatment, in his final chapter, of the position urging all-out war
against the Soviets is exemplary.[52]

The achievement of tolerable coexistence among parties at this
level would also be forwarded if all hands were to work toward more
semantic clarity, less obscurantism. I say all hands, but because the
Ultra-Hards and partisans of chiaroscuro are particularly to blame in
this case, the exhortation should be directed to them in particular. It

51. *Manchester Guardian,* June 1, 1920, p. 6, quoted in W. P. and Zelda
K. Coates, *A History of Anglo-Soviet Relations* (London: Lawrence and
Wishart, 1944), pp. 26–27.
52. George F. Kennan, *Russia and the West,* pp. 388–95.

just won't do, to cite perhaps the most acute case of such obscurantism, to use the term "war" as cavalierly as some have done: to call "World War III" the condition between West and East that has prevailed since 1945; to speak of Khrushchev's communism as *The War Called Peace;* to say of the United States that it is, because the Communists have so willed it, in a bitter, unending war to the finish.[53] (That the Communists sometimes do the same, seeing war and peace as continuations one of another, is no defense, being utterly beside the point.) As Kennan rightly suggests, there are very real and considerable differences between what Russia and the West were doing to one another during the postwar years of tension, or what the Soviet government has been doing to its people, and what Russia and her Western allies, on the one hand, and Germany on the other were doing to one another in World Wars I and II.[54] And to call these various relations by the same name is to conceal these differences, to the discouragement of clearheaded analysis. If, despite this, "war'" is to do double duty, let it at least be qualified as "hot" or "cold," as the individual case requires. And so with similarly rubbery terms. The elimination or qualification of such terms will measurably improve communication.

The second of the steps to be taken relates to a deeper level of intellectual activity. There is, I surmise, a radical difference in philosophic or epistemological outlook which in part underlies and explains the differences of image and world views under discussion. This, too, needs to be recognized and taken into account in discourse, each participant examining with particular care his own outlook.

The difference between partisans of views 9 and 1, on the one hand, and those of view 5, on the other is not just, I believe, a difference between one, on the one hand, who sees a threat to peace and justice correlated sharply with social structure and thus readily and permanently concretized and one, on the other hand, who does not see it thus correlated but sees it dependent rather on other variables or contingencies of time and place. George Kennan distinguished Soviet

53. See Anthony Bouscaren, *Soviet Foreign Policy: A Pattern of Persistence* (New York: Fordham University Press, 1962), p. 4; Harry and Bonaro Overstreet, *The War Called Peace: Khrushchev's Communism* (New York: Norton, 1961), Chapter 13, "The Party's War Against the People"; and Wolfe, *Communist Totalitarianism*, p. 305.

54. *Russia and the West*, pp. 388–89.

from Western conceptualizations of the international order in the between-war period on the ground that the former were concerned with what Western states and governments *were,* while the latter were concerned originally, if not subsequently, with what Moscow and its leaders *did.*[55] This reading of the original difference-in-general between viewers East and West, can, it seems to me, be fairly applied also to the variants of Western conceptual schemes that developed later and, particularly after the Second World War, became differentiated: variants that are represented by the views at points 9 and 5 on my scheme.

Partisans of chiaroscuro commonly (though not always) focus hard on what Communist and democratic states *are,* partisans of the multitoned view on what they *do.* The former look first to the presumed inner nature or essence of the type, Communist, totalitarian, or democratic, as the case may be; then, and then only, do they look to particular month-by-month and year-by-year moves; and, finally, in cases of apparent conflict they adjust the second to the first, rather than the other way around.[56] For example, finding the essence of the totalitarian state to be egotism unlimited, driven by an unquenchable thirst for power and conquest, yet finding particular moves on the surface moderate and reasonable (such as the moves of the post-Stalin "thaw" of 1953–55), they overcome the apparent discrepancy not by modifying or calling into question the notion of power lust, but rather by reinterpreting the moderate moves, reading them as tactical maneuvers or deceptions designed to put the rest of the world off its guard and make it more vulnerable when the attack is renewed.[57] A similar discrepancy in the democratic case, between bellicose moves and the high-minded devotion to peace descriptive of the type, is dismissed as a temporary blurring of principle.[58] The various means by which consistency is brought into the picture I have dealt with above at length under the name "sifting devices."[59] One implication of this procedure is that the status of a given statement as factual or not is not

55. Ibid., p. 190.
56. For comment on these essences or their equivalents, see, for example, Strausz-Hupé, and others, *Protracted Conflict,* pp. 125, 133, 143.
57. For example, ibid., pp. 70–71.
58. Ibid., p. 144.
59. Cf. Chapter 3, above, pp. 74–75, 98.

of much consequence, and a change in such status as may be dictated by later evidence in no way affects something called the "internal logic" of the functioning of the type.[60]

At the other end of the spectrum, American Communists commonly proceed, of course, in the very same way. To preserve their diametrically opposed concept of the essences in question they too explain away inconvenient data on grounds of deceptiveness, tactical maneuver, and what all. All this certain opposite numbers at point 9 recognize, report eloquently, and condemn—blissfully unconscious of the fact that they are doing the same.[61] In the case of both extreme groups, one is reminded of medieval scholars' handling of the challenge to received opinion on the number of planets that was presented by Galileo's discovery of Jupiter's moons. Received opinions that there were seven such planets (sun, moon, Mercury, Venus, Mars, Jupiter, and Saturn) was preserved inviolate by the simple expedient of denying as evidence anything perceived through a telescope.[62]

Partisans of the pluritoned and multitoned views, on the other hand, pay more attention to particular moves and the conditions environing them. "Handsome is as handsome does," or more nearly so, at any rate. Gehlen's call for more attention to actual behavior reflects explicitly the general position.[63] There is little emphasis on the type and its differentiae. In the case of apparent conflict between particular moves and the presumed essence of the type—or, more precisely, conduct deducible from the latter—the latter may as soon be adjusted

60. Cf. Strausz-Hupé, and others, *Protracted Conflict*, p. xviii. In the preface to the 1963 Harper Colophon edition, the authors inferentially dismiss their erroneous conjectures about certain facts that were contained in the original edition on the grounds that "the essential thesis embodied in *Protracted Conflict* was based"—and the implication carried is that this is the way it should be based—"upon the consistent internal logic of Communist strategy, not upon *mere ephemeral impressions of world events"* (italics mine).

61. See, for example, Chapter 3, pp. 96–97, above, for a discussion of Wolfe on this point. The Overstreets make the same indictment of Communist reasoning in *The War Called Peace*, pp. 18–20.

62. John H. Randall, Jr., *The Making of the Modern Mind*, rev. ed. (Boston: Houghton Mifflin, 1940), p. 233.

63. Michael Gehlen, *The Politics of Coexistence: Soviet Methods and Motives* (Bloomington: Indiana University Press, 1967), p. 207.

to the former as the other way around. In the example cited in the previous paragraph, wherein a presumed essence of unlimited egotism is challenged by moves of moderation, rather than interpret the moves as maneuver or deception, the partisans in question tend to call into question or reinterpret the egotistic tenet—or to raise the question of significant change in the particular. Tucker's attribution of post-Stalin liberalization to a transmutation of the totalitarian genius from one species (Führerist) to another (non-Führerist) is a case in point.[64]

One can overdo the point, no doubt. Behavior is not meaningless to the adherent of chiaroscuro.[65] Nor is it everything to adherents of more moderate view. Halle, for instance, seems to conceive a balance of power as the "essential" nature of the international order, and the process of redressing temporary imbalances as an automatic, regulatory device quite the equivalent of Wolfe's notion of a built-in mechanism for restoring autocratic rule to a totalitarian state.[66] But the point remains generally valid. A marked difference of emphasis does exist along the lines named, and it correlates in some significant degree with the images that result.

This difference in emphasis may be seen as one manifestation of a difference that John Dewey and others see as marking the change in the nature of inquiry which took place in the natural sciences at the start of the modern period, and which only in the last half century or so has begun to make headway in the social sciences—namely, the change from preoccupation with essences and final causes to preoccupation with relations and efficient causes.[67] F. Sherwood Taylor, describing this change as it occurred in the field of chemistry in the days of Robert Boyle, writes:

> Thus Boyle would say that iron is hard, not because the substantial form of the iron is the cause of the hardness in it, but

64. Robert C. Tucker, *The Soviet Political Mind: Studies in Stalinism and Post-Stalin Change* (New York: Praeger, 1963), Chapters 1–3.

65. See, for example, Strausz-Hupé, and others, *Protracted Conflict*, Epilogue, wherein the authors do take serious cognizance of various developments subsequent to the date of the original publication that seem to call the thesis of the work into question—as, for instance, the Sino-Soviet split.

66. See above, Chapter 5, p. 150.

67. For fuller statement, see John Dewey, *Reconstruction in Philosophy*, enl. ed. (Boston: Beacon Press, 1948), Chapter III.

because the shape and motion of its parts render them deformable only with difficulty.[68]

Taylor is saying, in this peculiarly appropriate passage, that chemistry in Boyle's day was shifting the grounds on which it framed its definitions and made its descriptive and explanatory judgments from prime reliance on postulates about essences presumed to be self-evident to prime reliance on observable behavior. These observations suggest that the interests of improved consensus in the field of Soviet external conduct would best be served by urging all hands to adopt the second approach and henceforth concern themselves solely with relations and efficient causes. And so this writer would argue—in fact, will argue before closing.

However, since this more stringent measure may be too impracticable, one is content within the immediate context to advocate the less stringent one already mentioned—namely, the heightened awareness of the epistemological differences and allowance for them in discourse. The specific requirement here is that partisans of different approaches become thoroughly aware of the differences, that they keep discussion on one plane at a time and, should this not prove possible, that they at a minimum avoid the unnecessary confusion (and sometimes bitterness) that comes from talking at cross purposes. We should at least be able to steer clear of false comparison—of comparing Soviet practice with American ideal (or, of course, vice versa), the facts of Soviet tyranny with the open, tolerant, and generous essence of the American system.[69]

The last and perhaps most important step relates to a third level of activity—a level deeper than that of the intellectual usually understood. There are, I surmise, differences of bias or basic emotional commitment which also in part underlie and explain the differences of image and world views under discussion. These differences of bias need also to be recognized and taken into account, each inquirer starting with a careful search for and examination of his own.

Bias I define as an emotional predilection for reaching one as against another of the possible conclusions on a subject under investigation.

68. *The Alchemists, Founders of Modern Chemistry* (New York: Schuman, 1949), p. 210.
69. For example, Strausz-Hupé, and others, *Protracted Conflict*, p. 143.

A bias distorts, I say, to the extent that the emotional commitment interferes with the execution of such steps concerning conceptualization, scrutiny of the record, etc., as have been taken to define correct method, interference taking the form, for instance, of provoking some fault in the assembling and interpretation of the data, or in the reasoning thereon. The demonstration of the existence of a bias and distortion, let it at once be said, cannot be perfect or, at least, cannot be perfect absent testimony based on introspection from the inquirer involved. For one cannot inspect directly the mental condition of the person concerned, nor trace directly a particular procedural defect to a particular mental condition rather than to sheer inadvertence. But presumptively sound demonstration is possible. And in the case of the works of the sample, taken collectively rather than severally, there is a good case for affirming that biases exist and a fair one for affirming that they have sometimes skewed results, thereby contributing to the end differences between images.

The case for affirming their existence is twofold. There is, first, the sheer inconceivability of the opposite—it is unbelievable that any American inquirer these days would be absolutely indifferent on the point of what he would like to find out to be true about such important and controversial subjects as the Soviet Union and the global scene as a whole. There is, second, the fact, elaborated in Chapter 1, that there are among the works of the sample many passages of high polemical content, of high frequency of colorable language, of strong emotional tone—extrarational passages eliciting the reader's affections for one conclusion on the data over another which, it is not unreasonable to suppose, reflect a similar preference on the part of the writer.

The case for affirming the disturbing influence of bias on proper procedure, hence conclusion, also has two strands, both of the nature of circumstantial evidence. There is, first, the juxtaposition of colorable language bespeaking strong emotional attachment to a given point of view and procedural errors bending the conclusion toward that point of view. Such juxtaposition, while most frequently found in works of Ultra-Hard persuasion, is not exclusive to them. There is, second, some correspondence between occupational, class, national, and other affiliations of traditionally anti-Communist or anti-Russian character and Ultra-Hard and chiaroscuro views, between affiliations not of that character and more moderate views. Instancing this correspondence is a rather clear correlation, with resultant image, of an author's national origin. Of the 21 major authors, 6 come originally from tsarist Russia or traditionally anti-Russian (and authoritarian) countries of central Europe, the remaining 15 coming from the not traditionally anti-Russian and freer societies of the United States, or, in one case, Czechoslovakia. Of the first group of 6, 4 (67 percent) reach Ultra-Hard conclusions, while of the second the number is only 5 out of 15 (33 percent).[70] Although not impossible, it is difficult to account for this correlation on other grounds, as, for instance, chance. One may add to the above the consideration that some other observers who have attempted to assess the condition of Soviet studies have reached a similar judgment.[71]

The corrective I advocate is not that possible biasing forces be eliminated at the source, through the expunction of the conditions that give rise to them. Even if this were possible, by the eradication of memory or by psychoanalysis, it might well be purchased at the exorbitant cost of draining out of personality everything that is original and individual. I am suggesting only that the potential effects of the forces be recognized and conscientiously offset—in short, controlled through an effort of intelligence and will. I am suggesting that the inquiring mind take the imaginative leap required to become aware of the peculiar perspective from which it views the world and to allow for this peculiarity in making and reporting its observations. For instance, for students of Central European origin who hold the Ultra-Hard view of the Soviet Union and world politics, this means asking themselves whether antipathy toward Russia in the country of their origin or an earlier antipathy toward communism associated with class or party do not in part account for their conclusion. For students of Western or American origin who reach the more middling position, and read Soviet behavior as more moderate, this means asking themselves whether they have not tended to project too readily upon

70. The six authors in the first category are Dallin (Russia), Kulski, Librach, and Ulam (Poland), Lukacs (Hungary), and Strausz-Hupé (Austria). All but Lukacs and Ulam qualify as indicated. Triska is of Czech origin.

71. See, for example, Alfred G. Meyer, "The Comparative Study of Communist Political Systems," *Slavic Review* 26, no. 1 (March 1967): 12.

the Soviet and international scene the less bitter-end character of
American politics. For all Americans, it means continuous awareness
of and attempt to allow for the fact of American allegiance—the fact
that while students of a world of bitter contestants for power and of
states divided into two sharply distinguished categories, they are also
bound by emotional ties to one of the contestants and one of the structural types—in short, that they are parties to the dispute as well
as observers and recorders thereof. It means, first, awareness of these
allegiances but, then and more difficult to bring about, it means
strenuous attempts to offset them. The Platonic figure of the charioteer
(Reason or Intellect) in full control of his horses (Emotion and Will)
epitomizes the proper attitude of mind, or mind-set.[72]

There may be some who challenge the possibility of developing
such control. But the matter is not that difficult. One can recognize a
commitment to reaching one conclusion on Soviet conduct rather than
another—for instance, that it is more addicted to violent than nonviolent means—and then deliberately set about looking for all evidence to the contrary, as Darwin did in order the more fully to test
his hypothesis about the origin of species. Or, distrusting the force of
one's precommitment, one can deliberately seek a check on one's procedure from someone not so precommitted, or oppositely committed
—as did Newton when, fearful of the potential falsifying effect upon
his calculations of his burning desire to find a figure for the distance
to the moon that would confirm his inverse-square law, he entrusted
the calculations to an assistant. One can, and some have. In the writer's
judgment, as earlier noted, in Chapter 1, Mosely and Schwartz, Gehlen,
Shulman, Triska and Tucker are in respect to the defect at issue largely
above reproach.

These steps and the self-awareness and self-control which they
mainly imply will not, of course, lead to lasting peace and concord
among adherents of the various images and world views, even when
augmented by the expansion of systematic inquiry called for by the
preceding chapter. (And this, one would add parenthetically, is probably all to the good; for on the analogy of the legitimacy of seeing

72. On this point cf. William Welch, *The Possibility of a Science of
Politics: Recent Expressions of the Affirmative View* (Ann Arbor, Mich.:
University Microfilms, 1951), Chapter 3, esp. pp. 77–85.

Light sometimes as a wave, sometimes as a stream of particles, it is probably good that the profession continue to entertain more than one image of Soviet conduct, peering at its subject, as it were, through bifocals.) But they can reasonably be expected to narrow differences, and mitigate acerbities, to some degree, and so to lead to a degree of consensus more appropriate to the academic ideal. Beyond this what is needed is a lowering of Soviet-American tension and the inauguration and preservation of milder international weather. For it seems almost self-evidently true that the chances of reconciling diverse views, even as the moderateness of the median view, vary inversely with the tension level. Given a rise in that level toward a point close to war and the disposition to examine critically one's own view, and to be tolerant of others', declines. Given a fall in that level, and the disposition rises.

The Essay Recapitulated

This essay on American images of Soviet external conduct that have come out of the academic community in recent years has two simple messages, one negative, one positive. The negative message is that these images are neither uniform in content nor well developed. The positive message is that much can be done to improve them and bring them more nearly into a common focus, the principal means of doing this being the expansion of systematic inquiry and the cultivation of attitudes of self-awareness.

The images in question are diverse. Although they all see Soviet conduct as militant rather than peaceable, and almost all fall into the upper half of a spectrum defined in terms of a synthetic property I have called hardness, they agree on little else. Rather, they group fairly cleanly into three disparate types. In descending order, these are egotism limitless and invariant, egotism limited and substantially moderating, and egotism restricted and defensive, zoological analogues being respectively the Great Beast, the Mellowing Tiger, and the Neurotic Bear. With exceptions in respect to particular tenets, the elements of which they are made meet indifferently the tests of well-disciplined learning. General characterization is not always explicit, nor, when it is explicit, clear. And when it is both explicit and clear, it is rarely well substantiated: the data offered are too few, are incon-

sistent with the general proposition, or are made consistent by reinterpretation on unexamined and undefended principles. In consequence,
none of the three images (but especially the first) can be considered
firmly grounded. In further consequence, whether the USSR in its
relations with the outer world is more accurately visualized as the
Great Beast of the Apocalypse, a Neurotic Bear, or a Mellowing Tiger,
the academic community has yet rationally and fully to decide. To
vary the simile, we are still close to the condition of the blind men
trying to determine whether the elephant is wall, spear, snake, tree, or
what.[73]

This is not to say good work has not been done. It has. Besides the
few well-documented generalizations, Wolfe's hypothesis about the
perdurance of totalitarianism and Schuman's about the reactiveness
of Soviet expansion and resort to arms; Goodman's monumental com-
pendium of Soviet dicta related to objectives, and Triska's demonstration of the selective impact of ideology; *Protracted Conflict's,* the
Overstreets' and Gehlen's conceptual frameworks, Tucker's and Shulman's suggested differentiations of kinds of objectives and policies—
all represent significant contributions. So too do the narratives and
interpretations thereon provided by those of the works that are pri-

73. The "Hindoo Fable" of "The Blind Men and the Elephant" *(The
Poetical Works of John Godfrey Saxe* [Boston: 1885] pp. 111–12) ends
with these stanzas:

> And so these men of Indostan
>   Disputed loud and long,
> Each in his own opinion
>   Exceeding stiff and strong,
> Though each was partly in the right,
>   And all were in the wrong!

> Moral

> So oft in theologic wars,
>   The disputants, I ween,
> Rail on in utter ignorance
>   Of what each other mean,
> *And prate about an Elephant
>   Not one of them has seen!*

As applied to the dispute among imagists of Soviet conduct, these lines,
though decidedly on the severe side, nevertheless contain a kernel of truth.

marily histories. Kennan in his treatment of the earlier part of the
story, and Shulman in his treatment of a more recent part, Halle and
Lukacs in their handling of the Cold War, Mosely in his accounts of
particular events and developments, and Ulam in his panorama of the
entire span—all have something provocative and thoughtful to say,
and all say it well. Nor is it yet to say improvement must await the
future. Works published near the end of the time span defining the
sample, and, as pointed out at the close of Chapter 1, works published
subsequently, do reflect movement in the desired direction. It is to say
rather that the in-no-sense inconsequential contributions of the sample
have been more often of the character of insightful hypothesis, fuller
and more accurate narrative, more illuminating commentary, or the
first promise of an adequate system of concepts and terms, than the
kind of rigorous definition and application of concept most needed
to supply the substantiation of clear-cut characterization that marks
well-disciplined learning. It is to say rather that improvement has
barely gotten under way.

The broadened systematic inquiry I advocate as corrective may be
characterized as the way of Science and justified in that holy name.
But names and affinities are not important. What is important is the
process answering to the name. Whether answering to the name
"scientific" or not, the claim to be made for the care in small things
I understand by systematic inquiry is that it is the most effective
way of getting at such truth as is publicly available to us. For we use
and shall continue to use, come what may, adjectives like "active" or
"reactive," "coercive" or "persuasive," "moral" or "immoral," etc., to
describe conduct of a given state or person. And in so doing we take
note of some general standard of distinction held by our minds, and
of something in the particular conduct under scrutiny that causes us
to place it in one category rather than the other. The only intelligent
issue of method, then, is whether we perform these operations cavalierly and carelessly, only dimly conscious of what we are doing, or
deliberately and carefully, fully conscious of what we are about. Is it
a question of whether the Soviets are unfaithful to their pledges?
Then let us not fudge meanings or gloss over parts of the record. Let
us rather, as outlined in the preceding chapter, be clear as to what acts
we shall call breaches or violations, what we shall not call breaches or

violations. Let us further define thoughtfully the record in terms of the time units and the pledge units we are going to examine. Let us meticulously search that record for the violations and nonviolations as defined, finally devising and applying some sensible mathematical operation for striking a balance between the two. For what third possibility is there? What more rational way is there of resolving the issue and such conflicts of view between different students as may have arisen over it? What more can the mind do?

In criticism of the foregoing some will urge that all we have when we are through applying the procedures indicated is a record of the fleeting and superficial aspects of conduct, not the reality of its permanent, hard core. Assume perfect data, impeccable conformity to the canons of procedure outlined, and 10 years of hard labor on the part of top minds, and, at the most, they will urge, we shall have: a series of graphs comparable to the economists', measuring the rise and fall over a 60-year period of the expansiveness, militancy, and other facets of Soviet conduct; a series of correlations between these and, say, the tension level of the world environment, the militancy of American policy, the messianic content of ideology, etc.; and a series of projections of the above into the next 60-year period. Assume, furthermore, that all the above support unequivocally the Mixed image of conduct, and we shall still, they will urge, not have proven the case for this view. It will still be entirely legitimate, they will urge, for the authors of some future *Protracted Conflict* to reaffirm the Ultra-Hard image on the grounds that the graphs, the correlations, the projections deal with the ephemeral only, the essential drive beneath remaining egotism unalloyed and limitless. The Wolfes of the future still, they will say, may with complete propriety urge that the totalitarian core has remained unchanged, and that the Great Beast has simply chosen for the time being to masquerade as the Neurotic Bear. In other words, they will say, the Wolfes and authors of *Protracted Conflict* may still have the truer grasp of reality.

The critics will urge all this, and they will be right.

Yet their case fails. Their unspoken assumption is that what we all agree is the kind of truth we should ideally like to have—Truth with a capital "T," Truth about essences, the Truth as the Good Lord sees it —is within our reach, or, to be more precise, within our reach in a form that can be communicated and shared. And this I cannot grant. The question of method won't go away, and I can see no way of determining when one has caught the essence of a thing, when one has not, nor any way of deciding between conflicting accounts of essence, between the confirmed anti-Communist's Great Beast of the Apocalypse and the Communist's Lamb of God. The only form in which the question before us can be intelligibly discussed, in my view, is therefore that of the least unsatisfactory of imperfect alternatives, and my answer—namely, care in small things—remains undisturbed by the criticism.

As with advocacy of systematic inquiry, so with advocacy of self-awareness: it too can be justified in the sacred name of Science. For what one is asking for here is the control of bias that has, on the whole, long characterized the operations of our brethren in the so-called natural sciences and figured prominently in their acknowledged successes. In a special, more contemporary, and more illuminating form, it is the kind of control that distinguishes the theory of relativity. Perhaps because of an unfortunate choice of names, many people, Bertrand Russell points out, "imagine that the theory proves *everything* in the physical world to be relative."[74] But, he continues, "on the contrary, it is wholly concerned to exclude what is relative and arrive at a statement of physical laws that shall in no way depend upon the circumstances of the observer."[75] The basic idea, he further explains, is the systematic taking into account, in the reporting and communicating of observations, of the particular physical vantage points from which those observations are made. And substituting psychological and/or sociological for physical vantage points, this is precisely what I understand by the consciousness and control of bias in the social realm. It is in this sense that one can rightly and validly say not only of Soviet studies in the United States, but of international relations and political science throughout the world as well, that one of the most pressing demands is for an equivalent of the Einsteinian revolution, the greatest single mark of which would be the sys-

74. *The A.B.C. of Relativity*, rev. ed. (New York: New American Library, 1959), p. 16.
75. Ibid.

tematic taking into account and systematic offsetting of ethnocentric or national bias.

However, justification in the name of Science is not the important thing here either. And if justification is needed above and beyond what is almost self-evident in the operation itself, I would appeal rather to Holy Writ. It was taught long ago that he who would take the mote out of his brother's eye should first take the beam from his own. The empirical relation given as reason for the teaching—namely, that only by removing a defect in one's own eye can one see the defect in someone else's—this is true, true literally and unequivocally. An analogous relation for the realm of scholarly inquiry is also true, true literally and unequivocally. For, literally and unequivocally, we American academicians who are students of Soviet conduct will not individually develop a true image of that conduct, in the measure of that truth which is given us to attain; nor will we collectively develop an image of that conduct upon which all can agree, unless we first learn to recognize the psychological, the sociological, and above all the ethnocentric emotional commitments that are part of our makeup —and, having recognized them, allow for them in our study.

Index

Academic views of Soviet conduct. *See* American academic community; Soviet academic community

Activism. *See* Addiction to initiative

Addiction to initiative: defined, 39, 40; proposed method for study of, 198–99, 207

—Soviet: variation in, established, 173, 174; as determined by proposed method of study, 198–99. *See also under* individual imagists

Ambition. *See* Offensiveness of motive

America, Russia, and the Cold War, 1945–1966: grounds for exclusion from study, 11 n.

American academic community: adequacy of treatment of Soviet external conduct, 27, 178; distribution of imagists on hardness scale, 51; clusters of traits in images held by, 51, 54–56; reasons for differences among, 266

—agreement among, on: major events in Soviet history, 21–25; periodization of Soviet history, 25–26; Soviet external conduct, 26, 28

—world views: relation of, to image of Soviet external conduct, 266–75; consensus, 280–81; relation of, to views of American officialdom, 281; relation of, to views of Soviet academic community, 282–85. *See also* individual imagists

American officialdom: supporters of various images among, 58; consensus on world view, 281; relation of world views to those of American academic community, 281; relation of world views to those of Soviet officialdom, 282–83

Armstrong, John, *The Politics of Totalitarianism:* grounds for exclusion from study, 8 n.

Beyond the Cold War. See Shulman, Marshall D., *Beyond the Cold War*

Bibliographies on Soviet external conduct: listed, 4 n., 5; aim of Hammond, 8–9; value of those used, 9

Bouscaren, Anthony T., *Soviet Foreign Policy: A Pattern of Persistence,* 6, 19, 21, 25, 270, 289 n.; author's credentials, 9; subject matter, 12, 13; time span covered, 12, 14; approach, 12, 19, 62; tone, 16; organization, 19; proposed classificatory scheme applied to, 44

—view of Soviet: offensiveness of motive, 200; successfulness, 203

—adequacy of: general characterization, 62; substantiation by historical record, 62. *See also* Ultra-Hard imagists

Brzezinski, Zbigniew, *The Soviet Bloc:* grounds for exclusion from study, 8 n.

Cautiousness: method of study, 195–96

—Soviet: established, 174; as determined by proposed method of study, 196. *See also* Militariness. *See also under* individual imagists

Change. *See* Invariance

Characterization: clarity of general, in images of sample, 174–75. *See also under* individual imagists